Developing Professional Knowledge and Competence

Acknowledgments

To John Burke who persuaded me to write this book.

To Malcolm Clarkson and Jackie Day at Falmer Press who responded quickly and positively at every stage and progressed the manuscript into print with remarkable speed and accuracy.

To Donald McIntyre who kindly wrote a preface at short notice.

To Liz Williams and Hayley Kirley who transformed difficult manuscript into elegant copy.

To Heather Nicholas for her expertise and persistence in finding and getting hold of relevant literature.

To colleagues, practitioners and students who have helped shape my thinking over the years.

To Ablex Publishing Corporation, Carfax Publishing Company, the UK Employment Department, Open University Press, Routledge and Studies in Education Limited, for permission to reuse material published by them.

To my wife and family for coping with the consequences of workload overspill during the last few months of writing.

Developing Professional Knowledge and Competence

Michael Eraut

UK   RoutledgeFalmer, 11 New Fetter Lane, London EC4P 4EE
USA   RoutledgeFalmer, 29 West 35th Street, New York, NY 1001

First published in 1994
Reprinted 1996, 1997, 1999 and 2000
Reprinted 2001, 2002 by RoutledgeFalmer

RoutledgeFalmer is an imprint of the Taylor & Francis Group

A catalogue record for this book is available from the British Library

Library of Congress Cataloging-in-Publication Data are available on request

ISBN 0 7507 0330 X cased
ISBN 0 7507 0331 8 paper

Jacket design by Caroline Archer

Typeset in 10/12pt Bembo by
Graphicraft Typesetters Ltd, Hong Kong

Printed and bound in Great Britain by Biddles Ltd, Guildford and King's Lynn on paper which has a specified pH value on final paper manufacture of not less than 7.5 and is therefore 'acid free'.

Contents

Tables and Figures

Tables

Figures

Preface

This is an important and timely book. It deals with issues which in recent years have generated much heated argument; and it throws much needed new light on these issues. Those of us concerned with the study of professional work and with the education of professional workers have become accustomed to benefitting from Michael Eraut's incisive scholarly thinking, through reading his articles published in journals. This Book offers us considerably more: it brings together his arguments on different topics and shows the connections among them; it substantially extends his previously published work; and it includes significant critiques of some influential theories of professional knowledge, education and work, such as that of Donald Schön.

On the first page of his introductory chapter, Eraut informs us that he will treat 'professionalism' as an **ideology**; and perhaps the most fundamental matter that this book helps us to consider is how to think about that ideology. Like all effective ideologies, the ideology of professionalism embodies appealing values, in this case those of service, trustworthiness, integrity, autonomy and reliable standards; it works in the interests of certain groups — those occupations recognized as professions — while winning the consent, most of the time, of others whose interests are less certainly served by it; and it is effective in so far as its representation of reality is accepted as obviously correct. It is the increasing lack of acceptance of the obvious correctness of the ideology of professionalism, partly but not entirely because of attacks from other ideologies such as that of 'the market', that presents us with a need, and an opportunity, to reappraise the idea of professionalism. For example, the undermining of the ideology of professionalism with regard to parent-teacher relationships over the last two decades has created a situation in which new thinking about the terms of collaboration between schools and families is much needed, but also more possible. Eraut's discussion of professionalism provides us with some of the tools needed for such new thinking.

The two interacting most central theme of this book, however, concern on one hand the nature of professional knowledge, competence and expertise and, on the other, the development of these through professional education. The need for the kind of penetrating cross professional treatment here provided of the development of professional knowledge and expertise is very clear. International and cross-professional comparisons of professional education provision seem to show a widespread sense of crisis but no coherence or consistency in the solutions being promoted. Thus the British government's current attempts to remove initial teacher education **from** the higher education sector contrast not only with the French government's radical moves in the opposite direction but also with the British government's own support for the movement of initial nurse education **into** higher education. Such apparent erraticism on the part of government is not, however, the only or even the primary cause for concern. More worrying is the readiness of those engaged in professional education to rely so heavily on slogans such as 'reflective practice' and, for example, to assert uncritically the need for university lecturers as agents, and university campuses as sites, for fostering reflection. Gross as the politicians' interventions have been, they have revealed a superficially in the theoretical rationales of many of these engaged in professional education which inevitably leave their practice open to attack. Eraut's wide-ranging, informed and above all deeply questioning discussions of professional expertise and of how the development of such expertise can be facilitated, gives a necessary lead in the required direction.

A third matter of great importance is how the competence necessary to qualify people as members of a profession should be described and assessed. How this is related to the profession's control of its affairs and its accountability to clients, and how it relates to conceptions of the knowledge and expertise used in professional work and of professional learning, are among the complex and contentious issues involved. Eraut offers an informed and thoughtful analysis of current government moves in Britain to exercise administrative, methodological and ideological control over the description and assessment of professional competence. He sets this analysis in a broader historical and conceptual context than others have to my knowledge provided, and he relates it to this own studies of the assessment of competence within a number of different professions. I found my own understanding of the issues greatly enhanced.

What I like especially about Eraut's writing is the vigour and enthusiasm which he communicates, the passion to understand and thereby to achieve practical improvement, but also the way in which passion is combined with a cool concern for clarity and clear judgement rather than extremes or distorting simplifications. This book shows these virtues in abundance, and demonstrates impressively the achievements to which they can lead.

Donald McIntyre
Oxford
June 1994

Chapter 1

The Context for Professional Education and Development

Professions, Professionalism and Professionalization

The professions are a group of occupations the boundary of which is ill-defined. While the most powerful professions of law and medicine are commonly perceived as the 'ideal type', few others even approach their degree of influence. Public-sector professions with significantly less power, such as teachers and nurses, were described by Etzioni (1969) as 'semi-professions'; but this simply added one further ill-defined category. Several scholars have approached the problem of definition by compiling lists of professional 'traits' (Millerson, 1964). Though not without interest, such lists have not solved the problem of definition for three main reasons:

- Without any clearly argued justification, each list appears to be based on its author's view of the most salient characteristics of high-status professions.
- When Hickson and Thomas (1969) applied a list of thirteen commonly agreed traits to forty-three qualifying associations, they found a continuum of scores from 0 to 13 without any clear cut-off points and little evidence of some traits taking precedence over others.
- Several traits are culturally specific, with greater significance in some countries than others.

Nevertheless, discussion of such traits has drawn attention to those characteristics of the most powerful professions which others seek to emulate; and fuelled the debate between advocates and critics of professional power. Since this debate is most clearly focused around the concept of an 'ideal type' profession, we shall follow Johnson's (1972, 1984) approach and treat 'professionalism' as an ideology without attempting to distinguish 'true' professions from other contenders. Johnson then goes on to define 'professionalization' as the process by which occupations seek to gain status and privilege in accord with that ideology.

Most accounts of the ideology of professionalism follow the functionalist models developed by Goode (1969), Merton (1960) and Parsons (1968) which accord primacy of place to the professional knowledge base. The problem to which the concept of a profession is said to provide an answer is that of the social control of expertise. Experts are needed to provide services which the recipients are not adequately knowledgeable to evaluate. So how can clients be protected against incompetence, carelessness and exploitation? If state control is unacceptable, as it was when the ideology of professionalism first developed in nineteenth-century Britain and America, then control has to be vested in the experts themselves. Hence the emphasis put by the professions on moral probity, service orientation and codes of conduct. The central assumption of this functionalist model is succinctly summarized by Rueschemeyer (1983):

> Individually and, in association, collectively, the professions 'strike a bargain with society' in which they exchange competence and integrity against the trust of client and community, relative freedom from lay supervision and interference, protection against unqualified competition as well as substantial remuneration and higher social status. (Rueschemeyer, 1983, p. 41)

The argument for relative freedom from interference is based on unique expertise, moral integrity, confidentiality and protection from political abuse. The protection against unqualified competition is to prevent clients from being deceived when they lack the knowledge to discriminate. The higher social status is probably linked to class-based notions of trustworthiness. However, there have been occasions when it became the cause rather than the effect of joining a profession: social status has affected both recruitment and preferment in many professions; and entry requirements were often arranged to favour those who already had the appropriate social background. Thus professions guarantee the efficacy of their self-regulation by undertaking careful recruitment and training, promulgating codes of ethics and setting up committees to deal with any breaches of these codes.

Against this ideology of professionalism, the conflict sociologists of the 1970s simply reversed most of the arguments, accusing the professions of using the power they derived from their superior knowledge to justify their sheltered market.

> According to these sociologists, the strong professional associations, which were established in the age of organized interests to fight for autonomy in all professional questions, exploited their collective power in the market place and prestige in the eye of the public for selfish professional goals. (Siegrist, 1994, p. 5)

Proponents of both the ideology and its counterpart regard expertise as the prime source of professional power and influence, but hold different views about how it is and should be controlled. Empirical studies by historians and sociologists have focused mainly on the older and more prestigious professions, revealing significant changes in systems for controlling them over time and between countries. In particular, as Burrage (1994) points out, the establishment of the older professional associations in Britain preceded the establishment of formal professional education in universities, while in France and the United States periods of deregulation in the nineteenth century led to the reverse process. The foundation of 'professional schools' in universities almost always preceded the development of practitioner associations in their current form. This is reflected in Wilensky's (1964) account of the professionalization process in America.

Occupations such as teachers and social workers have a long history of professionalization in which their number, salary level and social status have constrained their progress. They have had some difficulty in articulating a distinctive knowledge base, and have also suffered from being under much greater government control. Their lack of self-regulation (except in Scotland) had led some to exclude them from the ranks of the professions, but this does not accord with popular opinion.

Less attention, however, has been given to more technically-oriented occupations which have emerged under the control of other professions. For example, the occupations of architectural technician, accountancy technician and engineering technician have developed to undertake the more routine or mechanized aspects of what used to be professional work and require training in higher education which currently stops just short of degree level. But the analogous occupation of medical laboratory scientific officer (the technician title was dropped in 1975) is now regarded by many as having attained professional status. It has a stronger scientific base, operates more independently of its controlling professions (pathologists and haematologists) and now employs a majority of graduates. Much of this development has been very recent but an important milestone was the creation in 1960 of a government Committee for Professions Supplementary to Medicine to oversee the registration of eight health-related professions. This officially recognized MLSO aspirations to professional status but also confirmed their subordination to medicine.

Johnson (1972) interpreted this in terms of the power of physicians to delegate rather than the power of MLSOs to develop their status:

> The emergence of a succession of subordinate 'professions auxiliary to medicine' in Britain is the history of how physicians have been able to define the scope of new specialised medical roles and cannot be regarded as a hierarchy of semi-professions based upon the inherent potentialities for professionalisation of each occupation, or even as the product of the most rational utilisation of human resources. (Johnson, 1972)

However, this preceded the rise to graduate status of most of the 'supplementary professions'. Nevertheless Katz's (1969) comment is still valid today.

The caste-like system puts an unscalable wall between the physician and the semi-professional in the hospital. The legitimacy of the professional guardianship of a body of knowledge depends not only on having a distinct body of knowledge, but also on acceptance of that guardianship by those beyond as well as those within the ranks. In a hospital this means physicians. (Katz, 1969)

Interprofessional relations are strangely absent from accounts of the ideology of professionalism except insofar as that ideology is used to assert the supremacy of the 'true' professions over the newcomers. Although doctors have remained firmly in the ascendent in the health sector, power relations in the construction sector have been changing quite rapidly. Traditionally, architects were in charge of building projects and engineers of bridges, etc.; and they employed other professionals such as surveyors, service engineers and builders as subcontractors or consultants. But the increasing financial power of developers and construction companies has redefined interprofessional relationships in larger projects, so that architects are contracted by companies rather than clients and provide services without necessarily assuming any managerial control. In some cases, architecture is 'little more than just another works package' (Winch and Schneider, 1993). This raises the question of whether subordination to another profession entails less autonomy than subordination to a manager or a politician. Closer examination of professionals at work suggests that many members of higher-status professions have no greater freedom in these respects.

The ideology of professionalism appears to assume that professionals are self-employed or partners in small practices. However, while many professions retain a minority of self-employed members, very few indeed have a majority of members in such independent forms of employment. Hence ethical codes need to take into account the organizational context of professional work. When the legal relationship is between the client and the organization and the organization employs several professionals in the service of a client, there must be an ethical dimension to the roles, conduct and responsibilities of professional workers which takes this into account (see Chapter 11). On the one hand, attention is given to unethical behaviour by organizations and the risks of professional workers 'blowing the whistle', while on the other there is a growing literature on the management of professionals deploring their opposition to organizational procedures which might benefit clients but threaten their own autonomy. In some sectors the managers of professional workers are promoted members of the professions being managed, yet this critical role is not formally recognized by the profession. It would be difficult in those professions which explicitly forbid criticism of fellow members.

Further signs that the traditional ideology of professionalism is becoming outmoded come from the changing attitude of clients. The professional – client relationship is influenced not only by the expertise of the professional but also by the pecuniary and social status of the client. Thus it is possible to distinguish between:

- a relationship of patronage by wealthy and powerful clients, for whom not only expertise but confidentiality and social acceptability are important;
- a commercial relationship, significantly affected by professional body agreements over fees and restricted competition; and
- a welfare relationship, in which clients perceived as 'needy' receive services funded by the State.

In general, the importance of the clients affects the status of the professional providing the service; and the significance of status hierarchies within professions should not be neglected when studying professional work. But, more important for our purpose is the professional concept of 'service' which historically has pervaded relationships with all but the most powerful clients. The traditional ideology of professionalism uses the notion of specialist expertise to justify the assumption that only the professional can determine the real needs of the client. The concept of service was profession-centred rather than client-centred, and clients did not have the social, pecuniary or intellectual resources to challenge the professional's definition of the situation.

This position has been increasingly under attack from several directions. Over the last two decades there has been a growing distrust of the supremacy of scientific and technical knowledge. In whose interests is it being used, and to what extent do these interests determine how it is represented and reported? Traditional professional attitudes are perceived as unacceptably patronizing. Monopolies are challenged and professional conduct sometimes seen as self-serving rather than altruistic. The concept of 'client rights' has increasingly gained acceptance so that the identification of need is beginning to become a joint endeavour. There are calls for the least powerful clients to be supported by 'client advocacy' arrangements. As politicians have sensed these changes in public mood, they have sought to increase the role of government in the regulation of professional work. Concern for both citizens' rights and the increasing cost of public services has given rise to prominent accountability measures to promote the potentially conflicting aims of efficiency, effectiveness, economy, responsiveness and quality.

Thus the work of the professions can be viewed in terms of several interconnected sets of power relations: with service users, with managers of service-providing organizations, with government, with a range of special interest groups and with other professions. Increasingly, however, all these relationships are being framed by a complex web of state regulation. Cynics might argue that, whereas previously the State sought to protect its citizens from the unqualified practitioner, it now seeks to protect them from the qualified.

Professional Preparation and Higher Education

The occupations now claiming to be professions have employed several modes of training and preparation, often in combination. These include:

- a period of pupillage or internship, during which students spend a significant amount of time (up to five years) learning their 'craft' from an expert;
- enrolment in a 'professional college' outside the higher-education system;
- a qualifying examination, normally set by a qualifying association for the occupation;
- a period of relevant study at a college, polytechnic or university leading to a recognized academic qualification; and
- the collection of evidence of practical competence in the form of a logbook or portfolio.

Each of these modes makes a distinctive contribution to the student's knowledge base and to his or her socialization into the occupation.

When free of examinations or other forms of assessment, pupillage focuses on the gradual acquisition of craft knowledge through demonstration, practice with feedback and possibly even coaching. It also has a strong influence on the development of standards and values. It keeps occupational knowledge within the 'guild', does not require that knowledge to be presented in any publicly available form, and places the least demand of any training approach for explicit articulation of the knowledge base of the 'pupil master'. The students' access to training can depend on finding a pupillage or internship and their subsequent career may owe a great deal to the reputation, contacts and patronage of their 'master' or mentor. Students may also provide income, cheap labour and ultimately influence.

Professional colleges are of varied character, ranging from a private crammer or correspondence college, to a training organization set up by employers or a school set up by the occupation itself. Since the war many of them have sought validation of their awards by higher education and eventually merged into universities or worked under their aegis, partly to improve the status of their awards and partly in order to receive public money from the local or national-education budget. Such colleges, particularly in their early stages, relied almost entirely on part-time teaching from practising professionals, and focused very specifically on the requirement for entry to the occupation concerned. They might also act as placement agencies for periods of practice or even as employment agencies. According to the occupation the relative significance of the examination and practice-focused components varied; and the greater the practice component the more likely for the school to serve a socializing function rather than become a simple crammer. Colleges outside higher education are unlikely to develop new professional knowledge or deviate significantly from the occupational regulations; although they will respond vociferously to any proposed changes in the requirements for entering the profession.

Qualifying examinations rose to prominence in the latter half of the nineteenth century, in parallel with, and following, the introduction of examinations for receiving university degrees and for entering the civil service. At the same time they gave considerable power to the occupational organizations which introduced them, which Millerson (1964) therefore described as 'qualifying associations'. The change simplified entry into the professions and for the first time created national standards for the occupations concerned. These standards were important to maintaining the reputation of competent practitioners which was continually being undermined by underqualified non-members, and occasionally by members whose initial acceptance owed more to their connections than their knowledge. However, most examinations guaranteed only that knowledge they were able to test; and this seldom extended to practical competence. Hence one of the main consequences of their introduction was the transformation of large areas of the professional knowledge base into codified forms which suited the textbooks needed to prepare students for what were from the outset very traditional examinations. Another consequence was the opportunity for the qualifying association to function at a distance, not only nationally but internationally. Many of them developed quite a lucrative business, and income from student registrations and examination fees ensured the financial viability of the qualifying associations.

Examinations have also been an important factor within higher education, affecting how what is learned is selected from what is taught and what is taught is selected from what is known. There is also ample research evidence on the effect of examinations on the learning processes adopted by students (Snyder, 1971; Miller and Parlett, 1974). Universities have had more opportunity to introduce alternative modes of assessment, though changes have been rather slow. But the essential differences between university-based and other forms of professional preparation have been that:

- Universities form part of a recognized international system of education with clearly understood modes of entry and universally valued awards.
- The general education associated with universities e.g., maturity, intellectual development, pluralism, cosmopolitanism, has become increasingly valued, not least by students.
- Most universities now get their tuition subsidized by the State, thus reducing the cost of training.
- Universities have a recognized independent role in the creation and validation of knowledge.

Hence there are financial and attitudinal reasons why most students prefer universities to isolated professional colleges. Professional organizations increasingly cannot afford to ignore the talent which enters higher education; and increasingly need university validation to confirm the status, worth and complexity of their knowledge base. However, they also lose a significant degree of control over part of the professional preparation process. They can still influence university courses, some with more impact than others, but they cannot fend off university influences on staff and students. Universities will seek to broaden and academicize the knowledge base, and to challenge some cherished, long-established, professional practices. This tension between university and profession-oriented perspectives on knowledge is one of the main themes of this book.

In the international context, it is important to recognize that the process of incorporating significant parts of professional preparation into higher education has been much slower in Britain than in many other countries. Reasons include the greater power of the professional organizations in Britain, the persistence of élite rather than mass higher education and the concomitant lack of diversity in the higher-education system prior to the formation of the polytechnics. Only doctors were obliged to have degrees during the nineteenth century (by an 1858 Act of Parliament) but several professions (e.g., law, clergy, schoolteachers) recruited graduates for their élite. Although 70 per cent of practising barristers were graduates in 1875, degrees did not become compulsory until 1975. Solicitors still do not require degrees, though 90 per cent of their 1985 entry were graduates. Indeed the situation in law illustrates rather well the difference between higher education and an old-style professional college. To take a law degree takes three years, but graduates in other subjects can gain admission to the final 'vocational year' by taking a one year 'crammer-style' conversion course.

The process of acquiring graduate status for significant numbers of new entrants to occupations was considerably eased by the formation of the Council for National Academic Awards in 1964 to validate awards in the polytechnic sector. For this provided a mechanism for negotiating a mutually acceptable qualification system with half the higher-education system (and usually the more interested half) at once. Typically the compromise reached involved the professional organization approving higher-education awards (dual validation) or recognizing them as giving exemption from certain professional examinations, while higher education gained support for generic higher-education goals and for integrating significant parts of training into general higher-education provision. This latter usually involved foundation or contextual discipline-based courses in the natural or social sciences being taught by academics who were not members of the profession. Responsibility for the assessment of practical competence usually, but not always, remained with the professional organization. The principal landmarks for these later professional entries into higher education were the start of the first degree course in the field, reaching goals such as 25 per cent or 50 per cent graduate entry, the appointment of their first higher-education teacher on a full-time basis and the first doctorate to be supervised in the field by a member of the profession itself. While the first two indicate the changing composition of the profession, the last two indicate the development of a new specialism within the profession, that of the professional educator.

Once higher-education departments became established providers of initial training for the professions, it was only natural that they should also become involved in research and continuing professional education. But both these further roles are strongly influenced by other contextual constraints. A number of professional educators seeks to retain practitioner roles and some are obliged to do so. It is common for lecturers in practical arts — art, design, architecture, music, etc. — to continue in professional practice for part of their time; and the same is true for medicine. This has clear benefits for the authenticity of their contribution to initial training for their professions, providing their practice retains its quality. But it limits the time available for research or continuing professional education.

Another defence of the joint appointment philosophy could be the recognition that 'leading-edge' professionals develop new knowledge in practice rather than through formally designed research; which raises the important issue, of the status accorded to professional knowledge as distinct from scientific knowledge. This is not to suggest that the development of profession-related scientific knowledge is unimportant, simply that professional educators cannot easily engage both in such scientific research and in extending their own professional knowledge base. The norms of higher education tend to favour scientific knowledge rather than professional knowledge, and to encourage different research priorities from those likely to be espoused by the professions, thus helping to widen the gap between professional educators and their erstwhile professional colleagues.

This emphasis on discipline-based knowledge also affects post-qualification courses at postgraduate level. Typically such courses serve three constituencies. First there are professionals who wish to take up a specialism and/or engage in advanced study to improve their knowledge base. Second there are aspiring or recently appointed managers who need some form of management qualification, normally generic but sometimes specific to their own profession. Then third, there are the professional educators themselves who have responsibility for preparing the 'new generation'. In each case the course combines the development of new knowledge with socialization into a new role; and there is a natural tendency to emphasize the new rather than build upon the old, thus subtly devaluing both the prior experience of these advanced students and the status of the average practitioner's knowledge base. The extent to which this occurs will depend both on the design and pedagogy of the course and on whether, as in most management courses, it is shared with people from other professions. In the case of professional educators, there is also a tension between the further development of specialist knowledge and the research skills expected of teachers in higher education and the policy and practice of professional education itself.

Another effect of the changing relationship between the professions and higher education has been the increasing need to divide professional courses into separate credit-bearing units. While introducing greater flexibility and possibly enhancing access, such segmentation also affects the teaching and the nature of the knowledge being mediated and assessed. Professions like law, which conducted multi-subject qualifying examinations, are less affected. But those like nursing or primary-school teaching which used to be based on an 'integrated code' for relatively small groups of students have been radically changed by the introduction of unitized systems based on a 'collection code' system of disparate pieces of discipline or subject-based theoretical knowledge (Bernstein, 1971). Such segmentation and packaging of knowledge for credit-based systems seems inappropriate preparation for professional work which involves using several different types of knowledge in an integrated way; and the pedagogic approaches needed for linking book knowledge with practical experience are almost impossible to implement when there is little continuity in the membership of the student group.

In conclusion, we may note that historical, political and sociological factors have resulted in initial training for the professions being increasingly based in higher education under the leadership of academics recruited from these professions. However, these professional educators are likely to experience considerable role conflict as the norms of higher education take precedence over those in the professions. In particular, the knowledge-base is likely to be segmented and framed in technical/scientific rather than practical terms, rendering the nature of professional knowledge highly problematic for aspiring professionals.

The Learning Professional

Professionals continually learn on the job, because their work entails engagement in a succession of cases, problems or projects which they have to learn about. This case-specific learning, however, may not contribute a great deal to their general professional knowledge base unless the case is regarded as special rather than routine and time is set aside to deliberate upon its significance. Even then it may remain in memory as a special case without being integrated into any general theory of practice. Thus according to the disposition of individual professionals and the conditions under which they work, their knowledge base may be relatively static or developing quite rapidly. There is little research evidence to indicate the overall level of work-based learning in any profession, but individual examples of both extremes are frequently cited.

During the last two decades, the need for at least some off-the-job learning has been recognized by most professional workers. The term 'Continuing Professional Education' (CPE) usually refers to formally organized conferences, courses or educational events rather than work-based learning, while the term 'Continuing Professional Development' (CPD) refers to both. Most

Academic Award

Professional Qualification

Short Courses

Specialist Qualification   Higher Academic Awards

Short Courses

Figure 1.1:   Qualifications Affecting a Professional Career

professional codes of conduct refer to an obligation to engage in CPD, and some professions have now made attendance at CPE events mandatory for continuing registration. This raises important questions (to be addressed later) about how CPE is conceived. To what extent is it a substitute for work-based learning, a kind of insurance that certain important areas of learning will definitely be covered? To what extent is it a catalyst for work-based learning, providing the psychological support and incentive, assisting with the integration and organization of previous experience, alerting people to new sources of information and work-based learning opportunities? To what extent is it a complement to work-based learning, providing knowledge not readily accessible in the workplace, but not attempting to link it too closely with existing practice?

There can be as many as four different kinds of qualification affecting a professional career in addition to non-award bearing short courses; and these are depicted in Figure 1.1. Some professions, such as nursing and social work, integrate the academic award with the professional qualification, while others such as law and accountancy operate a dual-qualification system. The proportion of a cohort that proceeds to take a specialist qualification is very low in some professions and very high in others; and the propensity to take higher academic awards is also very variable.

Research into professional development, however, suggests that the initial period during which novice professionals develop their proficiency in the general professional role continues well beyond their initial qualification. Indeed, the first two or three years after qualifying are probably the most influential in developing the particular personalized pattern of practice that every professional acquires. There is a highly significant mismatch between policies for Initial Professional Education (IPE) and the experience of Initial Professional Development (IPD).

While policies for Initial Professional Education have developed through a series of mutual accommodations between higher education and professional organizations, the linkage between IPE and CPE has been almost totally neglected. IPE syllabi are notoriously overcrowded because they attempt to include all the knowledge required for a lifetime in the profession, almost regardless of students' ability to digest it and use it. There is little sign as yet of IPE being conceived in a context of lifelong professional learning, in spite of increasing evidence that the frontloading of theory is extremely inefficient. Many IPE courses exacerbate this situation by frontloading theory within the IPE stage itself, thus maximizing the separation between theory and practice.

Looking at professional education from the perspective of lifelong learning makes some of the current assumptions about IPE and CPE seem even stranger. The critical questions concerning IPE are the stages in a 'learning career' at which it should start and finish. What should be the modes of entry, the prior knowledge required and the criteria for selection for each mode? At what levels of capability and competence should registration be granted? Currently entry is determined by historical tradition, by the need to attract new entrants of the right calibre, by manpower needs and by assumptions about the importance of general education for subsequent professional learning and understanding. There is little attempt in some occupations to match qualities needed in a particular profession with admission decisions, so that calibre is construed largely in terms of formal academic qualifications. Nor, at a time when mature entrants are increasingly welcomed, is there much thinking about the proportion or type of mature entrants that would be most desirable; and how their previous experience might affect the curriculum or its delivery. Exit points are also determined by historical tradition, the attraction of a graduate profession, the technical requirements of the profession and the way professional work is organized for the exploitation, support and supervision of students, interns and newly qualified recruits. Many alternative arrangements are conceivable for the period of initial professional development from entry to proficiency, which might better accord with what we know about professional learning. But if it is difficult for higher education to break with tradition, it is even more difficult for employers and work-based supervisors to countenance radically different kinds of arrangement. Moreover, government financial support is often directed towards higher-education degrees, which may or may not incorporate large sections of IPE, not towards IPE itself. Professions are understandably wary of making any change which might offer a pretext for reduced government funding at a time when no proposed increase in cost would even be contemplated.

If IPE suffers from too much tradition, CPE may well suffer from too little. While some professions require attendance at CPE events, none require any continuing demonstration of competence to practice. The best employers give considerable support to CPD through management and appraisal and through funding attendance at CPE activities. The worst discourage both attempts to initiate peer-group learning and interest in external CPE courses and events. Even, where CPD and CPE are strongly supported the emphasis is likely to be on preparing for organizational change or career development and new aspects of professional work rather than improving the quality of current professional performance. This continual focus on the new rather than on renewal promotes new knowledge which comes from outside rather than

new knowledge arising from the distillation of personal experience; thus indirectly discouraging learning from experience and CPD activities which attempt to reorganize and share the accumulated experience of problems and
cases. The potential of work-related, if not always work-based, mid-career
professional education is underestimated. Instead of helping professionals to
reformulate their theories of practice in the light of their semi-digested case
experiences and under the stimulus of collegial sharing and challenging, CPE
all too often provides yet another strand of separate, unintegrated and therefore minimally used, professional knowledge.

Underpinning this discussion of the learning professional has been the
recognition that learning relies on three main sources: publications in a variety
of media; practical experience; and people. Each may be used for a variety of
purposes, often in combination with the others. Thus publications may be
recommended as reading for a course, regularly consulted as databases, referred to when tackling a problem or getting briefed on some issue of concern, scanned for new items of significance, or studied for personal interest.
People may be sources or interpreters of public knowledge, purveyors of
vicarious experience, or supporters of learning from any available and appropriate source. In this latter role (often referred to as tutors in educational
settings or mentors in work settings) they may suggest objectives, advise on
sources, challenge interpretations and provide feedback. Colleagues or
colearners may also take up any of these 'people roles' by bringing different
knowledge and perspectives, by sharing the burdens of finding, scanning and
degutting learning resources, and by providing the mutual psychological support and motivation so often engendered by group work. Learning from
experience is more problematic. In spite of its popular appeal, there is much
less evidence available about precisely what is learned from experience and
how. What we do know, however, is that such learning depends on what is
perceived, itself dependent on perceptual/cognitive frameworks and expectations, and on time devoted to reflection, making sense and linking specific
experiences with other personal knowledge. The relationship between learning from books, learning from people and learning from experience is a major
theme of this book, which is given particular attention in Chapter 6.

This brief overview suggests that any framework for promoting and
facilitating professional learning will have to take into account (1) an appropriate combination of learning settings (on-the-job, near the job, home, library, course, etc), (2) time for study, consultation and reflection, (3) the
availability of suitable learning resources, (4) people who are prepared (i.e.,
both willing and able) to give appropriate support and (5) the learner's own
capacity to learn and to take advantage of the opportunities available. While
planning will always be severely constrained by time and money, there is little
reason to believe that the policies for IPE and CPE which have evolved historically are optimal within these constraints. My own view is that changes
will come partly through growing recognition of other possible arrangements
but mainly because people begin to understand more about professional

learning and to further develop their own capacity to learn. As people become more professional about the way they approach, manage and pursue their own learning, they will be better able to assess the way learning is supported by IPE and CPE programmes. Hence the need to be 'professional learners' in order to become more effective 'learning professionals.'

Characterizing the Professional Knowledge Base

Both apologists for, and critics of, the professions have been united in stressing the importance of a profession's knowledge base. The power and status of professional workers depend to a significant extent on their claims to unique forms of expertise, which are not shared with other occupational groups, and the value placed on that expertise. Moreover, the less accessible to lay understanding and the more individualized the client, the greater the power differential. The close relationship which has developed during the twentieth century between the professions and higher education serves to legitimate these knowledge claims, but also affects the way in which the knowledge base is represented. Indeed, the public representation of the knowledge base is a critical feature of a profession's public image. In these circumstances, professions prefer to present their knowledge base as:

- carrying the aura of certainty associated with established scientific disciplines (or, if that is unconvincing, establishing strong links with university-based social and behavioural sciences);
- sufficiently erudite to justify a long period of training, preferably to degree level for all with specialist postgraduate training beyond that for some; and
- different from that of other occupations.

To achieve this goal normally requires the establishment of a subject base within higher education specific to the profession concerned, while still retaining sufficient grounding in the established disciplines to uphold its academic status. The creation of such quasi-disciplines or applied fields of study as sections or departments within higher education can help to organize and codify much of the knowledge accumulated within the profession as well as facilitate the import of concepts and ideas from other subjects, hence accelerating the growth of the professional knowledge base. But the selection and framing of this reorganized and newly created knowledge will be strongly influenced by the norms and expectations of the higher-education environment, possibly at the expense of needs identified within the profession.

An alternative approach to characterizing the knowledge base of a profession is to ascertain the personal knowledge of working professionals. But in pursuing such an approach we must be careful not to forget that higher education has a strong interest in the 'sale' and 'production' of knowledge as a commodity; and user-derived standards threaten its hegemony. Many of these important epistemological issues have only recently begun to attract widespread attention among those engaged in professional education.

The first such issue can be crudely expressed in terms of the distinction between propositional knowledge which underpins or enables professional action and practical know-how which is inherent in the action itself and cannot be separated from it (for example knowing how to swim or to play a musical instrument). This distinction has been articulated in several different ways, which are not epistemologically equivalent but represent different perspectives on a problem that has yet to be fully clarified. Aristotle made a distinction between 'technical knowledge' and 'practical knowledge' which was further developed by Oakeshott (1962). Ryle (1949) used the terms 'knowing that' and 'knowing how'. Polanyi (1967) invented the term 'tacit knowledge' to describe that which we know but cannot tell. All these ideas are discussed in later chapters. Here, we need simply note the increasing acceptance that important aspects of professional competence and expertise cannot be represented in propositional form and embedded in a publicly accessible knowledge base.

Recent attempts to capture such knowledge have cast considerable light on the nature of professional expertise and Schön (1983, 1987) in particular has highlighted the value of reflection in raising awareness of tacit knowledge and transforming knowing-in-action into knowledge-in-action. However, there are limits to how far such transformation is possible. Critics may illuminate the knowledge embedded in a piece of music, a painting or a dance but they cannot fully represent it in words. The instant recognition of a person or rapid reading of a situation involves digesting more information than could possibly be described in any brief, propositional form. There are important distinctions between awareness of tacit knowledge, subjecting it to critical scrutiny and being able to articulate it in propositional form. Workers in artificial intelligence have striven to create representations of professional expertise for some fifteen years, sometimes contributing new ideas but also revealing how much professional knowledge is not amenable to capture for representation in current computerized formats. The result has been the development of 'knowledge elicitation' as a new area of research, expressly devoted to developing methods of characterizing what experts know. One of its best established findings, which is of considerable significance for our study is that people *do not know what they know*.

A particularly confusing aspect of these epistemological discussions is the wide range of definitions accorded to the term 'knowledge'. For example, the frequently cited triumvirate — knowledge, skills and attitudes — assumed that skills, which Ryle would regard as part of 'knowing how' are something separate from knowledge itself. This restricts the meaning of the term 'knowledge' to propositional knowledge; which includes propositions about skills and procedures, for example sets of instructions about how to dress a wound or ride a bicycle, but excludes the practical know-how needed to perform these operations. Narrower still is the use made of the term 'knowledge' by Bloom and the co-authors of the *Taxonomy of Educational Objectives* (1956), who used it to characterize the lowest level of their cognitive domain, calling the second 'comprehension', the third 'application' and so on. By implication this kind of knowledge is something you have to remember but may not even comprehend. It has its everyday analogue in the term 'general knowledge', a compendium of facts for use in quiz-games and 'Trivial Pursuits'. Echoes of this narrowest of definitions also appear in the regulations of the National Council for Vocational Qualifications which refer to 'underpinning knowledge and understanding' as if it was possible to have underpinning knowledge which one did not understand. *The Shorter Oxford English Dictionary* gives a range of meanings for the verb 'to know', including 'to be cognizant of' (the Bloom meaning) 'to understand', 'to have personal experience of' and 'to be conversant with', which take us well outside the realm of purely propositional knowledge. Its broadest definition of knowledge is 'theoretical and practical understanding', which goes beyond propositional knowledge but still excludes knowing how in the sense of being able to do something, a central requirement of professional work.

For the purposes of this book, which is concerned with developing professional knowledge in its fullest possible sense, I intend to use the term 'knowledge' to refer to the whole domain in which more specifically defined clusters of meaning reside. Thus all the different forms of knowledge discussed above — procedural knowledge, propositional knowledge, practical knowledge, tacit knowledge, skills and know-how — are included. This enables the relationship between these types of knowledge and their significance for professional work to be discussed without repeatedly getting embroiled in definitional issues.

A second epistemological issue concerns the truth or validity of professional knowledge. To put it simply, can we refer to something as knowledge if we do not know it to be true? To apply such a truth test seems eminently reasonable within the realm of easily verifiable statements, but becomes quite impracticable in areas of complex theory. The truth of some of the best-known and most used theories, such as Keynes' theory of macroeconomics and Freud's theory of personality, is still hotly debated. Newtonian mechanics is now regarded as only approximately true. To treat such theories as outside the domain of 'genuine' knowledge would make thinking about the world virtually impossible. It is normal to accept new ideas and theories as at least temporary contributions to knowledge in order to discuss the extent of their truth and validity without engaging in unnecessary semantic circumlocution. In particular, when explaining the personal knowledge of experienced professionals, I prefer to follow the advice of George Miller: 'If someone tells you in good faith that something is true, you should always assume that they are right. The problem is to find out what it is true of.'

Allied to this problem of truth is the problem of uncertainty which pervades a great deal of professional work. Not only do predictions about human beings contain an element of unpredictability, sometimes a very significant element, but so also do predictions about the physical world. Weather is a notorious example. Even in the more concrete world of civil engineering, after precise calculations of the strength of a structure have been used to calculate the thickness of load-bearing parts, a large safety margin will be added. For behind almost every precise calculation or logical deduction lies a set of assumptions that conceals doubt and uncertainty. Indeed, most research findings in complex areas of applied knowledge are expressed in terms of probabilities. This can offer only limited guidance to professionals making decisions about individual cases unless further evidence is available about their typicality. In these circumstances, great weight is attached to professional judgment, the wise decision made in the light of limited evidence by an experienced professional. The assumption is that the wise professional has somehow managed to organize his or her personal experience of a large number of cases and use it to make 'good' judgments; though getting a 'second opinion' may still be recommended. This image of wise judgment under conditions of considerable uncertainty stands in marked contrast to the preferred public image of a reliable, quasi-scientific knowledge base.

In general, many differences can be found between the personal knowledge of working professionals which informs their judgment or becomes embedded in their performance and the public knowledge base of their profession as represented by publications and training courses. In particular:

- A personal knowledge base includes notes and memories of cases and problems which have been encountered, reflected upon and theorized to varying extents and with varying significance for current practice.
- The public knowledge of which a professional worker has cognizance will be an individual selection from a much larger public knowledge base, influenced by public knowledge encountered during professional education and independent reading, by personal interest and experience, and by social interchange with fellow professionals.
- Only a portion of this public knowledge which is potentially available to a professional has a significant chance of being used in practice. This portion, sometimes referred to as 'action knowledge', comprises knowledge which has been sufficiently integrated into or connected with personal practice to be either automatically or very readily called into use. Only when problems are difficult and time is available to work on them will searching beyond the domain of action knowledge be likely.
- Such action knowledge may include all the types of knowledge referred to earlier. Some of it will have been thoroughly thought out and used in a deliberate manner that can be justified and explained. Some of it will be used intuitively with varying degrees of self-awareness.
- Public knowledge which gets incorporated into action knowledge

undergoes a process of personalization in which some interpretations and uses become prominent while others get neglected. Hence its personal significance and meaning will show some variation between one professional and another.

All these phenonema will be discussed at some length in the chapters which follow. At this stage we need only note that characterizing the professional knowledge base in terms of what professional workers know presents many difficulties. Not only does it include tacit knowledge which has not been, and may never be, clearly articulated, but explicit knowledge which remains 'in store' and never gets used. Differences between individual professionals are likely to be considerable, raising questions of whose knowledge it is that is being described. Will we include knowledge of which there is some cognizance or only action knowledge which is used in professional practice? These questions, moreover, do not only apply to the characterization of a professional knowledge base. They also concern what is to count as *competence* and what is to count as *expertise*.

Professional Knowledge: Its Character, Development and Use

The six chapters in Part 1 progressively elucidate a complex tapestry of issues concerning the nature of professional knowledge, how it is used and how it is acquired. Thus the nature of professional knowledge is explored from several perspectives, and commonly cited dichotomies are examined in depth. These include the contrasts between theory and practice, public knowledge and personal knowledge, propositional knowledge and process knowledge, analytic and intuitive thinking. In each case the contrast tends to be taken to extremes which serve to disguise rather than elucidate the nature of professional thought and action. Moreover, in practice different types of knowledge and modes of cognition are integrated into professional performance in ways that are difficult to unravel, either conceptually or empirically.

Five of the chapters are based on previously published work but significantly revised. The sixth and largest is entirely new. They represent the progressive development of my thinking over a substantial period of time, being written in 1981, 1984 (2), 1987, 1992 and 1994. However while themes are revisited, there is very little duplication and nothing which I would not want to defend. Other work written during this period which overlaps with these chapters has been excluded. The advantage of this arrangement for the reader is a kind of spiral curriculum in which each time a theme is revisited new insights are gained because other related themes have been further developed and new aspects of the theme are introduced. Given the complexity of the territory this approach has significant advantages. Three of the six chapters are situated in the field of teacher education, where most of my work in the early 1980s was based; but each is focused on a theme of general interest to most professions: Chapter 4 on theory-practice relationships in pre-qualification training, Chapter 2 on incorporating new knowledge into practice in mid-career, and Chapter 5 on the nature and development of management knowledge as exemplified in the professional learning of headteachers. Chapters 3, 6 and 7 are multi-professional with a preponderance in Chapter 7 of examples from health professions.

An important argument developed throughout these chapters is that professional knowledge cannot be characterized in a manner that is independent of how it is learned and how it is used. It is through looking at the contexts of its acquisition and its use that its essential nature is revealed. Although many areas of professional knowledge are dependent on some understanding of relevant public codified knowledge found in books and journals, professional knowledge is constructed through experience and its nature depends on the cumulative acquisition, selection and interpretation of that experience.

Chapter 2 focuses on the influence of context on knowledge use, arguing first that the nature of the context affects what knowledge gets used and how. Three types of context are distinguished: the academic context; the organizational context of policy discussion and talk about practice; and the context of practice itself. New concepts and ideas brought into these contexts have to be transformed in order to become usable in contextually appropriate ways; and this transformation can also be viewed as a form of learning which develops the personal knowledge base of the professional concerned. Therefore it is inappropriate to think of knowledge as first being learned then later being used. Learning takes place during use, and the transformation of knowledge into a situationally appropriate form means that it is no longer the same knowledge as it was prior to it first being used. It also follows that learning to use an idea in one context does not guarantee being able to use the same idea in another context: transferring from one context to another requires further learning and the idea itself will be further transformed in the process. The practice context poses a special problem because practical knowledge integrates complex understandings and skills into a partly routinized performance, which then has to be deconstructed and deroutinized in order to incorporate something new.

Chapter 3 introduces the idea of different types of professional knowledge, distinguishing between the portrayal of knowledge in curriculum documents and evidence directly obtained from the observation of practice and discussion with practitioners. Particular attention is given to the issues of generalizability (of particular cases, of methods and of theory) and explicitness (codified technical knowledge, practical knowledge embedded in tradition and experience, tacit knowledge). Next it addresses the question of modes of knowledge use by adopting Broudy's fourfold typology of replication, application, interpretation and association (briefly introduced in Chapter 2) to illustrate the varying degree to which theory gets modified in practice. Thus theory and practice are shown to have a symbiotic relationship which varies with both the mode and the context of knowledge use.

This analysis is then extended to the process of knowledge creation. New knowledge is created both in the research community and in each professional community. But each places different valuations on different kinds of knowledge in a way that minimizes their interpenetration. The particularistic nature of knowledge gained by practising professionals presents yet another barrier to knowledge creation: both its exchange with other professionals and its incorporation into theory are limited by its specificity, and often by its implicitness. Hence higher education needs to develop an additional role to that of creator and transmitter of generalizable knowledge — that of enhancing the knowledge creation capacity of individuals and professional communities. This implies recognizing that much of the relevant expertise lies outside the higher-education system, but its development is limited by the lack of appropriate structures for knowledge exchange between higher education and the professions. This is matched by the lack of appropriate opportunities for mid-career professional education, whereby professionals can (1) reflect on their experience, make it more explicit through having to share it, interpret it and recognize it as a basis for future learning: and (2) escape from their experience in the sense of challenging traditional assumptions and acquiring new perspectives. There is a need, therefore, to see how Continuing Professional Education can provide a bridge between the continuing development of the personal knowledge of individual professionals and that of the knowledge base of the whole profession.

Chapter 4 inquires more deeply into the related questions of how theory gets used or fails to get used in practice and how theory is derived from practice by a process of reflection on, and theorizing about, practical experience. The context is that of the acquisition and use of theory by beginning teachers, for whom the introduction of theory is juxtaposed with practical experience and theorizing about that experience is strongly encouraged. However, the effectiveness and the authenticity of this approach depend on the pedagogic skills of teacher educators, the mentoring skills of teachers in practice schools and the dispositions of both. The changing concerns of student teachers are discussed in this context. Then finally it is argued that the whole process of professional learning needs to be explicitly discussed with students, together with teachers' moral duties and the disposition to theorize.

Chapter 5 introduces the common phenomenon of experienced professionals who take on significant management roles in mid-career. New headteachers in particular combine the state of being expert teachers with that of being novice chief executives. Then the situation is further complicated by them being accorded expert status in their new role and treated as being out of touch with their more familiar roles as teachers. The chapter starts in an analytic mode by examining the nature of a headteacher's knowledge. Six categories are distinguished: knowledge of people, situational knowledge, knowledge of practice, conceptual knowledge, process knowledge and control knowledge. The factors affecting the acquisition or learning of each type of knowledge are discussed with special attention to the often undetected bias and fallibility of what is assumed to be true. In spite of these validity problems and a tendency to rely on knowledge that has been only partially reflected upon and digested, on-the-job learning is the normal mode of acquiring knowledge; and attempts to introduce off-the-job learning have to take this into account.

Moving into a more developmental mode, the particular circumstances affecting management courses are then discussed. The focus of this discussion, however, is how to establish links between off-the-job activities and on-the-job learning which maximize the advantages of the off-the-job component, minimize the disadvantages and provide a significant pay-off for the investment of valuable time. Priorities are suggested for continuing professional development in each of the six types of knowledge; and appropriate learning activities for achieving these goals are discussed. Many fruitful ideas are put forward for the design of CPE activities which promote continuing professional development in important and often very difficult areas.

Chapter 6 returns to a multi-professional context and a more sophisticated analysis of the knowledge used in professional processes. Ryle's distinction between 'knowing how' and 'knowing that' is transformed into a distinction between process knowledge and propositional knowledge, whilst also recognizing that professional processes make considerable use of propositional knowledge. A third category 'personal impressions' is added to account for memories which are insufficiently reflected upon to have given rise to propositional knowledge. The development of personal knowledge which incorporates all three of these categories is discussed with particular reference to Schutz's account of learning from experience. The subsequent analysis of professional processes then gives considerable attention to the respective roles of learning from experience and learning from books, while still emphasizing both the fallibility of experiential knowledge with its use of partly tacit assumptions and frameworks and the need for book knowledge to be reinterpreted in use and personalized as a result.

Five types of professional process are examined in this way: processes for acquiring and interpreting information, skilled behaviour, deliberative processes, giving information and metaprocesses. The first of these categories is the least coherent because it covers a wide range of methods ranging from intuitive pattern recognition, through reflection on impressions, to study skills and the recognized inquiry methods of academic disciplines and technical professions. Skilled behaviour in the professional context is rarely automatic because routines are punctuated by myriads of rapid decisions, rather like riding a bicycle (pure skill) in heavy traffic (with constant adjustment in speed and direction based on constant monitoring). Deliberative processes include planning, evaluating, problem-solving and less rapid forms of decision-making. They normally involve a range of types of thinking and require a balance between analysis/reasoning and synthesis/creative invention. They often involve group processes which introduce another dimension of complexity. The difficulty of giving information in a manner which promotes understanding is underestimated by most professions. Both more imaginative representations of information and greater awareness of respondents' concerns and likely misunderstandings are important. The short section on metaprocesses briefly reviews the discussion of 'control knowledge' in Chapter 5, as the terms are used with almost identical meaning.

The final section of Chapter 6 discusses the implications of this analysis for professional education. It recommends greater interweaving of learning in academic and professional settings, avoiding too much frontloading of theory, a strong emphasis on process knowledge and a system of initial and advanced qualifications rather than a single qualification.

Chapter 7 reviews some of the major theories of professional expertise, using the analysis of Chapter 6 as a framework for characterizing their nature and disclosing some of their key assumptions. It begins with the Dreyfus Model of Skill Acquisition which characterizes expertise in terms of increasingly intuitive modes of cognition, then moves on to review theories of clinical decision-making. These theories seek to explain the accumulation of clinical knowledge and its use in either intuitive or analytic modes of cognition. Analytic approaches, it is argued, are often oversold but nevertheless offer greater opportunities for taking client values and preferences properly into account. Cognitive explanations of intuitive modes of cognition in terms of templates, frames, scripts or critical exemplars are also discussed at some length. This leads to a framework which incorporates both a continuum of cognitive modes and their integrated use in mixed models.

Schön's 'Reflective Practitioner' model is the next to be discussed, though with more difficulty as so few of Schön's examples seem to fit his own model. Reflection has a wide variety of meanings and Schön's work has not been well-served by its later advocates' neglect of whether their own meanings had much in common with his. I conclude that Schön's important insights are most usefully clarified by regarding his theory as a theory of metacognition rather than a theory of reflection. The concept of reflection-in-action only carries a clear meaning when the action is fairly rapid; because once the pace becomes slower there can be no clear distinction between when reflection is in action and when it is on action. Thus speed of thought and action emerges as a critical variable when considering the nature of expertise. Several reasons are given why deliberation is important in professional work, indeed essential for maintaining its quality. Hence a major problem for all professionals is making sufficient time to engage in deliberative as well as rapid and intuitive modes of thought and action.

Chapter 2

The Influence of Context on Knowledge Use: What Is Learned from Continuing Professional Education and How?

Introduction

One central purpose of continuing professional education is to bring practising professionals into contact with new knowledge and ideas. Sometimes this is conceived in terms of general updating, sometimes as a stimulus to critical thinking and self-evaluation, sometimes as the dissemination of a particular innovation, sometimes as part of the process of implementing a new mandatory policy. The evidence that subsequent practice is affected by CPE is scanty and more often negative than positive. Indeed, evidence of what has been learned has rarely been collected, as most evaluations have focused on the perceived relevance of the content and the perceived quality of the processes. Having been engaged for some time with practice-oriented Masters courses for mid-career professionals and shorter in-service programmes for school-teachers, it became clear to me that the whole question of professional learning during and after CPE had been little examined. Even in the education sector, empirical research was limited and the whole field appeared to be underconceptualized.

This chapter addresses two problems at once.[1] The first is the problem of how theory gets to influence practice, a preoccupation in both the literature on innovation and that on professional education. The second is the problem of how people use the knowledge they have already acquired. Both are central to the goal of developing professional practice. The key to unlocking these problems was my realization that learning knowledge and using knowledge are not separate processes but the same process. The process of using knowledge transforms that knowledge so that it is no longer the same knowledge. But people are so accustomed to using the word 'knowledge' to refer only to 'book knowledge' which is publicly available in codified form, that they have developed only limited awareness of the nature and extent of their personal knowledge. When it comes to practical knowledge acquired through experience, people cannot easily tell you what it is that they know. With these constraints in mind, the chapter approaches the question of what is learned from CPE from a knowledge use perspective. What has to happen for knowledge presented during CPE sessions to get used in practice; and what factors are likely to affect the necessary knowledge transformation process?

In order to get some grip on possible forms of knowledge transformation, Broudy's typology of knowledge use has been adopted, first to illustrate the different modes by which theoretical knowledge may be used in practice, then by reversal to illustrate how practical knowledge may be used in theory. This leads us to consider how theory is usually explicit in 'book knowledge' but implicit in 'action knowledge'.

The context of the discussion is that of the In-Service Education of Teachers (currently referred to INSET), as the original paper was presented to a conference on that topic. This is an occupation about which most people have sufficient knowledge to follow the specific arguments and examples which help to illustrate the more general theoretical framework being developed. Three contexts of knowledge use are depicted: the academic context, which can be found in all professions; the school context, which corresponds with discussion and policy-making contexts in other types of professional workplace such as a practice, department or project team; and the classroom context, which corresponds with more private contexts in which normal professional practice is produced in a relatively routine manner without questioning the assumptions on which it is based. These contexts can be distinguished by the way in which people learn to operate in them (by writing, talking or doing) and by the way knowledge is validated (by expertise, by stakeholders' support, or by personal judgment). Thus personal knowledge is significantly shaped by the context in which it has been and is intended to be used, and transfer of knowledge between contexts is limited by the different forms in which that knowledge has to be present in order to be usable.

The problems of introducing new knowledge are greater in contexts of normal professional practice, where work is likely to involve behavioural routines which are difficult to deconstruct and reassemble without causing disorientation and the threat of a temporary (and the fear of a more than temporary) inability to cope. Supporting such change is difficult not only because practical knowledge is implicit and less understood, but also because it is not awarded the high status of technical knowledge.

Modes of Knowledge Use

Broudy's typology was originally developed as a form of utilitarian justification for a liberal rather than purely vocational approach to secondary education by elucidating the different and complex ways in which school knowledge was used in subsequent life (Broudy, Smith and Burnett, 1964). Broudy then used it again much later in the context of Continuing Professional Education (Broudy, 1980) where it has helped to focus attention on the problems of how theoretical knowledge gets used in practice. The basis of his analysis is the distinction between four modes of knowledge use:

- replication;
- application;
- interpretation; and
- association.

In applying this typology to the continuing professional education of teachers I shall be primarily concerned with the interpretative mode, because teaching is too complex and unpredictable an activity for the *replication* of a blueprint or the *application* of a simple set of principles to provide a sufficient foundation for good practice. There may have been occasions during initial training in higher education when replication of theoretical knowledge was encouraged by traditional examinations; but in practical contexts theoretical knowledge has to be adapted to suit the particular demands of each situation. This requires more than the simple application of theory. Theories have to be *interpreted* in order to be used. However this raises further questions. On what grounds does one select from a large number of possible interpretations? If the grounds for selection are not in the domain of theory, does this put them purely in the domain of practice? Does one then select interpretations according to personal preference, or utility, or ethical principles? What implications does this have for learning to make interpretative uses of theoretical knowledge?

The *associative* use of theory has not, as far as I know, been much explored in education, in spite of the long history of association as a psychological concept. So let me provide some examples. One pervading metaphor which assumed increasing significance in public discussions of education during the 1980s is that of the market. While there exists a body of applied economics which attempts to use market theory to analyse resource allocation problems in the public services, political discussions have been far from theoretical. The market metaphor has been used to conjure up images of people going from stall to stall comparing the goods on sale and making their choice accordingly. But schools hardly conform to this image. Limited information is available. Choosing a school does not enable one to choose any particular teacher. There is little choice in rural areas. Variations in cost are limited to transport. Over-supply of school places is regarded as uneconomic, yet without it choice is heavily restricted. Nevertheless, some degree of competition is common; so the metaphor of a market continues to have political currency, both as a symbol of giving priority to the consumer and in shaping thinking about school-community relations. It competes with concepts of 'parent power' and 'parent rights' as an approach to empowering parents.

Another example arose during my recent research on accountability. We found that teachers never discussed children's work in isolation but always in context. What came before and after, how long it took, how much help they had, whether the child was highly involved or affected by some unusual circumstance, how it matched their expectations of the child, etc. Other classroom incidents deemed relevant to assessing the child's potential were also cited. This can be developed into a theory of how teachers collect and organize information about individual children which has considerable significance for classroom accountability, particularly because of its incompatibility with the theories underlying most testing and record-keeping systems (Becher, Eraut and Knight, 1981). What made the theory communicable, however, sustained its vividness in our minds and helped us to convince people of its validity was a metaphor. A teacher's store of information about a child is like a collection of film-clips, each clip portraying a separate incident, usually fairly brief but rich in contextual and interactional detail. Thinking about the child involves reviewing some of these clips, and records and questions serve primarily as *aides-mémoire* to stimulate recall. When one then compares a standardized test-score to a single still picture and a record card to a stereotyped film review, the impossibility of producing a short summary of a child's abilities and progress becomes obvious.

While ostensibly about standards, much of the recent public debate about education has been about images. What is less readily recognized is the extent to which this is also true of much professional discourse. Progressive education, in particular, has been powerfully presented in terms of images: and accounts of progressive classrooms were notable for their image-making as opposed to analytic qualities. Successful advocacy depended on the capacity to create images that excite and inspire teachers rather than prescriptions for classroom practice. Similarly, the contrasting appeal of the 'back to basics' movement has depended on its ability to conjure up linked images of order in the classrooms, at home and on the streets.

This associative use of theory is rarely made explicit, but one might expect it to be linked quite closely to teachers' personalities and their own experience as pupils. Not all teachers I suspect, have the romantic temperament identified by Jackson (1971); but most are more strongly influenced than they realize by images of a diffuse nature which have important consequences for knowledge use. INSET motivates teachers when it taps these emotional roots but possibly helps them more when it challenges and refines them.

A second perspective on the Broudy typology can be obtained by reversing our previous procedure and applying his categories to the use of practical knowledge in theory. *Replication* of practical knowledge is essentially atheoretical and is usually criticized on the grounds that contexts and conditions perpetually change and that mindless repetition is unprofessional and unethical.

The *application* mode is perhaps best conceptualized as the derivation of theory from practical knowledge to get what is commonly referred to as 'grounded theory' (Glaser and Strauss, 1967). Although it is improbable that any theory can be based purely on practice without there being some extraneous theoretical influences, the basic goal of grounded theory remains worthwhile. Perhaps it could be reinterpreted as giving the implicit theoretical knowledge of the participants precedence over that of the observer.

It has long been argued by psychologists that the understanding of a concept lies not in its definition but in knowledge of a range of examples and non-examples. This emphasis on use, however, is usually modified by the assumption that there is a correct meaning, independent of any particular user. Against this it can be argued that, particularly in a field such as education, the meaning of a concept is distinct for every user. Part of the meaning is generally shared by users in the same linguistic community, rather more is shared by close colleagues who regularly converse, but some will always be idiosyncratic. An individual's understanding of a concept is expanded, perhaps even altered by each new example of its use. Practical knowledge is used interpretatively to modify theory; and this can be as true for the academic theorist as for the classroom teacher. The *interpretative* mode of knowledge use necessarily implies an interplay between theory and practice. Indeed the balance between using existing theory to interpret practice and allowing practice to reshape theory is nicely expressed by Piaget's twin concepts of assimilation and accommodation.

That new theoretical ideas can arise by *associative* use of practical knowledge is also well documented, particularly in the literature on creativity. Contact with practical problems and situations can 'spark' ideas that are later found to have theoretical value. This is a powerful argument for involving theoreticians in practical affairs, but one has to take care to see that the resulting ideas are not presented as empirically derived without proper attention to the validity of the evidence.

As I have already hinted, the picture is further complicated by the existence of different kinds of theory. The first kind of theory is set in the context of a discipline and embedded in a network of concepts and ideas that form part of a system of thought. The second kind of theory is best described as a set of generalizations, precepts or maxims about an applied field. This can range from what some would call 'atheoretical' empirical research — found in the academic context — to 'craft knowledge' which is found in the practice context. Then, thirdly, there is the theory that is implicit in all purposeful actiön but rarely articulated or communicated; what Argyris and Schön (1974) call a theory of action. All these forms of theory get used, but not necessarily in the same way or in the same context. In particular the explicit use of the first form of theory may conflict with the implicit use of the third; and the source of the problem may not be readily understood.

Three situations can readily arise:

- The more academic theory may be adopted at the level of talk, what Argyris and Schön call an espoused theory, while the implicit theory of action remains undisturbed.
- The academic theory forms what Fenstermacher (1980) calls a 'set of intentions in storage' for some possible future occasion when circumstances will demand its use.
- The academic theory may be dubbed as 'impractical'.

Hence the pejorative connotation for teachers of the term 'theoretical'.

Contexts of Use

At the risk of oversimplification I wish to distinguish three main contexts for using knowledge about education: the academic context, the school context and the classroom context. Knowledge gained on award bearing CPE courses may be used in all three contexts, but the formal assessment requirements give priority to the specific expectations of the academic context. Knowledge use in the school context, which I have defined as excluding classroom teaching, is similarly influenced by institutional norms. Knowledge use in the classroom context, however, is usually a private affair. This section explores the situational factors affecting knowledge use in each of these contexts before concluding with a brief discussion of how such knowledge is validated.

The first characteristic of the academic context which an outsider will notice is its specialized language. A second is the high value placed on theories rooted in traditional disciplines or established fields of academic study. A third is the obligation to place one's ideas in close relationship to those of other writers by profuse citation. A fourth is the authority structure whereby the epistemological authority upheld by institutional norms and practices is reinforced by the positional authority of assessment. These characteristics limit the ways in which knowledge can be used in academic contexts with important consequences for knowledge acquisition. But these perceived constraints on those whose primary interest in knowledge use lies in other contexts need to be balanced against one major positive feature of the academic context. There is a strong expectation that new knowledge will be acquired by all members of the institution — staff as well as students — that knowledge acquisition is a continuing lifelong process, and that new knowledge will be put to good use. The significance of this expectation that teachers are learners should not be underestimated.

Schools, on the whole, do not share this expectation about new professional knowledge. New knowledge is increasingly sought to cope with external demands for change but rarely for the ongoing improvement of practice. A significant minority of schools attempt to develop or import new knowledge in response to perceived internal problems or new opportunities. But even in these schools it is only some teachers who seek any stimulus for change; others will resist it. In many schools the conservers of the status quo are dominant for long periods of time, and the general attitude towards introducing new knowledge is strongly discouraging (see Miles, 1981, for an excellent analysis of this issue). The extent of the problem is perhaps best understood through socialization theory. People adapt to organizational settings by being socialized into the prevalent norms, thus reducing the uncertainty of not knowing how to behave. The perpetual threat of instability at classroom level creates a strong need for maintaining stability at school level, unless prevailing institutional conditions are perceived as a cause of classroom problems. Thus changes which affect institutional norms and routines will only take hold if accompanied by a degree of resocialization; and the normal response to externally initiated change will be to attempt to minimize its effect. Institutional change is an enormous task, and the introduction and use of new knowledge by individuals is extremely difficult in this context.

One form of knowledge, however, is acquiring increasing importance in the school context: the language of policy. The accountability movement of the last few years and recent legislation have together created an expectation that schools have explicit documented policies. These documents appear to serve a number of purposes including: justifying what the school is doing; indicating that management is in control; informing the general public; and maintaining coherence between the individual actions of staff. Anyone in a position of responsibility likes to have a policy when it comes to interaction with superiors or externals. Without a policy, one is apt to be regarded as irresponsible. Yet the need for such a policy to correspond at all closely with reality is quite a different matter. The language of policy can be used to give the impression of control just as it can also be used to justify real control. Similarly, with coherence. A policy can give people a sense of collective purpose, when expressed with appropriate charisma and conviction, even though it may be dubious whether the policy is in fact being implemented. Thus it is possible for new policy statements to be 'developed' for changing circumstances without disturbing existing norms and practices. All that is needed are people who can speak the language of policy; and this is a purpose for which INSET courses on curriculum and management topics are well tuned. Indeed it can be argued that teachers seeking promotion learn to speak policy language in advance in order to demonstrate their promotion worthiness — an interesting example of anticipatory socialization.

Talking or writing about education is a dominant form of knowledge use in both the academic and school contexts; but the classroom context is fundamentally different. Though talk or writing may influence the perception or conceptualization of action, it does not itself constitute that action. A teacher is not so much in a 'knowing' environment as in a 'doing' environment. While classroom research may describe and interpret teaching activities, it still needs to acknowledge that seeing like an observer cannot be the same as seeing like a teacher. A teacher sees from within the action, not from outside it; and can only temporarily escape from a complex network of moral obligations to review selective aspects of his or her behaviour. Moreover, the classroom like the school is an ordered environment in which norms and routines play an important part. 'People have to develop implicit theories of action in order to make professional life tolerable. There are too many variables to take into account at once, so people develop routines and decision-habits to keep mental effort at a reasonable level. This evolution and internalization of a theory of action is one aspect of learning to become a teacher and coping in the classroom'. To change the routine or question the theory is to reverse the process, to 'draw attention once more to myriads of additional variables, and to raise the possibility of paralysis from information overload and failing to cope'. (Eraut, 1978).

Another important difference between contexts of use is the manner in which knowledge is validated. I have already referred to the high value placed on theory in the academic context, but not to fields of study where this practice is often modified. Debates on curriculum policy, for example, are largely conducted with reference to government reports and the views of curriculum experts. Each subject field has a small group of experts who work within established curriculum traditions and preside over their adaptation and occasional redefinition to fit changing circumstances. They cite research to gain credibility (Anderson, 1981) and may also engage in research themselves. But their policy recommendations do not depend on such research; nor indeed could they depend on it because there is rarely any one-to-one correspondence between curriculum decisions and research findings. Expertise is conferred by membership of a curriculum project team, by office within a professional association, by serving on a government committee or by writing an appropriate 'methods book'; and validation seems to be achieved mainly by citing other experts, though there is usually at least some attempt to establish links with a theoretical base.

Some vestiges of validation by experts remain in the school context, particularly at departmental level where autonomy can be partly protected by asserting subject-specific expertise. But the recent increase in accountability concerns has made validation a largely political process. It has always been important for new ideas to be incorporated into policies, activities and procedures which would gain the political support of a substantial number of teachers. Now the attitudes of parents and governors are also of considerable significance.

How will the school's reputation be affected, and what will be the consequent impact on recruitment? How will it affect the school's vital statistics — examination results, getting pupils into jobs, and places in higher education? Then, there is the effect on student flow into different subjects and the consequences for teacher workload and career prospects. The potential conflict between these increasingly dominant issues and any possible threat to established institutional norms is social and political; and the outcome will determine what kinds of knowledge will be perceived to have most value.

In the classroom context, however, the only significant validators of knowledge are the teachers themselves; and in the absence of any technical culture (Lortie, 1975) the validation process is individual rather than collective. Huberman (1983) argues that one teacher cannot *tell* another something; they can only exchange experiences. To assert unconditionally an idea or technique from another source is to imitate; and to imitate another is professionally unacceptable for all but beginners. Idiosyncracy and self-sufficiency are pervasive professional norms. Other teachers may have a degree of credibility but nothing is valid until one has tried it and, by implication, adapted it for oneself.

Knowledge Use and Acquisition

Professional Learning

Before proceeding to examine for each context in turn the connection between how knowledge is used and how it is acquired, I wish to make two claims about professional learning.

My first claim is that a significant proportion of the learning associated with any change in practice takes place in the context of use. It is customary to talk as if knowledge is first acquired and then subsequently, if circumstances permit, used. I would argue that this is a false assumption, even in the academic context. If somebody encounters a new idea in a lecture, book or seminar and then later refers to it in an essay or project, can we say that the learning takes place only at the moment of the original encounter? Some learning is associated with new input, some with new use; and some, no doubt with the period in between when there may be reflection on input or contemplation of use. Not only does an idea get reinterpreted during use in accord with the reciprocal relationship between theory and practice we discussed earlier, but it may even need to be used before it can acquire any significant meaning for the user. McClaughlin and Marsh (1978) for example report that successful innovations are not fully clarified until people have been using them in the classroom for one or two years; and argue that this clarity can only be acquired during use and cannot be provided by prespecified advice.

My second claim is partly a consequence of the first, that there is little immediate transfer of learning from one context of use to another. Using an idea in one context does not enable it to be used in another context without considerable further learning taking place. The ability to use certain ideas about teaching in academic essays or school documents does not greatly increase the probability of being able to use those ideas in the classroom. Moreover, the language and purpose of academic writing and school documents are so different that there is no guarantee that skills will transfer them from one to the other. A few people are bilingual in the language of academia and the language of school policy, but that does not make them good translators. Indeed it is difficult to translate writing that aims to be precise into writing that needs to be vague.

Learning Associated with Knowledge Use in the Academic Context

We have already discussed several important characteristics of the academic context; specialized language, preponderance of theory, citation of other work, epistemological authority and the expectation of learning. Two others need further explication. First, academic contexts are dominated by written work so knowledge use requires an ability to write. That people learn while writing is a well-known phenomenon, part of the evidence for my more general claim that learning takes place during knowledge use. However people also need to learn to write in an acceptable way; and this is a major preoccupation for students on award-bearing courses, for many of whom the hidden curriculum appears to be: it's not what you think or do but the way you write about it that counts. Yet this skill which much student time is spent in acquiring has relatively little value in the school context, still less in the classroom context.

Second, academic contexts are imbued with the ideal of openmindedness. Courses must not be too narrow. Students should acquire a broader vision, view issues from several perspectives, see many alternative courses of action, expect to handle multiple interpretations, etc. Where rival theories or explanations exist, academic staff are expected to give the student a choice and to avoid being prescriptive. Adhering to these norms, however, constrains a lecturer from spending much time on any one idea; and to focus on any one student's work-context to study the practical implications of an idea would be unfair to the other students. Hence the detailed working-out of an idea is left for students to handle on their own, unless there is strong support from individual tutorials. Though full-time students do at least get some time for this, staff time is primarily allocated to the 'front end' of the process. If discussions do take place it is usually soon after an idea has been introduced and long before it is first used in an essay or project. As a result, some students have considerable difficulty in moving beyond the purely replicative use of new ideas; and staff are cut off from opportunities to enrich their own understanding through dialogue with their students' practical experience. Academic freedom and breadth of study take precedence over knowledge use, and students get relatively little support for working with ideas and making them part of their own thinking.

Learning Associated with Knowledge Use in the School Context

Activities involving knowledge use in the school context include curriculum development and evaluation, management, public relations, development of policies and procedures, case discussions, etc. Unlike the classroom context and the relative privacy of student work for academic purposes, most knowledge use in the school context is visible to others; and validation, though often subtle and indirect, is still a largely public affair. As I suggested earlier, success depends on social relations and institutional micropolitics. Knowledge use for a teacher in this context means more than working out one's own ideas or even writing them down. One has to relate to other people's ideas, to make compromises and coalitions, to persuade people to think again about certain policies and procedures, even to move people to a new view of what they are or should be doing. Then there is a further crucial difference between seeing people persuaded or reconciled to some new policy and seeing that policy implemented at more than a superficial level. Thus one can argue that knowledge use at school level ultimately involves not one but several teachers coming to understand, accept and internalize some new ideas.

Advocates and providers of school-based INSET and post-experience courses with substantial school-based components recognize that knowledge use has to be integrated with ongoing institutional life, but have not always thought through many of the implications. Just as knowledge use in the academic context requires specialized writing skills, knowledge use in the school context requires specialized social and political skills. While some teachers have a natural flair for this, and a few seem forever destined to 'put their foot in it', most teachers have to learn the appropriate skills and attitudes. Moreover, the evaluative and problem-solving skills needed for much school-based development are rarely present to a sufficient extent. Initial training is too early to do more than familiarize teachers, and these skills are unlikely to be developed on the job. Much INSET, however, seems to assume that these knowledge use or process skills already exist; so the focus is on ideas which it is hoped the teacher will feel inspired to implement, without providing assistance with the process of implementation itself.

Another prerequisite for successful school-based INSET is that the ideas the teachers are working with have sufficient merit and practicality to be worth pursuing. Slogans, fads, careerism, and the 'change for its own sake' syndrome can all cause teachers to waste time on projects with little potential for bringing about worthwhile change. More common today is the fear that internally planned changes will be overtaken by external events; and that externally mandated changes will also turn out to have short half-life. Even before the current government tendency to impose wave after wave of change at a ridiculous pace, much school-based INSET tried to do too much too quickly. Perhaps the hurry is because when the pace is more realistic there is greater pressure on the ideas themselves having to be sufficiently attractive to justify the effort being devoted to them.

Finally, if we see knowledge use at school level in terms of teachers taking up new ideas, working with them and developing some new policy or practice, there remains the problem of the relationship between public statements in the school context and private action in the classroom. Even though public talk may be dominated by 'practical considerations', the link between talk and action will still be treated as unproblematic; because to do otherwise would be to threaten the autonomy of teachers within their own classrooms.

Learning Associated with Knowledge Use in the Classroom Context

The old adage is that we never really learn something until we have to teach it. When one is learning for oneself, one is always trying to convince oneself that one understands. Unless one is completely mystified, one prefers to go along with what is written or said in order not to seem foolish. But when one is about to teach, the possibility, indeed probability, of misunderstanding begins to arise. One has to struggle to find out what it really means and how to handle some of the questions and problems that are likely to arise. This is when one is left on one's own, one's confidence saps and one suddenly finds that the books which had previously seemed so adequate seem to gloss over the particular question that is worrying. Then beyond the problem of one's own understanding, there is that of the pupils. For perfect communication one needs to know each pupil's mind — what they already know, how it is structured, how they see this new idea, the nature of their misunderstandings. Impossible though this goal may be, the good teacher moves closer towards it through learning from experience. He or she also needs to find out which approaches to the topic arouse interest and develop understanding, and which pupil activities are productive. Thus a topic which may occupy one or two sessions on an INSET course may require several days of teacher effort and continued learning in order to be used in the classroom; and most of this will be in addition to the normal demands of the daily routine.

So far I have discussed only the simplest kind of change, that which involves teaching new content without necessitating any significant change in teaching style. Much INSET, however, is concerned with teaching processes rather than, or in addition to, changes in content; and it is this problem which I now wish to address. While the main emphasis of the discussion is on learning new processes, I would like to draw attention once more to the problem of unlearning or abandoning existing practices and routines. Changing one's teaching style involves deskilling, risk, information overload and mental strain, as more and more gets treated as problematic and less and less is taken for granted. In addition to practical help there is considerable need for psychological support (Day, 1981).

How then does one learn a new teaching process? One may receive a verbal description of it, written or oral; one may observe one or more people using it; or one may experiment with it oneself. In all three cases one may be learning in isolation, but there is the theoretical possibility of receiving considerable support. Ideas communicated in verbal form need talking through and working out. Observation is enhanced by access to the accounts of the people being observed, by reflective discussion, and by repeated viewing of live or recorded events. Learning from experimentation is dependent on feedback and access to a range of perspectives on what was going on; and will therefore be much facilitated by the accounts of pupils and sympathetic observers.

The limitations of written communication for guiding practice have been analysed by Harris (1982). She points out that it is only those aspects of teaching which are believed to be reliably based on technical knowledge and replicable with minimal adaptation to contextual variations that are capable of being guided by verbal communication alone. The most behavioural technology oriented innovation of the 1970s was probably Engelmann's Language Development at the University of Oregon, but even this project, which was one of the models selected for the 'Follow Through' programme, involved a substantial degree of site-visiting after the initial training workshops. Stallings (1979) concluded from her study of the INSET procedures of all seven Follow Through projects that only long-term interventions were likely to be successful. The sponsor had to be immersed in the field site over a period of years.

Joyce and Showers (1980), who take a more craft-orientated approach, recommend five components of training:

- presentation of theory or description of skill or strategy;
- modelling or demonstration of skills or models of teaching;
- practice in simulated and classroom settings;
- structured and open-ended feedback (provision of information about performance); and
- coaching for application (hands-on, in-classroom assistance with the transfer of skills and strategies to the classroom).

Moreover, their research on INSET indicates that all five are needed when mastery of a new approach is desired.

McLaughlin and Marsh (1978) concluded on the evidence of a major RAND Corporation study of educational innovation that professional learning is an adaptive and heuristic process. Skill-specific training workshops were important but had only a short-run effect unless backed up by longer lasting staff support for the 'mutual adaptation' of the new approach and the teacher's established practices. 'For teachers', they suggested 'the learning task is more like problem solving than like mastering "proven" procedures.'

The lesson from all three major studies of INSET in the United States is that effective INSET needs to be sustained and intensive and to provide individual support in the classroom. The concomitant teacher learning is a long-term process of up to two years' duration involving experimentation, reflection and problem-solving. The common practice of providing input without follow-up is almost bound to fail, both because it underestimates by an order of magnitude the amount of support that is needed and because it fundamentally misconstrues the nature of the professional learning process in the classroom context.

Another useful perspective comes from looking at other performing occupations. The perennial debate about whether teaching is an art, craft or technology neglects this dominant aspect of the teacher's life. The *actor* image is surely closer to classroom reality than that of the sculptor, potter, carpenter or even gardener. Technique is important for the actor but no performance can be analysed down to a set of distinct and separate skills. Interpretation and style are personal yet flexible, for the actor can play several different roles. Performance is improved by observation, discussion, reflection and experiment with only an occasional need for guided practice. Actors, however, have continuing opportunities to learn from each other; and even the most eminent members of the profession still get advice from producers. Perhaps it is no accident that two pioneering studies of INSET which attended to performance issues were written by people with training in drama teaching (Day, 1981; Verrier, 1981).

Most performing occupations offer considerable opportunity to observe master-performers at work both before and after initial training. The promising musician, for example, not only strives to see and hear famous players but deliberately arranges to study with more than one teacher for substantial periods, and to take master classes with yet others. Even after a long period of technical training, developing one's own style takes time; and one needs to see a range of other performers in order to learn, experiment, reflect and create one's own interpretations. In surgery also, practitioners have stated that learning to handle different cases is best accomplished in two stages: (1) watching several experts with differing approaches and having them explain their strategies and ongoing thoughts; and (2) practising while sharing one's thoughts with and receiving comments from an appropriately experienced mentor. Gaining access to experts' accompanying thought processes provides an essential new dimension to what would otherwise be pure observation.[2] While some teacher problem-solving is preactive, much of it has to be reactive with decisions being taken in mid-performance.

Why then, we have to ask, do teachers not get these kinds of opportunity? Several factors are probably important. First, teachers' career structures do not stress quality of classroom performance. There is a long history of debate in the Burnham Committee on this issue, but current pressures stress the managerial responsibility rather than the individual excellence of promoted teachers. Second, although many teachers are still personally motivated by the ideal of quality performance, INSET has rarely been presented to, or perceived by, them as 'a rather natural and on-going activity that is designed to help one to be very very good at something that is very very hard (challenging) to do' (Howey and Joyce, 1978), similar in conception to the musicians' master class. Third, as we concluded earlier, the short-term nature and input emphasis of INSET ignore the real problems of professional learning. Fourth, the notion of observation is alien to the essentially private nature of teaching as an occupation and a potential threat to teacher autonomy.

Beyond these more obvious factors, however, there may be still deeper cultural explanations for the lack of attention to the performance aspects of professional learning. Oakeshott (1962) distinguishes between technical knowledge, which is subject to precise codification and practical knowledge, which is expressed only in the practice and can only be learned in the practice. Performing occupations involve a large proportion of practical knowledge; and this is recognized in most of their training arrangements. Even medicine, which has a strong base in technical knowledge, gives its novices extensive periods of observation and guided practice. Its support for practical learning is far in excess of that accorded to teachers. The problem for teaching is that technical knowledge has much higher status than practical knowledge in schools and universities, so the primary purpose of teaching is perceived as the communication of technical knowledge. This interferes with giving priority attention during training to the acquisition of practical knowledge; and this state of affairs is upheld by the epistemological authority of higher-education institutions which is based on codified technical knowledge.

The learning of practical knowledge is little studied and little discussed. Indeed one probably acquires most of it without realizing that one is learning at all. The dominant conception of learning is our culture — so dominant that children have been socialized into it by the age of 7 or 8 — is that learning involves the explicit acquisition of externalized codified knowledge. My earlier claim that learning takes place during knowledge use as well as beforehand seems to go against the grain, however convinced I am of its validity. Perhaps it is not surprising after all that most INSET is based on the culturally prevalent view of learning.

Notes

1. Most of this chapter is based on the article 'What is learned in In-Service Education and How? A Knowledge Use Perspective', *British Journal In-Service Education* 9, 1, pp. 6–14, 1982.
2. The BBC has used this 'voice over' technique very effectively in programmes on chess and bridge.

Chapter 3

Kinds of Professional Knowledge: Modes of Knowledge Use and Knowledge Creation

Introduction

Hitherto, the debate about professional education has largely focused on the relationship between selection and recruitment, the process of initial qualification (comprising various mixtures of coursework, examinations and supervised work experience) and subsequent practice. Continuing professional education (CPE) has received little attention in many professions; and has only been seriously studied in medicine and schoolteaching. Apart from a natural conservatism, this is probably because the financial arrangements for post-school education are dominated by the presumed needs of 16–21-year-olds.

Behind the numerous policy issues, which have enlivened the debate about the appropriate form and structure for professional education, lies a remarkable ignorance about professional learning. Apart from the limited though valuable literature on professional socialization, we know very little about what is learned during the period of initial qualification besides the content of formal examinations. Still less is known about subsequent learning, how and why professionals learn to apply, disregard or modify their initial training immediately after qualification; and to what extent continuing on-the-job or even off-the-job learning contributes to their professional maturation, updating, promotion or reorientation. Yet without such knowledge, attempts to plan or evaluate professional education are liable to be crude and misdirected.

Moreover, the need to consider professional learning in all its various forms and phases is critical. The work context dominates professional socialization both during periods of practical experience prior to qualification and during the formative early years of professional practice. For every work setting that teaches and inspires the next generation of leaders for the profession, there are others that limit their development and perpetuate the weaknesses of the previous generation. There may be disagreement about where the best practice is to be found, but not about the limited proportion of young professionals who gain access to it. Moreover, even good practice is liable to decay over time, and the characteristics that bring quality to one generation of professionals may seem less important for the next. Both the ongoing development and the diffusion of good practice depend on the capacity of mid-career professionals to continue learning both on and off the job. Thus the quality of initial professional education and post-initial on-the-job learning depends on the quality of practice; and that, in turn, depends on the continuing education of mid-career professionals. The problems of initial qualification cannot be considered to be independent of those of post-qualification learning nor even of those of mid-career professional education.

This chapter provides a framework for studying and developing professional learning which recognizes and builds on the interdependence of its various aspects: — pre- and post-qualification, on-the-job and off-the-job, theory and practice.[1] The first part is about knowledge use and seeks to clarify issues concerning different types of professional knowledge, different modes of application of knowledge, and the influence of context of use on the kind of learning which occurs. The second part then goes on to consider the related problem of knowledge creation. To what extent is professional knowledge created by research or in practice; and what is the relationship between the facilitation of knowledge creation and the promotion of knowledge use? These questions have profound significance for the relationship between higher education and the professions, and hence for the practice of initial and continuing professional education. The principal argument of this final section will be that higher education should reconceptualize its role in professional education. Apart from playing some part in initial and continuing education and pursuing research that contributes to professional knowledge, higher education should aim to enhance the knowledge creation and utilization capacities of individual professionals and professional communities in general.

Different Kinds of Professional Knowledge

In normal circumstances, attempts to map out the knowledge requirements of a profession are associated with the design of training courses or the compilation of regulations concerning entry to the profession. The language of syllabus construction prevails, accompanied perhaps by some homilies about the aims of the profession. Knowledge of the kind that does not normally get included in syllabi will not be considered, as attention is focused on the listing of topics or specialisms. To questions about the significance of a quality like 'getting on with people', the usual response is to treat it as an unchanging personal attribute or to assume that it will be acquired on-the-job with no need for any special provision. In special circumstances it might be academicized and included as 'interpersonal skills' or 'psychology'. Thus knowledge is likely to be labelled and packaged according to traditional assumptions about where and how it will be acquired.

By abandoning such assumptions, it is possible for a researcher who studies the professional at work to draw up quite a different kind of map, and hence to put the problems of professional learning in a different perspective. Two examples of such maps are provided as appendices — one for headteachers and one for social workers. Both illuminate important aspects of the mapping problem. First, there is only limited overlap between such practice-derived maps and syllabi for initial training. Not only are large areas of know-how omitted from training, but where there is common knowledge it is structured, labelled and perceived differently. Secondly, where knowledge is outside traditional syllabi, its description is usually rather imprecise. One is reminded of a fifteenth-century Eurocentric map of the world, in which people and lands beyond the confines of Renaissance culture are barely acknowledged.

A further problem arises from the implicit nature of much professional know-how. Though analyses of such activities as problem-solving, decision-making and communication can be found in books, such codified knowledge is clearly different in kind from that experience-derived know-how which professionals intuitively use. The contribution of this particular kind of book knowledge may be increasing in significance as research into these phenomena expands, but it is still likely to remain subsidiary to the acquisition of practical know-how on the job. There is little evidence as yet that leading practitioners possess this book-knowledge, but what comes easily to some may need 'spelling out' for others. The question persists as to how much professional know-how is essentially implicit, and how much is capable with appropriate time and attention of being described and explained.

Oakeshott (1962), following Aristotle, makes a clear distinction between 'technical knowledge' and 'practical knowledge'. Technical knowledge is capable of written codification; but practical knowledge is expressed only in practice and learned only through experience with practice. Some kinds of practical knowledge are uncodifiable in principle. For example, knowledge which is essentially non-verbal: the tone of a voice or musical instrument, the feel of a muscle or a piece of sculpture, the expression on a face cannot be fully described in writing. Verbal performance, such as teaching or advocacy, which are not fully scripted beyond a brief set of notes, cannot be reduced to simple technical descriptions. Even scripted performances, like those of an actor or pianist, take on their special character because interpretations of quality require the repeatable elements such as the memorization of the script and the reproduction of the sounds to be reduced to instinctive routine.

However, to recognize that uncodifiable practical knowledge exists need not imply that stored written knowledge is irrelevant to such situations. Performances may be written about and discussed by critics and colleagues; and there is a tradition of criticism of non-verbal activities like art and music which, though perhaps overrated, is certainly not futile. The problem lies in the complex, often tenuous, relationship between comment and action. Moreover, as already suggested, the unscripted and intuitive nature of much verbal action makes attempts to describe or criticize it equally difficult. Argyris and

Schön (1974) have noted how divergence between comment and action still persists when commentator and actor are the same person. They argue that professional actions are based on implicit 'theories in use' which differ from the 'espoused theories' used to explain them to external audiences or even to the actor himself. Self-knowledge of performance is difficult to acquire, and self-comment tends to be justificatory rather than critical in intent. I shall return later to this problem of implicit theories, but here we should note that Argyris and Schön regard making such theories explicit and thereby open to criticism as the key to professional learning.

This brings us to two interrelated issues which are central to any general analysis of professional knowledge: the role of theory and the generalizability of practical knowledge. Let us begin with propositional knowledge, which comes closest to traditional academic territory, and explore the significance of the following threefold distinction.

- discipline-based theories and concepts, derived from bodies of coherent, systematic knowledge (*Wissenschaft*);
- generalizations and practical principles in the applied field of professional action; and
- specific propositions about particular cases, decisions and actions.

The validity of the first, discipline-based, form of knowledge, does not usually depend on the field of professional action; and the experts who teach it may not even be members of the profession concerned. Consider, for example, the role of psychologists in management education or the role of biochemists in medicine. However, the relevance of such knowledge to professional training is often difficult to decide, especially when crowded syllabi or job pressures force consideration of priorities. It may be easy to argue that an idea connects with a practical situation in the sense of contributing to some understanding of it or to one possible way of construing it; but difficult to persuade a practitioner that it is worth their while to use it. The process of becoming a professional involves learning to handle cases quickly and efficiently, and this may be accomplished by reducing the range of possible ways of thinking about them to manageable proportions. This leads to intuitive reliance on certain communal practitioners' concepts (Buchmann, 1980), while apparently more valid theoretical ideas get consigned to 'storage' and never get retrieved. Another difficulty, which I shall elaborate later, is that theoretical ideas usually cannot be applied 'off-the-shelf': their implications have to be worked out and thought through. The busy professional with an immediate decision to make or a job to finish by the end of the week is unlikely to find time for that. Thus the functional relevance of a piece of theoretical knowledge depends less on its presumed validity than on the ability and willingness of people to use it. This is mainly determined by individual professionals and their work-context, but is also affected by the way in which the knowledge is introduced and linked to their ongoing professional concerns.

The relevance of generalizations and practical principles in the applied field is rarely in doubt, but their validity is more problematic. The effectiveness of most professionals is largely dependent on the knowledge and know-how they bring to each individual case, problem or brief. Much of this knowledge comes from experience with previous cases, so its use involves a process of generalization. Some idea, procedure or action that was used in a previous situation is considered to be applicable to the new one. While most of the previous cases scanned for this purpose are likely to be the professional's own experience, some may be known only through the reporting of other people's experiences (formally in the literature or on courses, or informally via colleagues or social networks). The generalization used may vary in both scope and explicitness; at minimum Case A is perceived as being like Case K and handled in the same sort of way; at maximum, some practical principle is consciously applied, which is thought to be valid for all cases of a certain type. Semi-conscious patterning of previous experience may also occur, making it difficult for the professional to trace the source of, or even to clearly articulate, the generalization he is using. It might be argued that one way to develop the knowledge base of a profession would be to study this generalization process, to make it more explicit so that it can be criticized and refined, and to give close attention to specifying the conditions under which any given practical principle or generalization was held to apply. Such systematization of practical knowledge, however, is neither part of a practitioner's role nor a popular academic pursuit; and its feasibility may be open to question.

A useful discussion of this problem of generalization is provided by Buchler (1961), whose analysis of 'method' includes the following skeletal framework.

Whoever is said to act methodically (1) chooses a mode of conduct (2) to be directed in a given way (3) to a particular set of circumstances (4) for the attainment of a result. These four simple factors required by the conjunction of 'art' and 'method' can each assume different forms. The mode of conduct adopted may consist in (1a) established practice, in (1b) established practice modified by idiosyncratic technique, or in (1c) essentially idiosyncratic, private practice. Whatever procedure is adopted, it may be utilized (2a) strictly and in accordance with prescription, or (2b) loosely, variably, and with a discretionary relation to prescription, or (2c) uniquely, in consequence of predominant reliance on insight. The circumstances under which the procedure is utilized may be (3a) definitely classifiable circumstances, or (3b) circumstances ranging from the expected and classified down to the minimal circumstances that would allow the procedure. And the result toward which the activity aims may be (4a) an envisaged or familiar type of result, or (4b) an indefinite result accepted as such in terms of desirability, or (4c) a relatively novel result. These forms are not exhaustive, but their possible combinations help to explain the differences that prevail when we speak variously of the art of surgery, the art of writing fiction, the art of management, the art of building, or the art of swimming. (Buchler, 1961)

Commenting on Bentham's concept of a 'tactic faculty', Buchler distinguishes between two possible meanings.

One of these has to do with a prepared order eligible for application to appropriate circumstances; the other has to do with a power of adjusting practice to variable circumstances. The one emphasizes a fund or store of techniques whose function is anticipatory; the other emphasizes resourceful practice precisely in the face of the unanticipated. (*ibid.*)

According to the model of practice which is believed to be desirable, the process of professional education will need to take a very different form. A combination of (1a), (2a), (3a) and (4a) leads to an emphasis on methodic training, careful analysis and planned activity; while a combination of (1c), (2c), (3b) and (4c) leads to an emphasis on variety of experience, responsiveness, invention and quick reading of a situation as it develops. The former can bypass theory by teaching methodic procedures from an apparently atheoretical perspective, the latter is likely to emphasize the primacy of personal experience and lack of time for theoretical deliberation.

Many professions involve a combination of regular routine procedures of Buchler's first type and decision-making situations that more nearly correspond to the second. Proficiency on routine is essential for competence, but it is the handling of non-routine matters which is responsible for excellence. Not surprisingly, the balance of emphasis during professional qualification is frequently in dispute.

Another distinction, related to Buchler's but originating from medicine, is that between well-defined problems and ill-defined problems (Elstein, Schulman and Sprafka, 1978). For a problem to be well-defined, there must be one clearly preferable solution and a small change in the problem results in only small changes in the solution. Where the latter condition still holds but more than one potentially acceptable solution exists the problem is described as 'moderately well-defined'. In either case, there is wide consensus concerning the range of differential diagnoses and treatments and the principles underlying their selection. A formalized approach to teaching this kind of problem-solving is clearly appropriate, and one might expect computer-based simulations to be of considerable value. For ill-defined problems, however, there may be no solution; or there may be more than one solution, with small changes in the problem requiring large changes in the solution. Here the main pitfall is turning to tried and tested treatments without attempting to engage in more appropriate problem-solving strategies.

Returning to our original problem of mapping professional knowledge and know-how, one notable feature is the prominence of non-technical knowledge in practice-based maps as opposed to syllabus-based maps. Communication is perhaps the most widely acknowledged example, so it is worth considering at greater depth. Communication is often treated as a set of 'basic skills' or 'competencies', which are expected to be mastered at subdegree level. Thus the need for the further development of special qualities in communication is implicitly denied, and its academic status is correspondingly low. However, a map of the communications within a particular profession, which takes into account the full range of communication modes, purposes and contexts, will soon reveal how limited is the extent of what is taught in formal education. There is even a suspicion that some communication capabilities are worsened rather than improved by the process of professionalization. Much professional communication involves specialized knowledge; and the nature of that knowledge and its mode of organization constitute the principal difficulty. A science teacher is concerned not only with communication in general but with explaining concepts of particular significance and complexity. The interaction of a solicitor with a client involves not only ascertaining a client's wishes but translating them into legal form, translating the relevant legal knowledge back into everyday language, and confirming the client's choice against other carefully explained options (Cain, 1983).

Communication involves skills which can be improved by practice with feedback, but that is not all. It has to be tuned to person and context. The good communicator draws on 'knowledge of people' and has to be able to 'read situations'. We discuss the latter below, when we come to problems of knowledge use, but let us now consider 'knowledge of people'. This can be both particular, as with knowledge of individual colleagues or long-term clients, and general, as with characteristics of children of various ages, people from certain localities or members of distinctive cultural groups. With this more general 'knowledge of people', the problem is how to learn from experience without resorting to stereotypes. Such knowledge is merely contributing to the more central task of getting to know individuals. But how do people acquire the commitment and the ability to get to know individuals? What is the role in such learning of coursework in human relations, psychology or multicultural perspectives in society? What is the effect of different types of first-hand experience with people; or of the process of professional socialization?

Learning to work in teams and in organizations, is another area where professional education is often found lacking. It also raises problems of when the undeniably positive qualities of 'getting on with people' and 'fulfilling one's role' shade into undesirable attributes such as 'uncritical conformity' and 'value complacency'.

Professional ethics is a particularly difficult area of knowledge to handle. To discuss moral dilemmas arising from casework seems relevant and straightforward, until one recognizes that many proposed courses of action conflict with organizational policy or with professional norms. To discuss more strategic value issues about the role of a profession or the way in which it distributes its time and effort is even more threatening. These problems are exacerbated by a number of other factors. One is the implicit nature of many value assumptions: they are embedded in personal habits and professional traditions, and digging them out is difficult, painful and usually unpopular. Second, a particular feature of most professional work is the need for confidence and credibility: the professional has to believe that he is doing right. To challenge somebody's work may undermine their confidence without diverting them from following traditional courses of action. Yet clearly professional traditions have to be challenged on both technical and ethical grounds. Is a common practice still the most effective? Whose interests does a particular policy serve? Usually, technical and ethical questions cannot be wholly separated; but the timing and manner of their asking remains one of the most intractable problems of professional education. Perhaps this is an area where interprofessional groups have something special to offer?

Modes of Knowledge Use

Behind Oakeshott's distinction between technical and practical knowledge lies an assumption that technical knowledge is used systematically and explicitly while practical knowledge is used idiosyncratically and implicitly. This is true for some kinds of knowledge and some modes of use; but to deny other possibilities is to put unacceptable limits on the symbiotic development of theory and practice. If we create expectations that theory is only used systematically, we direct attention from learning to use it in other ways and encourage its early dismissal as 'irrelevant'. Non-systematic use of theory can be found if we look for it, for example in some of the 'theories in use' identified by Argyris and Schön or implicit in the way some professionals interpret situations. But this kind of use is rarely acknowledged.

Similarly, research into professional practice is beginning to explore the scope for making practical knowledge more explicit, and thus more capable of being disseminated, criticized, codified and developed. The availability of increasingly unobtrusive recording equipment has transformed the nature of reflective self-evaluation and peer-group analysis of professional activities. There will always be questions about authenticity when describing the ongoing thinking of the actor — crowded thoughts cannot be fully remembered, the tendency to reconstruct the logic of events after they happen is part of the way our minds work, quite apart from any possible intent to deceive. But such attempts at explicit portrayal of professional reasoning are important for the further development of professional knowledge.

Moreover, the distinction between technical knowledge and practical knowledge becomes virtually impossible to maintain in any linguistic analysis of professional discourse. 'Intelligent' as a technical concept is imported into practical situations where the term 'bright' is already in common use and the term 'wise' has a subtly different significance. The term 'average' cannot sustain its technical meaning because it has acquired a negative connotation, and because the reference group is rarely given.

These problems stem from trying to classify knowledge by its source alone, by whether it comes from books or from personal experience or even from books describing personal experience. It is equally important, for professional education, to consider the mode and context of use. The concept of 'mode of use' was introduced in Chapter 2 with a discussion of the typology developed by Broudy *et al*. (1964) which we will now elaborate further. This distinguishes between four modes of knowledge use i.e.,:

> replication;
> application;
> interpretation; and
> association.

The replicative mode of knowledge use dominates a large proportion of schooling and a significant part of higher education. It is characterized by close similarity between the epistemological context in which the knowledge is acquired and rehearsed and that in which it is used. Typically, the knowledge does not require processing or reorganization by the user, but gets presented for assessment in a form that differs little from the package received from textbook or teacher. Although memory is now increasingly recognized as a cognitive process and performance is known to be enhanced by reprocessing, the learning task is typically not treated in this way. Practical knowledge also gets used replicatively in routine, repetitive tasks; but it is argued that this is not professional work or that the professional aspect lies in the opportunity the task provides for professional communication with a client, e.g., when nurses and social workers assess clients' needs while performing routine caring or form-filling tasks.

To use knowledge applicatively is to do more than just use it in an applied setting. If a particular 'application' has been coached and rehearsed, then further repetition of it is purely replicative. But where such knowledge is used in circumstances at all different from those previously encountered, more than replication is involved. Application, however, still implies working with rules or procedures, even if occasionally these are of one's own devising. These enable one to translate knowledge into prescriptions for action on particular situations, and it is normal to describe their use as 'right' or 'wrong'. When people refer to technology as 'applied science', they imply that rules or procedures exist for applying scientific knowledge to certain practical situations and that these are clearly 'right'. Sometimes this claim is justified, sometimes it is only an attempt to give high status to a particular branch of technological knowledge.

When a distinction is made between technical or vocational education and professional education, appeal is made to terms like 'understanding' and 'judgment'. By implication, technical/vocational education is confined to the replicative and applicative modes while professional education involves something more. So let us attempt to unravel what is meant by 'understanding' and 'judgment'. Broudy identifies understanding with the interpretative mode of knowledge use. Concepts, theories and intellectual disciplines provide us with ways of construing situations; and our understanding is shaped by the interpretative use of such theoretical knowledge. Perspectives or 'ways of seeing' provide the basis for our understanding of situations and hence the grounds for justifying our actions, but cannot be simply designated as right or wrong.

The problem for professional education is twofold. First, certain systems of thought or paradigms dominate a profession's thinking in such a way that they are passed on unquestioned from one generation to the next. For example, the field of special education was conceptually organized for many years according to medically-derived categories of 'handicap'. Historically, this was advantageous in acquiring resources to cater for the needs of children; but it has hindered the development of ways of thinking that are more educationally constructive. Theories within well-established paradigms are found relevant because their concepts and terminology are widely used by practitioners, even though they may not offer any other practical advantage.

The second problem is the converse of the first. To make practical use of concepts and ideas other than those embedded in well-established professional traditions requires intellectual effort and an encouraging work-context. The meaning of a new idea has to be rediscovered in the practical situation, and the implication for action thought through. Yet instead of recognizing the significance of this intellectual task, students are led to believe that the use of theory is either simple and obvious or wholly impossible. No model of working with ideas is presented, nor do they find much evidence of it in the busyness of practice.

The interpretative use of knowledge also plays some part in that mysterious quality we call 'professional judgment'. But judgment is not the same as understanding: the brilliant political scientist or commentator does not often make a successful politician. Judgment involves practical wisdom, a sense of purpose, appropriateness and feasibility; and its acquisition depends, among other things, on a wealth of professional experience. But this experience is not used in a replicative or applicative mode; nor is it fully interpreted, for much practical experience accumulates with only limited time for reflection. On the one hand, we expect the wise judge to have had a sufficient range of experience to ensure a balanced perspective, to prevent 'overinterpretation' from the experience of only one or two previous cases of an apparently similar nature. While on the other we expect an intuitive capacity to digest and distil previous experience and to select from it those ideas or procedures that seem fitting or appropriate.

Broudy calls this semi-conscious, intuitive, mode of knowledge use associative and suggests that it often involves metaphors or images. These do not derive only from practical experience but also serve as carriers for theoretical ideas. For example, a group of orthopaedic surgeons who found that they could not make their theoretical knowledge of biomechanical engineering explicit, were shown to use implicit images to carry engineering principles. A ruler, for instance, bends along its flat axis but not along its thin axis; and the image of a ruler allows a surgeon to retain tacit knowledge of the engineering principles involved without having explicit understanding of the exact formulae (Farmer, 1981).

Another profession where imagery is important is schoolteaching (Buchmann, 1980). Progressive education, in particular, has been powerfully presented in terms of images: and accounts of progressive classrooms are notable for their image-making as opposed to analytic qualities. The success of influential educators has been in their capacity to create images that excite and inspire teachers rather than in their prescriptions for classroom practice.

I have used Broudy's typology, not because it is the only one available, but because it opens up the issue of knowledge use for wider consideration; and, I hope, empirical investigation as well. In most professions thinking about the theory–practice relationship is still dominated by the applicative mode of use and one or two dominant interpretative paradigms. This limits both the potential use of theory and our capacity to interpret, refine and improve practice. Moreover the whole process of practical reasoning is almost totally neglected. Is this because we cannot define it, we cannot find room for it, or we cannot decide whether it belongs with the theoretical or practical component of professional preparation? When a group of orthopaedic surgeons were interviewed about their own professional learning, they highlighted a need to observe a number of experts tackling ill-defined problems, each in their own style, and for an additional commentary by each expert explaining what he was doing and thinking at the time (Farmer, 1981). Resources of this kind are rarely put at the disposal of professionals in either initial or continuing education.

Contexts of Use

The third dimension of my conceptual framework for studying professional learning concerns the context of knowledge use. Together with an analysis of types of knowledge and modes of use, the careful characterization of contexts of use allows us to complete a users' map of the knowledge-base of professional practice.

One common assumption is that practical knowledge is context bound, while theoretical knowledge is comparatively context free. But is this true? Let us first consider knowledge of people as an example of practical knowledge, which figures prominently in the appended knowledge maps for headteachers and social workers. Can the acquisition of such knowledge be easily separated from its intended use? We may need knowledge of people in order to decide how to approach them (planning a communication), how to allocate tasks to them (delegation), how to interpret responses from them (understanding a client's concern or brief), how to motivate them (supervising or teaching) or whether to seek their advice (consulting). Ideally, each of these uses would draw upon a different set of encounters with the people concerned; but in practice there is likely to be some overlap. One has met a person only in different contexts from that now being considered, and is faced with the problem of generalization.

Of course, the idea that one first acquires knowledge of a person and later applies it is itself profoundly misleading. One accumulates knowledge of a person through a series of encounters without necessarily attempting to digest or summarize them. It is only when some action is needed that one rehearses one's memories of these incidents, deliberates upon them and decides what to do. This process of deliberation prior to action (or even inaction) is as much part of one's learning as the original encounters. The encounter probably determines how the knowledge is originally stored, but its later processing is mainly influenced by the context of use. Where notes and records are kept, they may serve as *aides-mémoire* as well as summaries, triggering the retrieval of further information from memory.

Our study of how primary schoolteachers make judgments about children revealed precisely this processorial quality (Becher *et al.*, 1981). Information about individual children was stored as memories of little incidents and brief encounters. Although notes appeared to give decontextualized information, talk about them inevitably began by supplying further information to set them in context. Where organized for use, knowledge of children was to guide the teacher's interaction with them and to inform practical classroom decisions about what to assign, how to give feedback, whom to group with whom, etc. The knowledge tended to be provisional and formative, and had to be completely reprocessed for inclusion in more definitive documents like records and reports.

In more bureaucratized professional settings, however, different people may see the client each time. Then there is no personal memory of previous encounters, only the file. Case records become more 'real' than the clients themselves, the need to complete them dominates the encounter and the types of knowledge they demand determine what the interviewer seeks.

I argued in Chapter 2 that the context of use also affects the learning of theoretical knowledge, and that it is misleading to think of knowledge as first being acquired and then later put to use. Not only does an idea get reinterpreted during use, but it may even need to be used before it can acquire any significant meaning for the user. Thus its meaning is likely to have been strongly influenced by previous contexts of use; and the idea will not be transferable to a new context without further intellectual effort. For example, the ability of a schoolteacher to use certain ideas about teaching in an academic essay, or even in a school policy document, does not greatly increase the probability of them being used in the classroom.

My analysis in Chapter 2 of knowledge use by schoolteachers identified three main types of context, each of which is also found in many other professions: an academic context, a policy-discussion context and an action context. Let us consider each in turn. The academic context is characterized by written communication in certain traditional formats: research papers and monographs for faculty; essays, examinations and dissertations, possibly even projects, for students. The demands of these formats determine the general pattern of knowledge use. The possession of knowledge is demonstrated by erudition and multiple citation of other work. Experiments are presented as standardized accounts. Action has no part to play, for only knowledge confers status. Students' demonstration of their knowledge through assessed work is private and its evaluation non-negotiable.

In policy discussion contexts, however, knowledge use is public, and the validity of knowledge can be a matter of public debate. Knowledge use means more than working out one's own ideas or even writing them down. One has to relate to other people's ideas, to make compromises and coalitions, to persuade people to think again about certain policies and procedures, even to move people to a new view of what they are or should be doing. Then there is a further crucial difference between seeing people persuaded or reconciled to some new policy and seeing that policy implemented at more than a superficial level. Thus one can argue that knowledge use by a team or organization involves not one but several people coming to understand, accept and internalize new ideas. Just as knowledge use in the academic context requires specialized writing skills, knowledge use in the policy discussion context requires specialized social and political skills.

An important point made by Cronbach *et al.* (1980), when assessing the impact of policy evaluation is that research findings and new ideas affect decision-making indirectly rather than directly, often without acknowledgment. They get used interpretatively rather than applicatively and influence people by changing the nature of discussion about a problem or by introducing new perspectives, not by persuading them that Option A is better than Option B. The language of policy, unlike academic language, has to be vague and general both to be widely applicable and to command consensus or at least general support.

Finally, there is a range of action contexts, which differ widely between professions but nevertheless share a few common characteristics. Unlike the academic, the practising professionals are in a 'what ought to be done' environment. The aim is not knowledge but action. Moreover they have to believe in what they are doing, rather than question it, because they take responsibility for the consequences. The result is an essentially pragmatic orientation which stresses first-hand experience in preference to abstract principles. So there is a certain subjectivism in the approach, a scepticism about 'book learning' and a belief in the individuality of each distinct case.

Freidson's (1971) assessment of the impact of the clinical consulting context on doctors includes the following comments:

One whose work requires practical application to concrete cases simply cannot maintain the same frame of mind as the scholar or scientist: he cannot suspend action in the absence of incontrovertible evidence or be skeptical of himself, his experience, his work and its fruit. In emergencies he cannot wait for the discoveries of the future. Dealing with individual cases, he cannot rely solely on probabilities or on general concepts or principles: he must also rely on his own senses. By the nature of his work the clinician must assume responsibility for practical action, and in doing so he must rely on his concrete, clinical experience.

Each man builds up his own world of clinical experience and assumes personal, that is, virtually individual, responsibility for the way he manages his cases in that world. The nature of that world is prone to be self-validating and self-confirming, if only because by hypothesizing indeterminacy the role of scientific (that is, generally agreed or shared) knowledge and the role of others' opinions in practice are minimized. This is not to say that such knowledge and opinion are not used, only that thinking in terms of unique individual cases places the burden of proof on the particular rather than on the general. (Freidson, 1971)

Jackson (1968) and Lortie (1975) have noted similar qualities in primary schoolteachers, particularly with regard to individualism, pragmatism and uncertainty. But other features of the classroom bear less resemblance to the consulting room. The doctor has a little, though not much time to reach a decision as the queue in the waiting-room lengthens. The lawyer preparing a brief has more time, as does the clergyman visiting a bereaved person; though both have to be prepared to meet the unexpected. But the teacher has no time at all to reflect: choices made during the preparation of teaching may be decision-governed, but those made during the course of teaching are largely intuitive. The pressure for action is immediate, and to hesitate is to lose. The whole situation is far less under control. To adapt a metaphor of Marshall McLuhan's, action in the classroom is *hot action*, while action in the consulting room is usually rather cooler.

Where the action is cool, the consideration of new ideas is much more feasible. There will still be pressures of time, but there is less direct interference between deliberation and action. There is more scope for limited trial and experiment. Personal style is less pervasive than in performing occupations like teaching, though still not unimportant. Where the action is hot, however, people have to develop habits and routines in order to cope; and self-awareness is more difficult as there is little opportunity to notice or think about what one is doing. Significant new knowledge about teaching cannot be used without being integrated into a person's overall teaching style, and thereby modifying both the most fundamental and the most intuitive aspects of their practice. The process of experiment, evaluation, adjustment and routinization takes considerable time; and it is psychologically stressful because it involves deskilling, risk, and information overload when more and more gets treated as problematic while less and less gets taken for granted. Yet professional autonomy/isolation limits collegial support and makes practical help in the action context extremely unlikely. Thus while there may be many attitudinal barriers to integrating new knowledge into cold action, improving hot action raises major practical barriers as well.

Knowledge Creation and Development

The literature on knowledge creation and development is organized around assumptions which I cannot wholly support. The principal issues addressed are (1) research policy: what kind of research should be funded and how should such funding be arranged; (2) the impact of research on policy: how can researcher links with policy makers be improved to make research both more useful and more influential; and (3) research utilization: how can the use of research findings be increased by practitioners 'in the field' (Rich, 1981). The principal actors are the research community, whose perspective dominates most of this literature, and the governments upon whose sponsorship they depend. By implication, other professionals are not only excluded from the knowledge creation process but assumed to suffer from knowledge deficiency, either because they ignore research findings or because their work does not fit the expectations or aspirations of government. Though there is now increasing recognition that knowledge may be used interpretatively (Weiss, 1977), knowledge is still defined according to the criteria of the research community alone — as codified, published and public.

A much broader framework is needed for studying the creation of professional knowledge; and the situation looks very different if we move the academic researcher from the centre of the universe. First we notice that new knowledge is created also by professionals in practice, though this is often of a different kind from that created by researchers. Moreover, in some professions nearly all new practice is both invented and developed in the field, with the role of academics being confined to that of dissemination, evaluation and *post hoc* construction of theoretical rationales. In others, knowledge is developed by practitioners 'solving' individual cases and problems, contributing to their personal store of experience and possibly that of their colleagues but not being codified, published or widely disseminated. Second, my earlier analysis of professional learning suggests that knowledge use and knowledge creation cannot be easily separated. The interpretative use of an idea in a new context is itself a minor act of knowledge creation, perhaps more original than one of the more derivative types of academic paper. Moreover these two creation processes may not even be distinguishable because new practice rarely gets invented from scratch: ideas from the published literature usually have an influence somewhere, even if it is not realized at the time.

Yet another perspective emerges if we look at the influence of practice on research, in particular at how problems for study are selected, defined and interpreted. Some of the possibilities are indicated by Weiss's three models of research use: decision-driven, knowledge-driven and interactive. In the first case research is primarily aimed at informing a particular decision: much commissioned research and evaluation is of this kind, so also is knowledge creation by practitioner problem-solving. Knowledge-driven research, however, aims to contribute to a specific discipline or field of study. It is judged less by utility than by theoretical significance and originality; and it carries the highest status in the academic community. The interactive model is less well defined, because,

> the process is not of linear order from research to decision but a disorderly set of interconnections and back-and-forthness that defies neat diagrams. All kinds of people involved in an issue area pool their talents, beliefs, and understandings in an effort to make sense of a problem. (Weiss, 1977)

Such interaction is rare because of the autonomous nature of research institutions and professional communities, but I shall return to this problem in my final section.

Finally we should not underestimate the degree to which unsystematized personal experience affects the knowledge-creation process. In talking to educational researchers, for example, I have often noticed how the influences of their own or their family's education, or their friends in the teaching profession, or the anecdotes of their students have subtly affected their work. It would not be unreasonable to suggest that the more time researchers spend listening to practitioners, the more their research will attend to practitioners' perspectives and concerns — even without any conscious intention that this should happen. Perhaps we could call this the 'implicit interaction model'.

Having thus broadened our view of the knowledge-creation process, let us examine some of the factors which constrain its ability to serve the professions and the public. First, there is the distribution and allocation of resources. Within higher-education professions like medicine are well resourced while professions like teaching are not. Banking and insurance are characterized by large firms whose research departments dominate the knowledge-creation process. In areas like planning and engineering there is a complex interrelationship between academic and commercial research. The least resources are found where there is no clearly defined commercial sector, e.g., social work, or where there is a preponderance of small practices, e.g., solicitors.

Secondly, the kind of research pursued reflects particular organizational interests. Though academic researchers are freer to choose what to do, they are still heavily influenced by prevailing norms and traditional sources of funding. The varied types of knowledge we reviewed at the beginning of this chapter are accorded differential status (Bergendahl, 1984); and some lines of research may never be developed because they are considered to contribute little to the standing of the department or the career prospects of the individual researcher. That research in commercial firms serves particular interests is more obvious, though here also the research may still be of considerable public benefit. The problem is not that existing research effort is harmful or wasteful but that, when seen from the perspective of professional practice, it looks unbalanced and likely to remain so. Some kinds of knowledge are developed while others are neglected; some people's interests are well served while others are not.

Thirdly, the knowledge-development potential of practitioners is under-exploited. Many of the reasons for this have already been discussed. Much of their knowledge creation is particularistic, transferred from one case to another only by associative or interpretative generalization. Further reflection and discussion can enhance the knowledge derived from case experience and organize it in ways that encourage its further development. But there is no tradition of engaging in such behaviour in most professional work contexts; and knowledge development receives little attention in an action-oriented environment. Moreover, communication between practitioners is such that only a small proportion of newly created knowledge gets diffused or disseminated. Thus there is no cumulative development of knowledge over time: the wheel is reinvented many times over.

Finally, the intellectual problems of attempting to describe, share and develop practical knowledge so that it becomes more widely available are formidable indeed. This in itself is likely to be offputting to researchers and practitioners alike. Practical knowledge is never tidy, an appropriate language for handling much of it has yet to be developed. Prolonged interaction between researchers and practitioners will probably be necessary, and that is not easy for either to arrange. The researcher–practitioner team will need to combine the analytic skills of the original researcher with the creative skills of the practical problem-solver, the observational skills of the naturalist with the communication skills of the novelist.

Higher Education and the Professions

To conclude this chapter I wish to present a case for reconceptualizing the relationship between higher education and the professions. This case rests largely on arguments already presented, so the outline is brief.

The quality of initial professional education depends to a considerable degree on the quality of practice; and that in turn is influenced by the continuing education of the practitioners. Continuing education needs to be viewed in the broad sense of all kinds of further learning beyond initial qualification, not in the narrow sense of attending courses. Thus it includes informal learning and on-the-job learning.

The improvement of both initial and continuing professional education is dependent on a broader view of what constitutes professional knowledge and know-how, more information about how professionals use and develop such knowledge, and a deeper consideration of how professionals learn.

Neither the creation of new knowledge outside traditional academic territory nor the redevelopment of syllabus knowledge for use in practical contexts are priority concerns among either the academic or the professional community. Responsibility for the development and diffusion of practice-created knowledge appears also to fall between two stools.

The kind of interaction that would be most likely to promote the development and diffusion of practice-created knowledge can be found in isolated examples of collaborative research and mid-career professional education. Thus it is suggested that knowledge creation, knowledge use and continuing education are highly interdependent. Such continuing education could be for the academics as well as the practitioners, feeding both into their research and into their contributions to initial professional education.

The barriers to practice-centred knowledge creation and development identified in the last section, are most likely to be overcome if higher education is prepared to extend its role from that of creator and transmitter of generalizable knowledge to that of *enhancing the knowledge creation capacities* of individuals and professional communities. This would involve recognizing that much knowledge creation takes place outside the higher-education system, but is nevertheless limited by the absence of appropriate support structures and the prevailing action-orientation of practical contexts.

Hence higher-education institutions and professional communities need to establish closer relations and to assume joint responsibility for knowledge creation, development and dissemination. The foregoing analysis suggests that some of the most fruitful joint ventures might be:

- collaborative research projects into the acquisition and development of important areas of professional knowledge and know-how;
- problem-oriented seminars for groups of researchers and mid-career professionals, including where relevant members of other professions;
- a jointly planned programme of continuing education opportunities for mid-career professionals which assists them: to reflect on their experience, make it more explicit through having to share it, interpret it and recognize it as a basis for future learning; and to escape from their experience in the sense of challenging traditional assumptions and acquiring new perspectives. The programme would also provide follow-up support with subsequent 'on-the-job' activities.

Finally it should be noted that throughout this chapter we have been primarily concerned with kinds of knowledge, qualities and skills which professionals might legitimately be expected to develop throughout their careers. While the updating of syllabus-type knowledge should not be neglected, I believe it is more likely to follow from, rather than lead into, a more general emphasis on continuing knowledge creation and development. In few areas of professional knowledge is it appropriate to talk of total mastery or a competence plateau, above which further development of expertise is unnecessary. Yet our qualifying system encourages the rigid separation of initial and continuing professional education. More interaction between the two and more explicit discussion of professional development during the post-qualification period would better prepare young professionals for their future problems and obligations; and awaken the interest of mid-career professionals in facilitating the 'on-the-job' learning of their younger colleagues.

Note

1. This chapter is based on the article 'Knowledge creation and knowledge use in professional contexts', *Studies in Higher Education,* 10, 2, pp. 117–33, 1985.

Chapter 4

The Acquisition and Use of Theory by Beginning Teachers

This chapter explores in some detail the problems and opportunities for acquiring and using theory during PGCE courses.[1] These one-year full-time courses are required for graduates wishing to become qualified schoolteachers. 60 per cent of the time is spent on school experience and teaching practice, so the course has a very practical orientation with theory being confined to a relatively minor role. Teachers' theoretical knowledge of the subject(s) they teach is not covered, though it is of course very important. But issues of how they represent and communicate subject matter are within its scope. Thus the theories under discussion will relate to classroom events, to school policy and practice, and to the effect of influences across the school's boundary with the community.

More heat than light is created by perpetually contrasting theory with practice, and by assuming that there is only one kind of theory. We need to introduce student teachers to different kinds of theory, to share with them the discussion about using theory in practice and deriving theory out of practice, and to develop their capacity to theorize about what they are doing. As Russell (1988) reports:

> We are increasingly convinced that the image one holds of the relationship between theory and practice can significantly influence understanding of the personal learning process, at every stage in one's development of the professional knowledge of teaching. (Russell, 1988)

Both the concept of theory and the process of theorizing must be demystified. I shall begin by providing definitions of two key terms; 'theory' and 'theorize', as these are fundamental to my analysis. Theory is used in both a public and a private sense. Publicly available theories — Piagetian Theory, Symbolic Interactionist Theory, Human Capital Theory, and so on — are systems of ideas published in books, discussed in classes and accompanied by a critical literature which expands, interprets and challenges their meaning and their validity. By extension, the term theory is generalized to include collections of such individual theories whose identity is proclaimed by the title of a course or a location in a library. Private theories are ideas in people's minds which they use to interpret or explain their experience. These may be private versions of publicly available theories, or they may not be traceable in any publicly available form. Their use may not be explicit, indeed they may only be inferred from observing someone's behaviour; but they must be at least capable of explicit formulation.

My definition of theory, therefore, is framed to allow for both public and private theories, and extended to include a valuational element in addition to interpretation and explanation: Educational theory comprises concepts, frameworks, ideas and principles which may be used to interpret, explain or judge intentions, actions and experiences in educational or education-related settings. This definition excludes the use of theory to mean something opposed to, or apart from, practice; because this leads all too easily to the absurd conclusion that an idea is only 'theoretical' if it never gets used.

My definition of the term 'theorize' also needs justification, because in common usage to theorize is to construct a theory. I shall be arguing below in some detail that both the complex and unique nature of practical situations and the manner in which publicly available theories are formulated makes the routine application of such theories to practice impossible. Using a theory involves giving it a contextually specific meaning, so there is always an element of reinterpretation or reconstruction; and the intellectual effort is often at least as great as in constructing a private theory. Thus it is unhelpful to suggest that the construction of private theory is significantly different from the reconstruction of public theory. Accepting this argument allows me to define 'theorize' in much more general terms: To theorize is to interpret, explain or judge intentions, actions and experiences.

Given the many ways in which people 'pick up' ideas, and their tendency to forget where they got them, it would be exceedingly impractical to adopt a definition of 'theorize' which depended on the nature of the source or even on knowing whether an idea was original or not. Both putting public theories into use and reviewing private theories already in use involve the process of theorizing; and the distinction between them is not always clear. Theory may be acquired from many different sources, for example pre-course experience, school experience, student colleagues, university teaching and reading. Teaching strategies of beginning teachers are generally acknowledged to be strongly influenced by their earlier experiences as pupils. People tend to teach, or in a few cases to avoid teaching, in a similar manner to that in which they themselves were taught. Similarly, student teachers already possess a considerable quantity of theory before they even begin their courses. Their reflections on their own experience of schooling are not the only important component of this theoretical pre-knowledge. Many other aspects of their lives will have contributed to their 'knowledge of people' and their 'theories of human behaviour'. Such theories need not be clearly formulated or even explicitly stated to influence their later behaviour as teachers. Moreover, there are many ideas about education freely circulating in the press, on television and in everyday conversation, to which they are unlikely to be immune. These last may have been subjected to at least some critical argument, but it is doubtful, apart from those cases where relevant material was included in first degrees, whether any of this theoretical pre-knowledge will have been subjected to any systematic reflection and scrutiny. To what extent, then, we may ask, should a PGCE course aim to make explicit this pre-course personal knowledge so that it may be criticized, built on or evaluated? At Sussex, this process begins with a student autobiography (see Grumet, 1989 for a more prolonged autobiographical approach) handed in on arrival and is linked to reflection on early observations in schools. However, the most extensive programme of reflection on prior experience is that reported by Korthagen (1988) from Utrecht where it is also linked to the concurrent learning of the main subject of mathematics:

> Two aspects are particularly noteworthy. First of all, learning to reflect is not limited to the pedagogical component of the programme. It is also a recurring principle on the mathematical side. Students are encouraged to reflect not only on the subject content, but also to consider the way in which they help or cooperate with others, as well as their awareness of feelings, attitudes and personal goals. Thus the mathematical side of the programme and the specific professional preparation are closely linked.
>
> A second major aspect of the programme is that reflection is stressed even before students embark on their practical teaching. The idea behind this is that student teachers can be armed against socialization into established patterns of school practice. The student teacher must first gain some idea of who he or she is, of what he or she wants, and above all, of the ways in which one can take responsibility for one's own learning. The first period of student teaching can be one of extreme stress, in which the prime concern is simply to 'get through'. This is not an auspicious moment for learning the art of reflection. Prospective teachers must already have at their disposal sufficient powers of reflection to enable them to evaluate the influence of these personal concerns on the way in which they themselves function in the classroom. (Korthagen, 1988, pp. 38–9)

Although most of this chapter is concerned with theorizing about one's own classroom experience, other school-based sources of theory should not be forgotten. Beginning teachers encounter other teachers' theories, even pupils' theories, whether or not they recognize them as such. These also could be examined with benefit. Clark (1986) reported that:

> Research on teacher thinking has documented the fact that teachers develop and hold implicit theories about their students about the subject matter that they teach and about their roles and responsibilities and how they should act. These implicit theories are not neat and complete reproductions of the educational psychology found in textbooks or lecture notes. Rather, teachers' implicit theories tend to be eclectic

aggregations of cause–effect propositions from many sources, rules of thumb, generalizations drawn from personal experience, beliefs, values, biases, and prejudices . . . And teachers' implicit theories about themselves and their work are thought to play an important part in the judgements and interpretations that teachers make every day. (Clark, 1986, p. 5)

Greater understanding of the origins and functions of teachers' theories about pupils, about knowledge, and about teaching and learning could help bring the process of socialization into the profession under greater critical control.

It would also be healthy if we regarded the acquisition of theory from books in a similar kind of way. We tend to take for granted that our students know what kinds of theory and theorizing are found in different sorts of text; and fail to help them evaluate the theories embedded in 'non-theoretical' curriculum and methods' books. Teachers tend to mine such books for practical knowledge and absorb without criticism the persuasive rhetoric in which such knowledge is often couched (Anderson, 1981). Surely the critical use of different kinds of books is important for beginning teachers' acquisition of theory?

If a major aim of PGCE courses is to enhance the theorizing capacities of our students, that is their ability to acquire, refine, evaluate and use theories for the improvement of their practice, then it is essential for them to have some knowledge and understanding of the theorizing process itself. Unless they can conceptualize the task of learning to theorize they are unlikely to develop the capacity to do so. Moreover, without some discussion and reflection on personal experience of professional knowledge and learning, the nature of the theorizing task may be misunderstood. Indeed there is a danger that it is perceived as other-oriented rather than self-oriented, completing written assignments to pass the course or talking in seminars to give the tutor a good impression and get good references. Beginning teachers also need to acquire some understanding of the role which theorizing can play in various aspects of professional practice, to have some knowledge of where and how other teachers have used it, for what purpose and with what effect. Such practical questions as when to theorize and for how long, what factors to consider, when and how to get another opinion, how to focus and organize one's thinking, what evidence to consider reasonable, when to trust and when not to trust one's early thoughts, have considerable influence on the benefits accruing from the theorizing process. These need to be discussed at some stage, because they affect people's ability to assert a useful degree of control over their own theorizing (their metacognition). It is also important to discuss the essentially practical nature of theorizing if students are to develop a sensible perspective on it (i.e., some practical wisdom).

It is misleading, however, to describe theorizing as a skill, because the repetitive element is far too slight. It probably improves with practice, but such practice is unlikely to be of a routine variety. Kuhn (1974) argued, in the case of science, that it is not by linguistic rules that science attaches its language to nature, but rather by means of exemplars. If this were also true of education, then students' knowledge of theorizing would consist primarily of those exemplars they had become familiar with. These would provide a knowledge of the theorizing process that could be applied through further intuitive generalization; and there would be no need to look for any special forms of reasoning that could be labelled as 'theorizing skills'. Indeed such is the power of conceptual frameworks that problems of theorizing are more likely to arise from the limited range of perspectives we bring to seeing practice and to representing what we see, than from any lack of ability to reason.

In order to extend the range of perspectives we bring to the interpretation of practice we need more concepts and ideas to think with. Although some may be derived from reflection and discussion of personal practice, others can be obtained from the domain of public theory. But what is the likelihood that public theory will be called upon in this way? This brings us to a practical paradox. If public theory is taught but does not get used it gets consigned to some remote attic of the mind, from where it is unlikely to be retrieved as it is already labelled 'irrelevant'. But if public theory is not taught, teachers' ability to theorize is handicapped by their limited repertoire of available concepts, ideas and principles. To resolve this dilemma, we must examine more closely the processes by which public theory gets used.

The Acquisition and Use of Discipline-based Theory

Traditionally higher education has accorded priority to discipline-based theories and concepts, derived from bodies of coherent, systematic knowledge. Historically, those disciplines regarded as relevant to education have been psychology, philosophy, sociology and occasionally history. The validity of these disciplines does not depend on their professional application, but their relevance to beginning teachers has been increasingly questioned. Though it is usually possible to argue that discipline-based knowledge connects with practical situations in the sense of contributing some understanding of them, this does not establish any priority. The problem with public theories in general is that they tend to remain in educational discourse, be discussed, criticized and written about without affecting practice. They may not ever get used. Hence, before we try to decide what theories should be included in PGCE courses, we need to understand rather more about how and when such knowledge might get used.

Broudy *et al.* (1964) defined four categories for describing how knowledge acquired during schooling is used in later life, namely replication, application, interpretation and association. These can also be applied to the use of discipline-based theories by beginning teachers. The replicative mode of knowledge use is rare in PGCE courses, being confined to derivative approaches to essay writing (strongly discouraged) and examinations (does anyone still have them?). The applicative mode has been long regarded as important, but support for the notion that theory derived within discipline-based enquiry can be directly applied to practice has dwindled over the last decade. Indeed many authors argue that such a relationship between theory and practice is impossible (Hirst, 1979; McIntyre, 1980; and Tom, 1980). Instead we are offered the notions of grounded theory, practical principles and craft knowledge, which are both directly derived from, and readily applicable to, practice. These ideas will be further examined in the next section.

The interpretative use of theory has become increasingly prominent in discussion of theory-practice issues, so let us consider some of its implications. First, the complexity of educational settings usually ensures that a very large number of concepts and ideas is potentially relevant. So on what grounds does a person select? Is it according to utility or ethical principles, or is it governed by more intuitive criteria like personal preference or fittingness? Second, how does a discipline-derived concept or idea come to be seen as relevant? Either because interpreters make their own linkages to practical situations, or because some previous user of the theory has demonstrated relevance for a situation construed as similar. Without such examples and without the ability or disposition to draw fresh concepts into their theorizing, beginning teachers are likely to relegate areas of theory to storage. Thirdly, both the selection and the use of ideas are likely to be influenced by existing conceptual frameworks. Some teachers will be more inclined to use certain ideas than others, and they may not be aware of the reason. Finally, the process of interpretation is reversible. The meaning of a concept is largely carried by knowledge of examples of its use; so that an individual's understanding of the concept is expanded, perhaps even altered by each new example of its use. The converse of using existing theory to interpret practice is allowing practice to reshape theory, a relationship that is nicely expressed by Piaget's twin concepts of assimilation and accommodation. Thus if we wish to encourage the interpretative use of discipline-based theories, we need to consider the following points:

- The use of an idea depends not only on it being 'in mind' but also on it being perceived as relevant because examples are known of its use in similar situations.
- The selection of an interpretation is influenced by existing conceptual frameworks that may derive primarily from prior experience and not be at all explicit.
- These frameworks may change through accommodation to new experiences, but the process is slow, gradual and uncertain.
- The interpretative use of theory necessarily involves theorizing, for which many beginning teachers may have neither the skill nor the disposition unless their training is somehow able to provide them.

The associative use of theory is rarely discussed but a few examples will illustrate how powerfully pervasive it can be. The accountability debate has been not only about power, but also about images: the school as a garden, the school as a club, the school as a factory. Progressive education, in particular, has been powerfully presented in terms of images and accounts of progressive classrooms are notable for their image-making as opposed to analytic qualities. Special education, on the other hand, is dominated by medical rather than horticultural images — classification according to handicap rather than need and the diagnosis-treatment approach to individualization. Still other images are conjured up by terms like 'core', 'basics', 'pastoral' or 'interface'. Even the process of learning itself is frequently discussed in metaphoric terms (Reddy, 1979).

> It is very difficult to put this concept into words. (Reddy, 1979, p. 312)
> Everybody must get the ideas in this article into his head by tomorrow. (*ibid.*, p. 315)
> You have to absorb Plato's ideas a little at a time. (*ibid.*, p. 319)

Practical Knowledge and Practical Principles

Those types of knowledge that are derived from practice and validated in practice are variously described as practical knowledge (Oakeshott, 1962) or craft knowledge (McNamara and Desforges, 1979; Tom, 1980). This encompasses process knowledge or 'know-how'; specific knowledge about particular people, situations, decisions or actions; and generalized knowledge of the type Hirst (1979, 1985) has called 'practical concepts and principles'. However the nature and status of this practical knowledge is by no means agreed, and its separateness from discipline-based knowledge may be more apparent than real. Four major issues for debate are the explicitness of practical knowledge, its generalizability, its scope and its morality.

Oakeshott (1962), following Aristotle, made a clear distinction between 'technical knowledge' and 'practical knowledge'. Technical knowledge is capable of written codification; but practical knowledge is expressed only in practice and learned only through experience with practice. Some kinds of practical knowledge are uncodifiable in principle. For example, knowledge that is essentially non-verbal — the tone of a voice or musical instrument, the feel of a muscle or a piece of sculpture, the expression on a face — cannot be fully described in writing. Verbal performances, such as teaching or advocacy, which are not fully scripted beyond a brief set of notes, cannot be reduced to simple technical descriptions. Even scripted performances, like those of an actor or pianist, take on their special character because interpretations of quality require the repeatable elements such as the memorization of the script and the reproduction of the sounds to be reduced to instinctive routine. Critics may write and talk about these performances or even provide detailed commentaries on video recordings. But, while usually not devoid of

Mode of Conduct	Established Practice	Established Practice Modified Idiosyncratically	Idiosyncratic Private Practice
Mode of Use	As Prescribed	Prescribed with Discretion to Adapt	Unique and Intuitive
Context of Use	Definable Expected Circumstances	Acknowledged Range of Situations	Any Situation where feasible
Expected Outcomes	Particular Outcomes Envisaged	Wide Range of Familiar Outcomes Expected	Relatively Novel Outcomes
	TECHNOLOGY	CRAFT	ART

Figure 4.1: Buchler's Typology of Method

meaning or relevance, such criticism cannot construct an authentic account of all the meaning embedded in a performance. Indeed the relationship between comment and action is distinctly problematic, even when the commentator and the actor are the same person.

Argyris and Schön (1974) argue that professional actions are based on implicit 'theories in use' which differ from the 'espoused theories' used to explain them to external audiences or even to the actor himself. Self-knowledge of performance is difficult to acquire, and self-comment tends to be justificatory rather than critical in intent. They also regard making implicit 'theories in use' explicit and thereby open to criticism as the key to professional learning. However, the question persists as to how much professional know-how is essentially implicit, and how much is capable with appropriate time and attention of being described and explained. Moreover it is easier to follow the Argyris and Schön model in their selected context of management than in classroom teaching. Most managerial decisions can be described as *cool* — there is time to reflect and deliberate; whereas classroom decisions are *hot* in the midst of the action, and intuitive (Jackson, 1971). The problem of making classroom knowledge explicit is clearly much greater.

A useful approach to the questions of the generalizability of practical knowledge is provided by Buchler's (1961) analysis of 'method'; which we discussed in Chapter 3. It is represented here in diagrammatic form (Figure 4.1).

Although it is possible for a method to incorporate elements from different columns I have chosen to treat the columns as archetypes and labelled them accordingly. Where practice is conceived in terms of technology, then preparation will emphasize demonstration and coaching. But if practice is conceived in terms of artistry, preparation will need to emphasize variety of experience, responsiveness, invention and quick reading of a situation as it develops.

Between these two extremes lies the possibility of a method that is adapted to suit both user and situation. Although teachers are expected and encouraged to develop their own personal method, this is usually viewed in terms of selection from recognized methods followed by adaptation to create a personal style. Only rarely would the method itself be seen as novel. The process requires that the student teacher be prepared to modify and experiment with the methods they have chosen to use, that they are encouraged to do this and that they are provided with appropriate feedback. Adaptation to situation, however, requires rather different treatment. It is little help merely to agree that it is desirable to adapt a method to suit particular pupils and particular circumstances; for there remains the problem of precisely how it is to be done.

This leads us back to decision-making as an aspect of teacher behaviour to which our attention is frequently drawn, and whose effectiveness dearly depends on the knowledge and know-how which the teacher brings to each individual situation. Because much of this knowledge comes from experience with previous situations, its use must involve at least some degree of generalization. Some idea, procedure or action that was used in a previous situation is considered to be applicable to the new one. The nature of this generalization process, however, may vary in both scope and explicitness: at minimum Situation P is perceived as similar to Situation Q and handled in the same sort of way; at maximum, some practical principle is consciously applied, which is thought to be valid for all situations of a certain type. Semi-conscious patterning of previous experience may also occur, making it difficult for the professional to trace the source of, or even to clearly articulate, the generalization he or she is using. In this context it is important to note that recent research on human inference (Nisbett and Ross, 1980) has shown that it has many limitations. For example, Tversky and Kahneman (1973) found that in judging the relative frequency of particular objects or the likelihood of particular events, people are influenced by their relative accessibility in the mind. In particular the immediate perceptual salience of an event influences the vividness or completeness with which it is recalled. Thus a teacher making a judgment about a child's behaviour or potential is more likely to remember some incidents than others and to attach more weight to some kinds of evidence. Learning to read a situation and adapt one's behaviour accordingly is likely to be promoted by reflective theorizing, whether or not the behaviour is perceived as principle-based or rule-following. But such reflection is also susceptible to error, unless it is brought under proper critical control.

Teachers are also particularly vulnerable to what Ross (1977) has called the 'fundamental attribution error' — the tendency to attribute behaviour exclusively to the actor's dispositions and to ignore powerful situational determinants of the behaviour. He suggests that this 'dispositionalist theory' is woven into the fabric of our culture, with 'situationalist' thinking being confined to social scientists. Hence we need to introduce beginning teachers to sufficient social-science theory to enable them to place teaching within its situational and institutional contexts, what Zeichner and Lipson (1987) refer to as 'second-level reflection'.

Another issue that remains to be solved is the scope of practical knowledge or, what matters more for many practical purposes, the scope of those practical principles that can be derived from it and made explicit. How feasible are the aspirations of those who hope to codify teachers' craft knowledge? It is not difficult to find maxims or practical tips to pass on to beginning teachers, but what do they all add up to? Can we envisage a situation where the sum of such advice specifies at all precisely what a teacher ought to decide, even if one assumes there is basic agreement on aims and values? Wittgenstein pointed out that no set of rules can completely prescribe a decision because there remain further decisions about when a rule is applicable and when it is not. But this theoretical limit of prescription seems very remote when we have nothing resembling a comprehensive set of rules. Can an amorphous collection of practical principles be said to constitute a grounded theory of practice, or is this mere wishful thinking?

Other philosophers have focused on the way in which practical knowledge incorporates moral principles. The Whites (1984) disclose the complex nature of the relationship when they define 'successful practice' as 'that practice which is achieving justifiable aims in an acceptable way'. However, although moral principles must be involved in deciding what aims are justifiable and what methods are acceptable, these may not be made explicit. As Petrie (1981) suggested 'Norm-regarding behaviour can be in accordance with implicit or unconscious rules, if we stand ready to correct deviations from the norm and recognize our mistakes' (p. 89). If one questions teachers about where and when they are called upon to resolve moral issues, they are likely to cite critical incidents involving the conduct of individual pupils and teachers; the moral principles underlying the teaching process itself are often taken for granted. Nevertheless, moral principles *are* embedded in practice; and it is because we believe teachers *ought* to recognize them, discuss them and evaluate them that we seek to include such activities in initial training courses.

The Influence of Context on the Theorizing Process

Theory is not stored in the mind in isolated and decontextualized form: it derives meaning and richness from connections with other ideas and associations with a variety of situations. The form the knowledge takes is strongly influenced by the ways in which it has been used, and this creates barriers to transfer between dissimilar contexts. We could ask, for example, whether the prolonged use of an idea in an academic context gives it a framework that inhibits its transfer to the school context — a mental analogue of that well-known phenomenon of 'functional fixedness'.

So let us consider carefully what learning to use ideas in various PGCE contexts involves. Within higher education, ideas may be used in writing, in formal discussion and in informal conversation. Where there is academic writing in essay format, both teachers and students (other than scientists and mathematicians) are well-used to the conventions — specialized language, profuse citation, validation according to traditional disciplines or established fields of study, attention to several perspectives, and so on. The purposes of other kinds of writing, for example extensive entries in course files may be much less clear; so too might the criteria by which such writing is to be judged. Could the hidden curriculum ever become: 'Provided you keep within acceptable limits, it's not what you think or do but the way you write about it that counts?' Theorizing in written form can also cause problems, because it leaves the students on their own just when they are most in need of help. Moreover, because the written form is rarely found amongst practising teachers, it appears inauthentic and is unlikely to be used after qualification. We tend to take it for granted that writing for a wider audience enhances the theorizing process, but this may not necessarily be true. Teaching is primarily an oral culture.

Similarly, the way in which theory is used in formal discussion is strongly influenced by the communication process involved. Both group pressures for consensus and arguments between opposing members can lead to ideas being clothed in emotional language and used for their immediate impact on the discourse, to justify a viewpoint rather than clarify a meaning. Good preparation for staff-room politics perhaps, but not good professional learning! Another problem arises when importing classroom experience into university-based discussions. To be anecdotal is easy, but to give sufficient contextual information for group theorizing is both time-consuming and risky for the individual involved. Not all students can provide the required quality of reporting, nor indeed can many experienced teachers. Given the personal nature of theorizing, we also ought to ask ourselves whether the group discussion provides the best way of developing it. For example, does it give all but one or two students sufficient practice in making it part of their own natural way of thinking? How about other forms of groupwork? Would it not be valid criticism to suggest that most PGCE courses give too much attention to the acquisition of theory and too little to helping students to use it?

Within schools, beginning teachers undergo three main kinds of experience which may or may not be closely related. They *listen* to, and sometimes *participate* in, teacher discourse about pupils, about school or department policy or about classroom practice. They *observe* teachers and pupils in classrooms, corridors, staff rooms and other settings. They *practise* teaching with some guidance, receiving comments on lesson plans, being observed, engaging in post-lesson discussion and contributing to a logbook or course file. In some PGCE courses they also have the opportunity within a day or two to *discuss* what they have heard, seen or done in school back in the university setting. All these experiences can promote theorizing, particularly when this is encouraged by school as well as university tutors; but there are major contextual constraints.

First, there is the comparative rarity of professional discourse in many schools, particularly about classroom matters. Indeed, in most staff rooms the hidden agenda seems to be how to talk about the classroom without giving away any information that could possibly be used as a basis for criticism. That generating such discussion is difficult has been noted by McNamara and Desforges (1979); although there have always been some schools and departments where talk about teaching is common. However the problem remains that the further away from the classroom, the more decontextualized such discussion becomes and the more difficult for the discussants to share meanings. In the absence of what Lortie (1975) calls a 'technical culture of teaching', there is no common language of talk about classrooms; and the communication of meaning is dependent on shared experiences which can provide common points of reference.

Discourse about pupils, however, has traditionally played an important part in the training of primary teachers; and it has been linked with classrooms through observational studies of pupils. One possible explanation is that discourse about pupils is acceptable, even common, in primary schools, perhaps because it carries less threat than talk about teaching. Another is that student teachers have excellent opportunities for collecting information about individual pupils and studying how they learn. There is probably scope for more such work in secondary schools. The main problem here is not so much the lack of theorizing — labelling is a form of theorizing, for example, but the need to bring that theorizing under proper critical control.

Students' access to policy talk is likely to be limited, unless there is a series of joint seminars with their school-based tutors. These days, however, they are increasingly likely to encounter policy documents. To understand the significance of both spoken and written policy discourse, they will need to know something of school micropolitics and of policy-related communication between the school and external groups. This is virtually impossible on a PGCE course unless students spend considerable time in one school. Moreover, do we not need to examine more carefully how theory is used in policy discourse: does it add meaning, does it mystify the audience, or is it simply a convenient source of justification? Another problem arises from the inevitable gap between policy and practice, between what people say and what they do. When policies are characterized by explicit reference to educational principles this difference between rhetoric and reality can lead to rejection of those principles or to a kind of cynical and amoral pragmatism.

The second major contextual constraint on theorizing in schools arises from the nature of teaching itself. Learning to become a teacher and cope in the classroom involves developing routines and short cuts, internalizing classroom decision-making and reducing the range of possible ways of thinking to manageable proportions. There are too many variables to take into account at once. This leads to intuitive grasping of certain communal practitioners' concepts (Buchmann, 1980) before they can be brought under proper control; although apparently more valid theoretical ideas get consigned to 'storage' and never get retrieved.

Another difficulty, which I discussed earlier, is that theoretical ideas usually cannot be applied 'off-the-shelf', their implications have to be worked out and thought through. The busy teacher or student teacher may not easily find the time. Thus the functional relevance of a piece of theoretical knowledge depends less on its presumed validity than on the ability and willingness of people to use it. This is mainly determined by individual professionals and their work-contexts, but is also affected by the way in which the knowledge is introduced and linked to their ongoing professional concerns.

The Disposition to Theorize

Finally, we come to the most important quality of the professional teacher, the disposition to theorize. If our students acquire and sustain this disposition they will go on developing their theorizing capacities throughout their teaching careers, they will be genuinely self-evaluative and they will continue to search for, invent and implement new ideas. Without it they will become prisoners of their early school experience, perhaps the competent teachers of today, almost certainly the ossified teachers of tomorrow. Calderhead (1988) wrote:

> Recent research on student teachers tends to suggest that their teaching relies heavily on the images of practice that are acquired from past and current experiences in schools. These images can be taken and implemented uncritically. The evaluation of practice might remain at a superficial level and knowledge bases which could potentially inform practice be little utilized. Furthermore, the school, and sometimes college, ethos might support a conception *of* teaching which does not encourage and may even impede an analytical response to one's own teaching, leading in some cases to opinionated or self-defensive approaches to professional learning. As a result, student teachers' learning could quite quickly reach a plateau where teaching has become routine, conservative and unproblematic. (Calderhead, 1988, p. 62)

So what factors are likely to affect the disposition to theorize; and what can we do to promote it? First let us consider Fuller's developmental model of the process of becoming a teacher, which she derived from a longitudinal study of the concerns of beginning teachers (see Table 4.1).

At the beginning student teachers' concerns may be distributed over stages 0–3, with attention to 2 when starting class teaching and attention to 3 when taking small groups of pupils. As and if they develop competence and

Table 4.1: Fuller's Model of Teacher Development

I	Early phase	0	Concerns about self (non-teaching concerns)
II	Middle phase (competence)3	1	Concerns about professional expectations and acceptance
		2	Concerns about one's own adequacy: subject matter and class control
		3	Concerns about relationships with pupils
III	Late phase (professionalism)3	4	Concerns about pupils' learning what is taught
		5	Concerns about pupils' learning what they need
		6	Concerns about one's own (teacher's) contributions to pupil change

Source: adapted from Fuller, 1970.

confidence, they begin to acquire significant concerns at stages 4–5; though the earlier stages are likely to remain prominent for some considerable time. However student teachers, or indeed qualified teachers, who are still struggling to manage their classes may be unlikely to accommodate these later stages of concern. Insofar as this model is true for British PGCE students, and I suspect it is true for many but not for all, there are important implications for theorizing about classroom practice. Neither public theory nor requests for experience-based theorizing are likely to be taken seriously unless they engage with student concerns that are current. Hence, one might argue that early in the course student theorizing will need to address competence concerns; whilst the more advanced professional concerns are considered later.

However, in addition to teacher development we have to consider the process of professional socialization. Beginning teachers may need to theorize about 'Middle phase' concerns, but competent experienced teachers cope with them semi-automatically. It is only the 'Late phase' concerns that demand theorizing from experienced teachers as well. But in many educational settings only minimal attention is paid to these professional concerns. So there is little demand for theorizing, which then gets identified with the 'Early phase', the beginning teacher phase — something to be grown out of instead of something to be grown into. How then do we prepare our students for continuing professional growth in unthinking schools?

First, I believe we have to share the problem with students from the outset. The nature of their moral commitment needs to be clarified and the issue of professional identity continually discussed. Second, they need to encounter theorizing in school settings and gain some understanding of its potential role — if not in their practice school, then in some other school. Third, they need to have some knowledge of alternative courses of action, without which planning or evaluating becomes a routine from which practical theorizing is likely to be excluded. To provide such knowledge should be the responsibility of the curriculum component of a PGCE course; though a discussion of the nature of a choice between two alternatives might well be part of a theorizing course. Fourth, they have to develop realistic views about theorizing, that are not impossible to realize when they become full-time teachers. Then, finally, they need to experience some success in theorizing, to be helped to see what and how they have learned, and not to see themselves as deficient in comparison with academic models. Both writing and formal discussion may easily acquire the negative significance of time away from practice, which will be exacerbated by any personal difficulties with these types of communication. Moreover, lack of self-knowledge may lead to students being unaware of the extent of their learning and assuming the least possible benefit.

The other main influence on the process of learning to theorize is the relationship between lecturers and mentors in the practice schools. Even on well-coordinated courses, students have to negotiate meanings and expectations with each group separately. Thus the institutional separation presents a structural symbol of what both sides tend to call a 'theory-practice gap'. Theorizing becomes what one does in university for the lecturers, not what one does in school. Is it not then important for there to be continuing discourse between teachers and lecturers on both sites to demonstrate their shared commitment to theorizing? Such discourse would also be a valuable staff-development activity for both parties, a necessary complement to 'recent and relevant experience'. At the end of an article describing the many problems of an experienced teacher-education programme, planned jointly by teachers and teacher educators, Lanier (1983) gave an attractive account of just such a process.

> Discussions sometimes grew out of material selected by teacher educators for its apparent general importance to education (for example, studies of child development, teacher expectations, the changing nature and structure of American families, the complex organisation of modern institutions including the school.) Other times discussions grew out of practical problems and interests of classroom teachers (for example, How can one motivate youngsters to read? How does one help apparent under-achievers? How can one encourage greater respect among youngsters of different races?). Thus, the teacher educators made the initial judgements about the formal knowledge that they thought might be worthwhile and then let their shared examination and discourse with teachers determine whether or not it was useful in helping them understand and think better about the problems and practice of teaching. The teachers, on the other hand, made the initial judgements about the concrete problems that they thought were worth serious attention, and then let their shared examination and discourse with teacher educators determine whether or not they could justify actions in light of public and general criteria, rather than by personal and unexamined preferences alone. The prevailing approach was continually to use conceptual tools in examining fundamental beliefs and ideas, whether they emanated from formal *or* practical knowledge. The movement was back and forth, from the

abstract to the concrete, and from the practical to the theoretic. Questions of how much attention and when to shift attention from one emphasis to another were continually open for consideration and negotiation. (Lanier, 1983)

Note

1. This chapter is a revised version of a paper given to a UCET conference in 1985 and subsequently udpated for publication in Harvard, G. and Hodkinson, P. (Eds) (1994) *Action and Reflection in Teacher Education*, New Jersey, Ablex Publishing.

Chapter 5

Headteachers Learning about Management: Types of Management Knowledge and the Role of the Management Course

Educational managers possess a great deal of knowledge. Some of it has been acquired in a formal manner through training, conferences, reading and so on. Most of it has been acquired through experience. Some of this experiential knowledge has been reflected upon and organized sufficiently to be talked about or written down. Much of it has hardly been reflected upon or organized at all. Such unorganized experiential knowledge gets drawn upon without people even realizing that they are using it. It is built into people's habits, procedures, decision-making and ways of thinking, without ever being scrutinized and brought under critical control. Thus, people are partly controlled by their own 'unknown' knowledge.

This situation is never static. Professionals continue to learn throughout their careers and this learning can take many forms. They can assimilate new information to their existing frameworks, neglecting those aspects that do not readily fit; and they can periodically adjust or accommodate those frameworks the better to fit their newly acquired information. Piaget describes the learning process as a balance between the two, between assimilation and accommodation. However, there is a tendency for assimilation to dominate for some people, particularly as they get older — you cannot teach old dogs new tricks — and more senior — you only tell your bosses what you think they want to know. Nevertheless, professional learning continues both on and off the job: in action, in discussion and in periods of personal reflection. Most of it is unplanned, even personal reflection taking place more in unplanned moments — when driving to work, talking to a friend or having a bath — than in periods deliberately set aside for the purpose.

A management course of a week or more in length is properly viewed as a significant episode in mid-career learning, but its significance will depend on the degree to which it can enhance or boost the ongoing off-course learning process beyond its boundaries. For this, it needs to capitalize on the special opportunities for learning provided by a course setting and not attempt things that can be better achieved in other ways. The aim of this chapter, therefore, is to discuss the kinds of contribution that courses can make to the lifelong task of learning to be a manager.[1]

The first section discusses the nature of management knowledge acquired; while the second looks at the opportunities and constraints offered by a management course. The middle of the chapter examines ways in which courses can contribute to different types of management knowledge. Then the concluding section looks at how a course can most usefully incorporate planning and problem-solving for the job context itself. The continuing theme throughout is the linkage between the temporary setting of the course and the more permanent setting of the school or college where course members normally work.

Management Knowledge and Management Training

Discussions about professional knowledge and learning tend to be based on a dichotomy between theoretical knowledge, which is codified in books and taught and examined on courses, and practical knowledge that is acquired 'on the job'. The organizational model for theoretical knowledge is the course description and reading list, while that for practical knowledge is the job description and job reference. Both education and management are applied fields of study, taught and examined in higher education, often at postgraduate level to experienced practitioners. However, management qualifications are still based in the education sector. Most 'good' educational managers are qualified in education but not in management. This preponderance of senior, experienced but 'unqualified' practitioners reinforces the supposed dichotomy between theory and practice.

This common distinction between theoretical and practical knowledge is not only unhelpful but misleading. When we talk about people's perspectives and preconceptions, we acknowledge that they perceive and think about the world in their own particular way. They have their own theories about what is out there and how the world works; and these theories affect their behaviour, even if they are only partly aware of them. Moreover, many ideas that are given special treatment in 'theory books' are in wide circulation within the educational community and often outside it as well. Consider, for example, ideas such as the democratic school, informal teaching, social disadvantage, the intelligent child, the committed teacher. It is only when ideas have not yet been integrated into people's thinking and conversation that they get labelled as 'theoretical'. Then people can consign them to storage in some remote attic of the mind or perhaps even exclude them from memory altogether. Thus, for practitioners, theoretical ideas are the ideas they do not use or think they do not use. If they start to use them then they cease to describe them as 'theoretical' and call them 'common sense' instead.

The other common mode of classifying knowledge is by its content. The educator will classify into subjects and topics because that is how educational courses and institutions are organized. Management theory tends to divide knowledge into key tasks and processes like planning, coordinating, administering or controlling, with the addition of a few key concepts like leadership or morale. Both approaches, however, lead to views of knowledge that are seriously incomplete. So I am developing a framework of my own to fill some of the more important gaps while still finding a place, albeit a diminished one, for those areas of knowledge commonly found in education or management books.

This map is still in an early stage of development, consisting merely of six knowledge categories. So I must begin with several provisos: few management tasks involve only one category of knowledge; the categories are interdependent in a complex variety of ways; some might benefit from further subdivision; and it might be better to map the categories in the form of a Venn diagram as sets of overlapping circles. However, I would make two positive claims. The map covers a much greater range of territory than is common in management education; and the topology serves as a powerful heuristic for thinking more deeply about the nature of a school manager's experiential knowledge and how it might best be further developed. My six categories are as follows:

- knowledge of people;
- situational knowledge;
- knowledge of educational practice;
- conceptual knowledge;
- process knowledge; and
- control knowledge.

Each of these knowledge types is explained below, together with a discussion of issues relating to how it is acquired or learned.

Knowledge of people plays an important part in a manager's life. It is often the major factor in a decision and it affects those myriads of personal encounters that fill a manager's day. Much of this knowledge is open to challenge, at least in principle. Judgments about people are generally recognized as somewhat fallible, but managers still have to make them. Some managers' knowledge of people appears both to participants and to impartial observers as more authentic, more thorough and more insightful than others. But although there is scope for improvement, managers are not offered much practical help in developing this aspect of their work. The territory has been explored by psychologists, but the results of such exploration have not been translated into the field of management education, except in areas where current concerns with gender and racial stereotyping have been prominent.

Knowledge of people is largely acquired unintentionally as a by-product of encounters that have other purposes. These may be direct encounters with the person concerned, or encounters with third parties, who provide indirect information about that person, often only incidentally. The information presented by these encounters will be affected during acquisition by such factors as the manager's knowledge needs at the time, the contexts of the encounters, varying from personal interviews to large meetings, and the manager's views of the people presenting the third-party accounts. On those few occasions when managers deliberately set out to get to know someone, they will try to find an occasion for informal interaction in a friendly, relaxing manner. In most cases, the acquisition of information about another person is relatively disorganized, somewhat random and even partly subconscious.

However, this subconscious acquisition of knowledge is often a more orderly process than one might think. What people perceive is largely determined by what they look for, that is, by their pre-existing cognitive frameworks, categories and expectations. This is especially true of personal relations, where what one person tells you about another often conveys as much about your informant as about the person being described. What you see as significant and how you interpret what others say and do are significantly affected by your own perceptual frameworks.

Selective memory also filters the information you gather about people so that more salient or unusual encounters feature more prominently than those that are merely routine. Indeed research suggests (Nisbett and Ross, 1980) that knowledge of another person is normally constructed in a manner that is largely intuitive, but occasionally reflective; is based on a sample of that person's behaviour, which is often extremely unrepresentative of his or her daily professional life; is characterized by typifications that necessarily oversimplify; and is often confirmed during further interaction in a way that is essentially self-fulfilling.

Situational knowledge is concerned with how people 'read' the situations in which they find themselves. What do they see as the significant features? Which aspects of a situation are more susceptible to change? How would it be affected by, or respond to, certain decisions or events? Much, but not all of this knowledge is consciously held, though it is rarely written down; and it will usually contain strong personal elements. Thus, one teacher's description of a class is unlikely to coincide with that of another, but it may contain quite a lot of common ground. Headteachers' descriptions of schools would probably be very different from those of most teachers, because their role, as well as their personality, would affect their perspective. But how is this perspective acquired?

Researchers apart, people normally learn about situations by being in them rather than by studying them. Thus, situational knowledge is acquired in a manner that is partly accidental and partly purposive; involving some discussion and deliberation but also a lot of intuitive assumptions. As with knowledge of people, the quality of the information will depend on how it is filtered through the receiver's perceptual frameworks and on whether it is based on an adequate sample.

Senior managers, however, have a special problem because much of the information that reaches a senior manager is second-hand, already shaped and filtered by the perspectives of the informants. Not only are such accounts affected by what informants consider significant, but also by what they consider fit to pass on. In particular, they will be concerned with how their accounts will reflect back on themselves. Hence there is a tendency to pass on only that information that they think is wanted and to organize it in a way that shows that they understand the senior manager's intentions and concerns.

Most information received by managers about their situations has to be interpreted and invested with significance either by themselves or by their informants. Little of it could be described as objective, the sampling will almost certainly be skewed and it will be acquired with a lot of unconscious filtering by perceptual frameworks of which they are only dimly aware.

Knowledge of educational practice lies at the heart of what is sometimes described as the 'leading professional' role of a head. It covers the whole repertoire of possible policies and practices from which, in an ideal world, educators are able to choose: teaching methods and approaches, curriculum strategies and assessment patterns, pastoral systems, organizational structures, staff-development activities, external relations and so on. The domain is large, but no one person is expected to have deep knowledge in all these areas. Hence the need for a senior-management team, for heads of departments or curriculum coordinators and for access to consultancy support. In recent years, there have been so many changes, especially in the role of educational management itself, that it has been difficult even for a team to keep abreast of current developments.

What, however, constitutes sufficient knowledge of any particular practice? Is it knowing that it exists, knowing enough to decide whether to adopt it, or knowing enough to implement it? The extent to which individuals take the trouble to brief themselves will depend on:

- whether they have any interest in changing from current practice;
- whether they consider the 'new' practice to be practicable; and
- whether they think the new practice is likely to be beneficial.

Practicality, in particular, is used both as a genuine factor in decision-making and as an excuse for not pursuing the matter further. Possible alternatives can be dismissed as impractical or non-beneficial on the basis of remarkably little evidence. Often it takes a very active desire for change, strong external pressure, or a strong recommendation from a highly trusted source, to get somebody sufficiently interested in a new practice to learn much about it; though there are some people who seem to be naturally innovative and tirelessly search for new ideas.

Even when people are well-informed about a new practice, their judgment is likely to be strongly influenced by their existing views on what is educationally worthwhile, what is likely to work and whether it is capable of being introduced into their own particular school. Thinking about educational practice involves not only situational knowledge, but also personal theories and values; and these in turn are likely to be informed by concepts and ideas from recognized educational theory, even though the thinker may not be aware of this influence.

Conceptual knowledge is defined as that set of concepts, theories and ideas that a person has consciously stored in memory. It is thus available for use in analysing issues or problems, or debating policies and practices. This explicit use of conceptual knowledge is easiest to describe. However, when describing knowledge of people and situational knowledge, we noted that information is filtered and shaped by perceptual frameworks. These frameworks are largely implicit; but if they were to be made explicit, the use of certain concepts would be revealed. The concept itself may be consciously stored in memory, but its use is unreflective. The consequent lack of critical control can be a serious cause for concern.

The opposite problem occurs with concepts learned in academic contexts. These concepts are more under critical control, but rather less likely to be put to practical use.

Two important reasons for this were discussed in earlier chapters. First, there is what I like to call 'the iceberg principle'. Most learning of a new idea does not take place when it is first introduced and 'understood'; that is, only the part 'above the surface'. The real work of learning comes when you try to use the idea. It is during the struggle 'below the surface' that you take ownership of the idea, link it to other ideas and acquire the capacity to use it for your own particular purpose. Second, and as a direct consequence of this learning during use, ideas become linked to particular contexts of use. Hence they are learned differently in each separate context, and have to be partly relearned when transferred to a new situation, for example, from INSET course to departmental meeting, or from curriculum guidelines to classroom practice. Such transfer of ideas is often difficult and requires much further thought and effort.

Whether concepts are already embedded in practice or deliberately introduced to help understand or rethink practice, they seldom achieve the ideal state of being both in practical use and under critical control.Hence the current interest in developments such as job-related inquiry, action research, school-based evaluation and reflective professional discussion. These show some potential for helping to solve the problems of using conceptual knowledge.

Process knowledge usually features prominently in management courses. Management is about getting things done and books on management are largely about managerial processes such as planning, organizing, monitoring, coordinating and team building. Even decision-making and problem-solving are sometimes treated as if they were pure processes in which the actual merits of the decision-makers' options or the problem-solvers' solutions were of relatively little consequence. To carry out these processes successfully is essential for good management, but what kind of knowledge is involved? Besides the kinds of knowledge we have already discussed — situational knowledge, knowledge of practice and conceptual knowledge — there is the knowledge of how to do things, what is often referred to colloquially as 'know-how'.

This process knowledge, or know-how, ranges from being able to carry through explicit rational procedures like timetabling or budgeting to intuitive skills like handling complaints in a meeting or making a visitor feel at ease. Although these may seem very different types of knowledge, most important educational processes involve their use in some kind of combination. For example, planning a meeting, an interview or a lesson is an explicit rational process conducted in one's own time. But the actual running of the meeting, interview or lesson is semi-intuitive: it involves routinized behaviour and the kind of rapid thinking on one's feet that can only be rationalized afterwards. This more intuitive behaviour is heavily characterized by personal styles, of which people are only partially aware. Thus, process knowledge is partly a matter of knowing all the things one has to do and making sensible plans for doing them; and partly a matter of possessing and using practical, routinized skills. The former can be grasped intellectually, though reading and discussion, though plans always have to be fitted to each individual context, so it is not just a matter of following simple checklists and algorithms. The latter, however, cannot be learned in this way: practical skills can only be acquired through practice with feedback — a learning opportunity that is often in short supply.

Control knowledge, my final category, is perhaps the most difficult to explain. The term 'control' is taken from cybernetics, not from management theory. Thus it refers to knowledge that is important for controlling one's own behaviour, and excludes that concerned with the control of others — that would be process knowledge. Control knowledge covers all of the following areas: self-awareness and sensitivity; self-knowledge about one's strengths and weaknesses, the gap between what one says and what one does, and what one knows and does not know; self-management in such matters as the use of time, prioritization and delegation; self-development in its broadest sense, including knowing how to learn and control one's own learning; the ability to reflect and self-evaluate, that is, to provide oneself with feedback; and generalized intellectual skills like strategic thinking and policy analysis, which involve the organization of one's own knowledge and thinking.

Although it is clearly important, because it incorporates the means by which one uses all the other forms of knowledge, control knowledge is rarely given much explicit attention. Indeed, many would be surprised to see it appear on the programme for a management course. If anything, the development of self-knowledge is hindered by the often implicit transmission of unrealistic, idealized models of managers who somehow seem to have everything organized and under control. This often creates a lack of confidence and thus inhibits any self-analysis. However, there are some signs that self-awareness and self-development are developing a higher profile in management education. Also, there is a growing interest in expert systems that can incorporate areas of professional knowledge into forms that can be consulted by computer; and this will draw attention to the significance of the strategic-thinking aspects of control knowledge. So it may yet be given the attention it deserves.

The Management Course as a Temporary System

Most learning about management takes place 'on the job', so a course is properly seen as a special kind of episode in the continuing process of becoming a better manager. There is danger that the significance of a course will be overestimated by those who consider that management knowledge is a packaged, transmittable commodity, for it would be difficult from that viewpoint to explain how anyone could manage without a course. But it is equally dangerous to underestimate the contribution which a well-designed course of significant length can make. As indicated above, much management learning is haphazard and semiconscious. It is easy for managers to become too reliant on past experience without examining it sufficiently critically; and they may also fail to draw on other areas of their experience that are relevant to the task at hand, because they did not perceive them as relevant at the time. Thus, providing an opportunity to reorganize one's experiential knowledge and bring it under greater critical control is an important aim for management education, to which courses can usefully contribute. Other, more obvious aims will emerge throughout the rest of the chapter.

First, however, we need to examine some special features of courses and the kinds of learning opportunity they can provide. The most obvious differences between being on a course and doing one's daily work are the distribution of time between various types of activity, the change in the company one keeps and that strange feeling that somehow life on a course is not real. For many managers, courses are negatively perceived for one reason alone: they take time away from the job. Senior managers cannot be spared, because decisions and tasks will be postponed and pile up to await their return, cherished initiatives will meet with disaster while they are away, serious mistakes will be made and so on. This is particularly true if people are recruited to courses with inadequate time to plan for their absence. With sufficient warning, however, an absence can be used to delegate tasks — at least temporarily and sometimes even for longer periods. It can also be seen as a staff-development opportunity for a teacher who takes on a new role for a while. Without such preparation, people come to courses in a state of guilt and anxiety about being away; and their natural reaction is to expect the course to compensate for this by being as much like work as possible, with a hectic pace and heavy throughput of relatively undigested information. But to make a course like work is to miss out on the advantage of a learning environment that offers other distinctive kinds of opportunity.

Some course activities — such as reading, reflection, consultation with colleagues and school-based tasks — are capable of being pursued in the normal school context; but do not get given the same degree of attention because they are crowded out by other urgent business. My own version of Parkinson's Law is that unavoidable decisions take precedence over avoidable decisions, regardless of their respective importance. Thus, many course tasks are commonly described by participants as 'things I ought to do and always wanted to do, but for which I never found the time!' Examples of such activities might be longer than usual talks with staff and students with a greater emphasis on listening, sorting out one's ideas about a seemingly intractable problem and formulating a proposal for dealing with it; getting oneself properly briefed about some new development. Often a major challenge of a management course is how to make more time for these kinds of activity in the ongoing job context by reassessing priorities for the use of personal time.

Other learning activities are specific to a course context: for example, group discussions of issues and problems and engaging in collective tasks with colleagues from other schools; a concentrated period of learning about other people's situations, perspectives and practices; listening to and questioning external resource people, followed by sufficient discussion time for ideas to be worked over. The special advantage conferred by a course is not only that these opportunities are provided, but that they take place in a context of group development. People are together for long enough to get to know and trust each other, and this is essential for proper sharing and exploration of experience and ideas.

Matthew Miles (1964) drew attention to the special change-inducing properties of various types of temporary system. Courses of a week or more in length bring people together for long enough for them to acquire a strong sense of group identity and for important behavioural changes to begin to occur — the unfreezing of attitudes, more careful listening to each other's views, a more innovative and inventive approach to issues and problems, a stronger resolution to act on problems that have been neglected. The enhanced level of communication and honesty about one's problems also bolsters people's confidence as they realize that others have similar difficulties. The psychology of such group development is extremely important for learning and course designers and tutors need to know how to promote it. There are few other situations so conducive to re-examining deeply entrenched attitudes and the effect is often more than temporary. People who have learned to work together on a course can become mutually supporting when they return to their separate schools, and continue to learn from each other and work in less isolation than previously.

One further feature of a course as a temporary system is that it confers legitimacy on activities that might otherwise be viewed with considerable suspicion. If a manager is pursuing some school-based task as part of a course, there does not have to be a hidden agenda as well. This helps set a good atmosphere for consultations and reviews; and the more the experience of the course is shared with colleagues at the time, the more the ownership of some of the tasks can be shared. Often new initiatives are expected from someone who goes away on a course, but these too can be discussed and planned in a more cooperative and consultative manner if the proper relationship between course and school is developed from the beginning.

The interface between course and school is the subject of the last section of this chapter, but it also forms a recurring theme throughout the next six sections. These are concerned with how best to develop each of the six kinds of knowledge we described in the preceding section; and they discuss the kind of contribution to that development that management courses can be designed to make.

Developing Knowledge of People

How are managers to change or develop their knowledge of people and what should be their learning goals? Their knowledge is likely to be changed by seeing a person in different contexts and situations, by encounters designed to enhance their knowledge of a person, by consulting with other witnesses and by greater awareness of the nature and precariousness of their own assumptions. Relevant learning goals are as follows:

- awareness of how one acquires knowledge of people (as discussed in an earlier section), of one's own categories and assumptions, and of the effect of one's own behaviour on interpersonal encounters;
- development of skills in acquiring knowledge of people in a more reliable and reflective manner (this is process knowledge); and
- experience of changing one's mind or greatly expanding one's knowledge about one or two particular persons (important for future attitudes).

Some of these goals can be pursued within the course itself. For there can be a great deal of interpersonal interaction in a variety of contexts: large group, discussion group, small task-group in the formal programme; small group and one-to-one in informal settings 'out of hours'. Awareness of the goal of developing knowledge of people, and time and encouragement to reflect on relevant on-course experience would promote the first and third goals above. An interviewing workshop would develop all three goals, especially the second.

For maximum impact, however, and an improved chance of transfer back to the school situation, it is imperative to engage in some school-based activities under the aegis of the course. These 'Course Activities Based in Schools' (or CABS) will often have more than one purpose and cover several types of knowledge. They must be seen as relevant in school terms, as well as in course terms; and their potential for learning is greatly dependent on good preparation and follow-up within the course itself.

For example, a primary headteacher is asked to carry out pilot staff-development interviews with two teachers. The explicit purpose is to gain experience that will feed into on-course discussions about staff development and teacher appraisal, in other words, developing knowledge of practice; but it is also recognized that the activity could form part of the preamble to any formal discussion of the issue in school, as there will now be teachers with experience of having been interviewed. A third purpose could be the development of interviewing skills (process knowledge), especially if there was prior discussion and an interviewing workshop and later reflection about the interview process itself as well as its content. However, the experience is also likely to develop their knowledge of the teachers they interviewed; and could even affect their management approach if, for example, they became convinced that they should spend more time listening to staff and talking to them as individuals for longer periods, rather than just 'on the wing'.

In another CABS, a group of primary headteachers is asked to interview their staff singly or in pairs about school–parent relations, using a common framework as a guide. The explicit purpose is again that of sharing findings on the course and hence developing knowledge of practice; but often policy discussions and changes in schools have resulted. At an experiential level, many headteachers who thought they knew their staff's views found this knowledge to be either simplistic or wrong. This learning experience of finding existing knowledge of people to be either inadequate or false is important, if they are to develop greater awareness of their own fallibility.

Developing Situational Knowledge

Situational knowledge is probably the least likely to figure in managers' pre-course expectations. Even if they have reflected on the nature of their own situational knowledge, they will perceive it as uniquely held by themselves and therefore unlikely to be further developed on a course. No other course member is likely to be sufficiently informed about other people's schools to be able to contribute knowledge of this kind. Yet, situational knowledge is clearly of enormous importance. It is necessary, if not sufficient, for good relationships and good decision-making; and it is the key to the connection between course events and concurrent or subsequent action in members' own schools. Indeed, some managers rate it so highly, that they doubt the value of management courses because they think management knowledge is ungeneralizable: it is impossible, some would claim, to transfer management ideas from one school to another. We shall examine this issue of transfer later. Meanwhile, it is reasonable to surmise that if changes in situational knowledge can be achieved through the medium of courses, they are likely to lead to changed behaviour in school. Conversely, lack of change would indicate a rigidity of perspective that does not augur well for the course having any significant impact.

In order to discuss how courses may develop the situational knowledge of their participants, it is useful to classify relevant course activities according to information source. The most obvious and authentic source is the situation itself. Hence the need to consider a range of CABS specifically designed for the purpose. This use of CABS as a means of collecting evidence for on-course discussion is significantly different from the more usual practice of using them as applied projects linked to course follow-up. We discuss this in our final section, but here we should note the danger of taking people's situational knowledge for granted when developing school-based action plans. Meanwhile, let us consider two examples.

One fairly common CABS asks a headteacher or a head of department to observe two or three pupils in a class or to shadow a pupil for a day. Commonly, they are struck by the lack of variation in activity, the limited access to teachers' attention and the spasmodic nature of pupils' interest in, and work on, assigned tasks. None of these is a surprising observation in itself, but the magnitude of the problem and the direct experience of observing it have considerable emotional impact. Its priority rating rises; and managerial attention returns to the quality of the classroom experience: the major goal from which it is all too easily deflected.

A perceptive tutor will point out at this stage that reading about the problem or being told about it would not have had the same effect as this first-hand experience. Should they not be devising means whereby teachers could have a similar experience, for only then would they also take ownership of the problem? Such a move would need to be accompanied by the acknowledgment that the problem was a general one, not specific to a few schools or a minority of 'weak' teachers. Otherwise, their actions could be seen as implying a deficit view of their teachers. In this particular case, the explicit purpose of the activity was indeed developing situational knowledge, but the management problem was represented as that of how to develop the situational knowledge of their teachers. At a more general level, it also helps to keep the interests of pupils firmly at the front of people's minds when they consider management issues.

Another very substantial CABS for heads of secondary science departments asks them to construct a departmental profile during the first phase of a management course. This involves them in two days of preparatory training, release days in school, two tutorial days for further advice and support and a substantial written report. The explicit purpose is a thorough situational analysis, and this is followed by a four-week block that relates to some of the problems and issues identified: then finally there is a school-based project with tutorial support. The profile comprises an introductory section about the school context and organization; a description of the department's structure, curriculum and management practice; staff profiles for every teacher in the department; pupil profiles for a small sample; and course profiles incorporating staff comments and pupil questionnaires. The department heads are encouraged to share some of these activities with their staff, sometimes giving them the allocated cover. This sharing of the situational analysis gives staff a stake in the course and provides a sound base for any consequent changes. Apart from

developing this wide-ranging and thoroughly researched situational knowledge, the profile often causes the head of department to tackle difficult relationships that had been allowed to fester.

Next, we consider information sources outside the situation. This can
come from other course members, course tutors, outside speakers or the
education literature. There is a danger of oversimplifying a complex learning
process, but it is still useful to distinguish two ways in which situational
knowledge can be affected by outside sources. These are intuitive generalization and conceptual generalization. Intuitive generalization is the process
whereby connections are made between one situation and another without
any attempt to analyse convincingly the similarities and differences.

At its lowest level, there is recognition that speaker and listeners or author and readers have had similar experiences and are therefore likely to be
useful to each other. This confers authenticity on the information source, thus
increasing the propensity to take their views seriously. Such mutual recognition of credibility is important between course members and plays a significant part in group development. The highest level of intuitive generalization
occurs when the speaker's and listener's situations are perceived as so similar
that identical courses of action are appropriate: the listener is moved to rep-
licate the 'successes' of the speaker. A medium level of generalization would
be when listeners accept the major part of a speaker's interpretation of his or
her situation as also applicable to their situation; so listeners interpret their
own situation in a similar kind of way and welcome the insights that result.

The dominant features of intuitive generalization are that the situation is
treated holistically and the learning experience is *gestaltic*, whereas the opposite
is true for conceptual generalization. Here, some concept or idea that is stated
or demonstrated to be useful in one situation is taken by the learner and
applied to his or her own situation. The idea may be acquired either from a
fellow-practitioner's theorized account of a personal situation, or from some
spoken or written theoretical discourse. Normally, it will not be in a form
that can be instantly applied, though there is usually some early recognition
of its potential. In order to make the idea useful, learners have to work it into
their own thinking, and this takes both time and intellectual effort. The thinking process may be initiated by on-course tasks or discussions but ultimately
has to be completed by learners on their own. Though there will probably be
'flashes of insight', the dominant mode of thinking is analytical. Many managers are unused to this style of thinking, even suspicious of it; but encouraging its development is important for future growth.

Certain government publications and research reports often alert people
to important aspects of their school situations, sometimes by providing new
information and ideas, sometimes by giving such prominence to familiar ideas
that they are taken much more seriously. For example, HMI's continuing
attention to the concept of match between pupil and task is given a strong
empirical base by Bennett's (1984) research on *The quality of learning experiences*. Bennett's examples are easily recognized by primary teachers, who are

thus strongly challenged to review their teaching from this particular stand-point. Similarly, at secondary level, the Rutter report (1979) *Fifteen thousand hours* provoked a great deal of constructive thought about school quality, whether or not one entirely agreed with his conclusions. However, for books such as these to invoke a significant contribution to people's situational know-ledge, their treatment has to be carefully planned. A simple 'read-and-talk' assignment is rarely as productive as a deliberate attempt to seek out key issues, prepare briefings on them, critique the author's views and present provisional thoughts on the implications for one's own school. The ideas of external speakers often require similar treatment if they are not to be rapidly erased by subsequent events. The typical 'lecture and questions after' session is insufficient if conceptual generalization is to result.

The third type of information source is oneself. A common feature of management courses is the time that members give to accounts of their own situations; briefly, informally and frequently in discussion, or in an occasional formal presentation. This rendering of accounts is a learning experience in its own right, because it stimulates the organization of one's knowledge and may even bring about a significant amount of rethinking. This learning does not require any new external input, because the concepts and ideas come from the course members themselves. However, the size of the group is an important factor in discussions. Situational knowledge is unlikely to be developed by personal reflection and accounting in larger groups, because there is no time for any account to be sufficiently developed to be helpful. Groups of three or four are best so that there is time for longer, more detailed accounts, and scope for the prolonged interchange of questions. Similar considerations apply to on-course, follow-up discussions of evidence from CABS.

Given the somewhat haphazard way in which situational knowledge is developed, one major goal of management courses must be to bring it under greater critical control. This and four other learning goals for developing situational knowledge are listed below:

- to bring situational knowledge under critical control;
- to see how others see a situation (this links with knowledge of people);
- to acquire a wider range of interpretative concepts and schemas (conceptual knowledge);
- to develop the ability to improve one's own situational knowledge (this is process knowledge); and
- to experience changing one's view of one particular situation as a result of such improved knowledge (important for future attitudes).

Developing Knowledge of Educational Practice

Knowledge of practice is defined for our purpose as knowledge of the reper-toire of possible educational policies and practices that could be relevant to one's school or college. This includes not only some awareness of the existence of each possible option, but also knowledge of its advantages and limitations in a variety of circumstances, and of opinions regarding its feasibility and its desirability. This category is confined to knowledge about practice, so it does not include the know-how to actually implement that practice: that comes under process knowledge. Nevertheless, the domain is quite large.

For members of management courses, the aim of developing knowledge of practice can be pursued at two levels. First, there is the task of developing knowledge of school-management practice. Second, there is the management task of overseeing the acquisition of knowledge of practice by the school community as a whole, thus ensuring that functional groups and individuals within the school are knowledgeable and up to date in those areas of practice for which they have some responsibility.

For any particular area of practice, the desirable knowledge would include all of the following:

- the approaches used in a range of different schools or colleges;
- other approaches advocated or currently under discussion;
- the principles underpinning and justifying each approach;
- evidence about the strengths and weaknesses of each approach and its appropriateness for particular types of context;
- key issues and arguments on which the choice of approach is likely to hinge; and
- problems likely to be encountered in implementing a particular approach and suggestions for overcoming them.

This formidable list raises the question of how a manager can acquire such knowledge, for it is neither readily available nor uncontested.

An overview or map of the main approaches, principles and issues is an excellent starting point; preferably more than one map if the territory is highly contested. Then concise accounts are needed of the various approaches, summaries of debates about principles and issues, and references to more substantial literature — if it exists. These provide the basic resources for learning. But they will only be useful if there is sufficient time for reading, discussion and reflection; and they may need supplementing by visits to see various options in action.

One problem for the course designer is to acquire the learning resources. If not readily available, they will require considerable pre-course preparation, though in some cases the development of a brief can be part of the members' coursework. This experience of developing a brief would be especially valuable for those who have little experience of thorough preparation of policy briefs — an important type of process knowledge. A second problem is to decide how much time is needed for proper discussion: the criteria for concluding such a discussion could be that most members feel that they have sufficiently used the resources of their course colleagues and they are fully prepared to brief their own staff back at school. The danger is that too many topics will be treated too quickly and too superficially with the result that course members are confirmed in the view that conversational facility with alternative policies and practices is all that good management requires.

This danger is often exacerbated by inviting speakers to come along and market particular policies and practices. This casts course members into a passive role, instead of assuming responsibility for their own continuing development of knowledge of practice; it also encourages the adoption of trends, rather than properly considered policies. The whole process may then be replicated by managers selling the policies to their staff, casting their subordinates into a similarly passive role and probably limiting their understanding of, and capacity to implement, the policy. The dominant metaphor for the approach we advocate is not pyramid selling, but consumer education.

To summarize, learning goals related to developing knowledge of educational practice might be:

- awareness of management's role in developing knowledge of practice in the school as a whole;
- recognition of a good brief;
- developing the capacity to get oneself briefed — process knowledge; and
- enhancing one's knowledge of practice in certain priority areas defined by oneself and/or the course.

Developing Conceptual Knowledge

As argued earlier, conceptual knowledge determines how people perceive and think about their world. The domain of education is no exception. Teachers' conceptual knowledge is developed in a number of ways. Apart from their formal training, many of their perceptual frameworks and values are well-formed by the time they enter the profession. Early socialization into classrooms and schools initiates them into its many unquestioned norms and traditions; and they learn to speak education in the distinctive dialects of their training institutions and local schools. Then consolidation follows during the first few years of teaching. There is a danger that such knowledge will remain static and unchallenged, for even controversial issues tend to be debated along familiar dichotomized lines. While newly appointed headteachers might be expected to show considerable flexibility, some areas of their knowledge will probably remain fairly fixed. Since much of this knowledge has been acquired more by absorption than by study, it will be used without stopping to question its validity or its relevance. A major problem in developing managers' conceptual knowledge is making them more aware of how they already think, so they can bring their knowledge under greater critical control.

The relationship between existing and new conceptual knowledge, policy and practice is best illustrated by some examples. Fifteen years ago, I co-directed a research project on accountability, which involved a great deal of conceptual sorting out and mapping of existing accountability practices, in addition to the examination of, and debate about, new policies. This project required a large number of interviews with different groups — parents, teachers, headteachers, advisers, officers, committee members, governors — reporting of findings, preparation of many drafts of discussion papers, meetings and so on. For those who participated, and also, one hopes, some who read the subsequent reports, the learning included: situational knowledge, because the mapping of practice gave them a much clearer picture of what they themselves were doing and how it was perceived by the various interested parties; knowledge of practice arising from the mapping but also from the discussion of a whole series of possible new policies; and conceptual knowledge. Not only did the development of their conceptual knowledge underpin the first two, but it enabled them to see the connections between a whole range of practices relevant to accountability that would otherwise not have been brought into a unified picture. Many existing ideas were clarified, for example, parent rights, school-based evaluation; and some new conceptual distinctions were made, for example, between monitoring and review. We would argue that this project gave managers conceptual knowledge that was essential for proper handling of accountability policies and issues, without pre-empting any decisions about their own or their LEA's policy and practice.

Another example, which has figured prominently in some management courses, is the concept of individualization. Within the classroom itself, it could apply to the setting of work, the pacing and control of work, teacher-pupil interaction and feedback on performance. Some of these depend on classroom organization, others on teacher interaction time. Similarly, at school level, there are arrangements for handling pupils as classes and arrangements for handling them as individuals. If we get away from the rhetoric and recognize that, with existing teacher-pupil ratios, individualization is only partly achievable, we can ask where it is most necessary and how it can best be made to count. Here, there are no new concepts, but reorganizing one's categories and asking different kinds of questions reshapes one's thinking and significantly affects the management agenda. Very similar treatment could be given to such concepts as communication or consultation, which are fundamental aspects of management practice.

Conceptual development is often best started by a short discussion paper, which seeks to clarify the field, sort out the terms and pose some important issues. Individuals note how they use the terms, or other similar terms, in their own current practice and add further issues to the agenda. Groups are then ready to discuss how they now conceptualize that policy area and what they perceive as the principal issues for their schools. During this process, it is important to develop managers' sensitivity to the role that certain words play in educational discourse. Their history can give them a symbolic meaning that is very different from their literal meaning; they may even be loosely associated with particular ideological positions. Their function, in the short-hand jargon of education-speak, may not be to clarify but to conceal and prevent certain issues from being properly examined. Awareness of education language helps managers understand not only how they themselves have perhaps unwittingly come to use certain words and think in certain ways, but also that the same is true for their teacher colleagues.

A rare example of a book that tries to show how training and socialization have burdened teachers with a series of conceptual assumptions that fail to stand up to critical examination and seriously impede constructive debate is Alexander's (1984) *Primary teaching*. The role of child-centred ideology in diverting attention from serious consideration of pedagogy is developed by Simon (1981); and Anderson (1981) examines the extent to which major curriculum documents trade on rhetoric instead of clarifying issues.

So far, I have stayed within a predominantly educational context, but there is also an area of conceptual knowledge about management itself. Concepts and ideas from management studies feature quite prominently on some courses in educational management, particularly in the areas of personnel, human relations and decision-making; and management literature on such themes as motivation, leadership and organization development is widely used. This importation of fresh ideas can be highly invigorating if properly handled. The worst situations are when management theory is presented as a fixed body of knowledge that will help education become more businesslike. Although unthinking adoption of management theory could well be disastrous in many schools, there is an equal danger that it will be totally rejected as irrelevant to educational contexts. For if theoretical knowledge is seen as a set of tools sitting on a shelf, waiting to be either applied or ignored, or as presenting some kind of complete account of management problems, then rejection is a likely consequence. New concepts and ideas should be seen not as immutable, but as offering fresh insights: starting points for further thinking and reflection that will ultimately result in different perspectives on one's own role and situation. This requires that particular attention is paid to the way in which management theory is introduced. Moreover, in my experience, it helps to be very explicit about the learning process and about both the difficulty and the importance of taking ownership of new concepts.

Given this view of theory as needing individual interpretation, we are concerned about the practice of using psychological instruments without also providing the opportunity to criticize the assumptions on which they are based. There is a plethora of questionnaires on issues like leadership style, learning style, motivation and decision-making, mostly derived from particular theories. But if this is not pointed out, and other theories are not also mentioned, people may feel that they are being brainwashed or being forced into a false position of either total acceptance or rejection of the exercise. Worse still, they might not even notice the assumptions being made.

Concepts can, indeed should, be introduced to help people acquire a range of different ways of perceiving and understanding phenomena. But they have to be worked into people's own individual ways of thinking before they can be properly used. Thus, even in the area of developing conceptual knowledge, on-course activities can only initiate the learning process. In any one course, a limited number of ideas can be examined; but it is nevertheless possible to raise awareness of the significance of conceptual knowledge and the process of developing it. Thus, reasonable goals for a management course might be:

- to make managers more conscious and more critical of their existing conceptual knowledge;
- to recognize the potential of new ideas; and
- to take responsibility for their own continuing development of conceptual knowledge in addition to some of the more obviously practical types of knowledge.

Developing Process Knowledge

Process knowledge is essentially knowledge of how to do things and how to get things done. As suggested earlier, this usually requires a complex combination of knowledge and skills. For example, to manage a process like the introduction of a new options scheme or a policy review involves thinking about the following:

- the division of the process into stages, albeit partly overlapping;
- the key decisions and transition points;
- the tasks to be done;
- the people who will accomplish those tasks;
- the people or groups who will need to be consulted at various stages;
- the approach to be adopted at each stage;
- the problems to be anticipated and overcome;
- how the process will be monitored;
- how the effect upon relationships will be handled; and
- how the concerns of individuals will be met.

This will necessitate drawing on a manager's situational knowledge, knowledge of people and knowledge of educational practice. But conceptualization of the process is not in itself sufficient; the manager also has to initiate and oversee its implementation. Many skills then become important, particularly interpersonal skills, communication skills and skills in planning and coordination.

Perhaps we should start our consideration of improving process knowledge with the development of these skills. This requires the opportunity both to observe the skills in action and to undertake practice with feedback. The special advantages of a course are that one can observe and discuss colleagues' performance, experiment in a less threatening situation and get good quality feedback on one's own performance. The main disadvantage is lack of authenticity. Course situations inevitably differ from school situations and, if that difference becomes too great, the validity of the exercise becomes unacceptably low. This is a particular danger with role-playing exercises. However, the difficulty can be eased if the activity has purpose within the course itself, so that its relevance is not dependent on it being a pale imitation of some similar event in school. Chairing a course meeting, leading a group preparing a policy brief, giving a colleague feedback on his performance and reporting a discussion are all genuine course activities that can be used for learning skills. We have found, for example, that giving opportunities to observe and then report on group processes has been invaluable, as many headteachers seem not to understand how groups work and operate.

Interviewing skills can also be developed by a series of course-relevant activities. For example, collecting accounts by mutual interview of headteachers' experiences as deputies could lead to discussion of headteacher–deputy relations and, if recorded, to analysis of the interviewing process itself.

Another approach is for the genuine task to be performed in school and observed by another course member or recorded for later observation and discussion. One could envisage providing feedback in this way on staff meetings, parents' meetings or even governors' meetings. To my knowledge, this approach has seldom been used. The nearest approximation to it would be rehearsals 'on course' for certain critical school events, for example, introducing a difficult item at a meeting or setting the scene at the beginning of an interview, with videorecording to assist with feedback.

A few skills, however, such as writing, or even telephoning can be practised for real in a course setting. People are used to mock in-tray exercises, but why shouldn't course members bring their own? Those involving phoning or writing could be dealt with in full, while other forms of responsive action could at least be planned.

In general, it is dangerous to cultivate the notion of disembodied skills that exist independently of context and purpose. Interviewing, for example, becomes a different process when the aim is information-seeking and there is only one interviewer from when the aim is selection and there is an interview panel. An appraisal interview would be different yet again. Logical and numerical skills like timetabling and budgeting, which are most prone to decontextualization, normally involve major policy decisions or nondecisions. But these are often hidden so that the aim is reduced to preserving the status quo with the minimum perturbation. Alternative timetables or budgets are particularly difficult to introduce without a great deal of consultation and hard work; and who is looking for that?

Possessing the skills, however, is only one aspect of process knowledge. One also needs to know when and how to use them. A sense of the stages and tasks in a complex change process can be communicated by experienced practitioners presenting case studies; but unless they have kept diaries or been followed by a researcher, much of their finesse may be lost. In particular, how their ongoing reading of the situation and interaction with staff led to adjustments in timing, modification of plans or trouble-shooting, is unlikely to be accurately recalled unless the case study was commissioned beforehand. Otherwise, the closest one can get is the sharing of particular accounts and experiences with the aid of a checklist. Listening to others' accounts can broaden awareness of the factors involved in change and possibly expand the tactical repertoire as well; but the application of this knowledge will still depend on people's ability to understand and perform in their own schools. Developing process knowledge depends not only on seeing or hearing about others' performance, but also on getting sufficient feedback on one's own. If this cannot be done by visiting outsiders, then managers are dependent for feedback on their own staff. Here, a CABS, which required a manager to collect accounts from subordinates about some particular change process, and how they perceived it at various stages, would be doubly useful. First, it would enhance their awareness of how their own actions were seen by others; and, second, it would establish a greater sense of the value of feedback and the feasibility of obtaining it — an important aspect of control knowledge that we shall return to shortly.

It is also important to gain a balanced view of different but complementary perspectives on the change process. In the technical-rational perspective, there are stages where information is sought and analysed, issues are discussed and argued through, decisions are made and plans are developed and implemented. From a political perspective, the same process becomes a power game, in which certain people influence others by a variety of means. Some see themselves as winners and others as losers, as the balance between authority, collegiality and autonomy is constantly renegotiated. From a social-psychological perspective, there are encounters over a period of time that affect teachers' personal relationships, their morale, their involvement with the school and their image of themselves and others. Then, finally, there is the learning dimension, which is our special concern. People learn as they collect or receive new information, rethink issues, and develop and work through ideas; and the quality of this learning is particularly important at the implementation stage of any change process. One cannot easily explain how these perspectives interrelate without an extremely detailed account of a particular case; and that would not be generalizable at a detailed level. What the analysis serves to demonstrate is the complexity of process knowledge and the need for a range of approaches to its development.

Developing Control Knowledge

Control knowledge is taken here to mean metaknowledge, that is, knowledge about knowledge and its use, which guides one's thinking and one's learning. In its most situational form, this might include self-awareness; in its most abstract form it covers thinking strategies and overarching theories that appear to govern one's behaviour. Its core is self-management.

Self-awareness is acquired through reflection and feedback. Courses have tended to use so-called 'sensitivity training' activities for this purpose, but again the transfer back to school is problematic. As suggested earlier, a key factor in such learning is the ability to get feedback within the work situation itself. The use of recording and mutual observation by course members was suggested earlier, perhaps using sensitivity exercises to establish initial trust between course members.

Self-knowledge is a wider term, which also includes knowledge of one's own knowledge and skills, when and how to use them and when to look beyond one's own resources. One problem is the apparently simple one of organizing one's knowledge for easy retrieval, otherwise it tends to get forgotten or ignored. Another, to which managers are particularly prone, is over-reliance on one's own knowledge and resources. Knowing how to get briefed by others is important, and this can be practised and taught. More fundamental still is the knowledge of one's strengths and weaknesses, which guides the way one delegates and the types of task one assigns to oneself. People often have such self-knowledge but do not think through its implications for how they define their management role. The contribution of courses here is to raise awareness of the problems, to provide an ambience which makes it easier for people to recognize and come to terms with personal strengths and weaknesses, and to encourage habits of organizing and noting thoughts before they get forgotten.

This brings us to self-management, the control of conduct in such crucial areas as use of time, prioritization of management resources and delegation. People's subjective impressions on such matters are usually inaccurate; so CABS involving data collection on use of time and multiple perspectives on prioritization and delegation are particularly important. Such data can then be discussed on-course with the issues linked together. Members may wish to develop action plans; and there are considerable advantages in phasing the course so that members can test these out — particularly those involving time management — and return to discuss the problems of implementation. Instead of a single course input on time management, with little implementation or follow-up, there needs to be a continuing dialogue between the ideal efficient suggestions of the 'management experts' and the ongoing practical problems of individual course members. Moreover, most of the key issues are not purely technical; they involve complex professional judgments about managers' roles and priorities.

Perhaps most difficult of all is the creation of time for one's own further learning and development; this is partly because few managers have attempted to formulate a self-development programme that is sufficiently precise to be a serious contender for their time. Where a course can help is first, by providing a wide range of learning opportunities, and CABS are an important element in this; and second, by deliberately seeking to raise participants' awareness of themselves as learners. Professional knowledge and professional learning should be an important part of the course agenda, so that members can critically assess what and how they have been learning, the learning opportunities that are available to them in the normal school context and how these might need supplementing in any planned self-development programme. This experience could also be generalized to reconsidering the nature of their managerial responsibility for the professional development of their staff, and the capacities of various types of staff-development policy for providing the kind of learning opportunities that they themselves have found to be the most productive.

The last suggestion above was an example of a particular kind of thinking skill — speculative generalization — in which ideas or experiences gained in one situation (their own course-related learning) are tentatively applied to another (their school's staff development policy), not with the intention of direct transfer, but rather to raise new questions and provide a different perspective. One could ask, for example, how many of the ideas that seem obvious during a discussion of team-building, actually get used when the process is school review or curriculum development. These are but some of a number of ways in which managers' ability to think analytically and creatively about their problems and policies could be developed. A course is an excellent context for developing strategic and analytic thinking, because time can be set aside for it and examples can be offered for discussion. It is also particularly important, if members are to develop action plans, that the considerable commitment of effort involved is directed towards a strategic priority for the school, not just a conveniently easy exercise.

Finally, we come to that aspect of control knowledge given particular attention by Argyris and Schön (1974), the theories that determine how managers manage. Argyris and Schön demonstrated that for most professional managers there is a significant difference between their espoused theories, their justifications for what they do and their explicit reasons for it, and their theories in use, those often implicit theories that actually determine their behaviour. This gap between account and action is a natural consequence of people's perceptual frameworks being determined by what they want or expect to see, and by subordinates reporting to managers what they think they want to hear. The solution Argyris and Schön recommend is to give priority, not so much to objectives — for then one reads situations purely in terms of one's own preplanned ideas of how they ought to develop — as to getting good quality feedback. Unless one is prepared to receive, indeed actively seeks, feedback that is from a different perspective and often adverse or distressing, one will continue to misread situations and to deceive oneself that one's own actions are the best in the circumstances. A major purpose for a management course, then, is to raise members' awareness of the gap between their espoused theories and their practices, to make their theories in use explicit and bring them under critical control, to equip them with the skills of getting good feedback and to commit them to continuing to seek good feedback on the job. According to Argyris and Schön, control knowledge, is the key to good management and continuing professional development, is critically dependent on obtaining and making proper use of good quality feedback.

The Interface Between Course and School

Throughout the chapter, the linkage between course and school has been a major emphasis. The assumptions have been: that most professional learning is 'on the job', and the role of the course is to enhance such on-the-job learning; and that where learning involves the introduction of new concepts or new 'management knowledge' there needs to be provision for transfer back into the school situation. The simplest examples of good linkage are those where CABS both foster in-school learning and provide evidence for discussions on course that further develop, broaden and enhance this learning. However, this simple sequence can sometimes be profitably extended by adding a further CABS and yet another on-course discussion after that. The merits of such a prolonged sequence are that it treats the topic with sufficient thoroughness and depth really to make an impact and that it is often at the application stage, rather than the gathering of relevant evidence, that many major problems arise. This makes it a priority stage for course support. It is also the stage when members can begin to give each other practical advice in addition to generally exchanging ideas.

It is common for periods to be set aside on courses for members to make action plans for their return to school. These can range from merely listing things to be done to producing substantial documents with a great deal of consultation with course colleagues and tutors. The former is like making New Year resolutions and probably has a similar chance of success. The latter frequently leads to subsequent action because the time, the support and the impetus have been given to getting over the initial stage. However, being out of school makes consultation with colleagues difficult, so there is a need to introduce consultation days back in school, or to phase the planning over several course blocks so there is plenty of in-school time available during the planning process.

There is a great accountability benefit in including such work on management courses, because the short-term impact on schools becomes more clearly demonstrable. But what is the nature of the learning process? Often it is seen as a culminating exercise bringing together a number of course topics — a synthesizing and consolidating activity. It could also be seen as training in planning and problem-solving, or as confidence-building. It could be showing people how much they can help each other, even when planning actions for their own particular schools. Whatever combination of objectives the course designer chooses, the tasks will need to be defined, phased and supported in a manner that reflects these intentions.

Yet another approach is to rely on subsequent meetings of course members to provide the necessary support. The most sophisticated form of this can be found in Revans' (1982) notion of 'action learning groups'; and members formulate their own action plans for their own situation; and the group meets regularly thereafter to report on progress and to question one another. Significantly, Revans worked with mixed groups of managers from different sectors, suggesting that school managers should not be segregated from those outside education for this particular kind of activity. He also used a trained set adviser to guide and catalyze the learning in each group. His groups did not arise out of a management course, though there was an induction process. However, we ourselves have tended to use them as an integral part of a course, which continues throughout the follow-up period.

Nearly all the procedures discussed above are time-consuming. We do not believe there are short cuts; the danger is usually a consistent underestimation of the requirements for effective learning. In our experience, a series of activities, both in school and on course, are needed if one is to achieve a significant impact on a particular issue or topic. Courses have to be designed to allow interplay between course and school; and the number of themes has to be restricted accordingly. Moreover, there are obvious limits to the number of CABS that any one person can undertake. In turn, this need for a limited focus for any particular course challenges the prevalent assumption that a management course, even a fairly long one of twenty days, should be a once-in-a-lifetime experience.

Note

1. This chapter was originally published in Poster, C. and Day C. (Eds) (1988) *Partnership in Education Management*, Routledge.

Chapter 6

Learning Professional Processes: Public Knowledge and Personal Experience

The Professions and Higher Education

The professions constitute a subset of occupations the boundary of which is ill-defined. Features such as length of training, licence to practise, code of ethics, self-regulation and monopoly feature in most discussions about the nature of professions but do not provide a workable definition nor remain stable over time. Hence Johnson (1972, 1984) argues that, instead of defining what constitutes a profession, we should regard 'professionalism' as an ideology and 'professionalization' as the process by which an occupation seeks to advance its status and progress towards full recognition within that ideology. Irrespective of what professionals actually do, their knowledge claims are strongly influenced by the need to sustain the ideology of professionalism and further the process of professionalization. Since higher education also derives its authority from knowledge claims, the history of the relationship between higher education and the professions has to be seen in this political context.

Since the war, an increasing number of occupations has taken advantage of higher education for two main reasons. First, getting a degree-entry route established validates the profession's claim to a specialist knowledge base, and hence to professional status. Second, recruitment through the higher-education system is critical for sustaining, let alone improving, the relative quality of a profession's intake.

Higher education has also derived considerable benefits from its relationship with the professions. The presence of professionally-focused courses has helped increasingly beleaguered institutions to argue that they do prepare students for employment and make a positive contribution to society. They have contributed to the expansion of student numbers, particularly in the public sector; and individual faculties and departments have been able to increase their relative power by incorporating areas of professional training which were previously outside higher education. Indeed, the widespread incorporation of paramedical training was strongly aided by the wish to sustain the number of science students at a time of declining recruitment for degrees in pure science (Jones, 1986).

Although both partners stood to benefit, there were many complicated negotiations between professional bodies and representatives of higher education, often involving other agencies as well. The professions sought to maintain their control over the licence to practise, while higher education sought to permeate new courses with its espoused aims of breadth, intellectual challenge and the development of critical abilities (Kerr, 1984). In a very real sense, these negotiations involved both partners in a reconstruction of the professional knowledge base. However, it is arguable how far this started from first principles. The resultant compromises could equally be described in terms of power-sharing between two distinct historical traditions.

The most obvious area of compromise is the structure of the training period. Three distinct patterns stand out. First there is the dual qualification system, favoured by law and surveying, in which a degree approved by the professional body is followed by a period of apprenticeship in professional practice and separate assessment for licencing purposes. This tends to be favoured by the more powerful professions, which can justify a long training period and argue that their knowledge base demands at least three years of full-time study. Its major disadvantage is the acute separation of theory from practice. Second, there is a concurrent system, in which periods of professional practice are built into the higher-degree course. The power of the profession is considerably less, but may be asserted in two ways: through the assessment of the professional practice component or through the course-approval process, although neither is guaranteed in all professions. Concurrent systems offer greater opportunities for integrating theory with practice, but this potential is still underdeveloped. Some sandwich courses fit this more integrated pattern, for example those in design. But others are only dual-qualification systems in disguise: in engineering, for example, there is little integration and undergraduate trainees are underused on many placements. Third, there is an increasing range of patterns associated with part-time study, some of which incorporate links with students' regular employment: personnel management and management accountancy use this as their major route to qualifications.

The negotiations over content have had equally pervasive results because the traditional higher-education concern with disciplined, codified, propositional knowledge has usually triumphed. Either degree courses have been heavily weighted by components from 'recognized disciplines', or professional departments have been influenced by higher-education norms towards giving research priority over developing professional practice. The result has been what Schön (1983) has called the dominant 'technical rationality' model of professional knowledge, which is characterized by a number of features:

> the systematic knowledge base of a profession is thought to have four essential properties. It is specialised, firmly bounded, scientific and standardised. (Schön 1983, p. 23)

> the two primary bases for specialization within a profession are (1) the substantive field of knowledge that the specialist professes to command and (2) the technique of production or application of knowledge over which the specialist claims mastery. (Moore, 1970, p. 141)

> the concept of 'application' leads to a view of professional knowledge as a hierarchy in which 'general principles' occupy the highest level and 'concrete problem solving', the lowest. (Schön, 1983, p. 24)

Schön goes on to argue that this definition of rigorous professional knowledge excludes situations and phenomena which many professionals perceive as central to their practice. Knowledge of central importance to providing services to clients is accorded low priority in higher education or omitted altogether.

Behind Schön's position lies the view that the term 'knowledge' should be interpreted with the broadest possible meaning. Thus it should not be confined to codified, propositional knowledge but should also include personal knowledge, tacit knowledge, process knowledge and know-how. All kinds of knowledge are necessary to professional performance; and they should therefore be accorded parity of esteem in higher education. Hence the fundamental issue of different kinds of professional knowledge will be explored at some length before I finally return to discuss the implications for professional education.

Towards a Map of Professional Knowledge

This chapter attempts to provide some guidance for those about to engage on the difficult task of determining the knowledge base of a profession.[1] At this stage, any map is bound to be fuzzy and incomplete but nevertheless it is needed for several reasons:

- to correct oversimplified views in current circulation;
- to illuminate the debate about theory–practice links and the role of experiential learning;
- to highlight aspects of knowledge that hitherto have been somewhat neglected in higher education; and
- to inform the growing debate about competence-based approaches to occupational standards and qualifications.

My task is complicated by the primitive state of our methodology for describing and prescribing a profession's knowledge base. Many areas of professional knowledge and judgment have not been codified; and it is increasingly recognized that experts often cannot explain the nature of their own expertise. A variety of methods and approaches has been developed by philosophers, psychologists, sociologists and government agencies, each with its own limitations. However, one central difficulty has been the lack of attention given to different kinds of knowledge. The field is underconceptualized.

Most of my attention, therefore, will be devoted to distinguishing between different types of knowledge, considering how they are acquired and discussing their role in professional action. I shall begin with 'propositional knowledge', the traditional basis of teaching in higher education; then move to consider the nature and role of personal knowledge, especially pre-propositional 'impressions'. The longest section, however, will be devoted to various categories of 'process knowledge', a term I prefer to the more limited 'procedural knowledge' and 'know-how'. This will include discussions about how different processes make use of propositional knowledge and personal impressions. Finally there are some areas of knowledge which are more than impressions yet different again from propositional knowledge or process knowledge. These include moral principles and knowledge embedded in literature and the arts, the particular characteristics of which I do not propose to address.

Propositional Knowledge

Higher education is accustomed to maps of propositional knowledge, which it uses for the construction of syllabi. So I will give it only brief attention and avoid repeating what is already well-known. Chapter 3 distinguished three subcategories of propositional knowledge:

- discipline-based theories and concepts, derived from bodies of coherent, systematic knowledge (*Wissenschaft*);
- generalizations and practical principles in the applied field of professional action; and
- specific propositions about particular cases, decisions and actions.

then went on to explain that such knowledge may get used in one of four modes — replication, application, interpretation or association — as a corrective to the common assumption that there is but one 'applied' mode of use. The last two modes, in particular, characterize the use of propositional knowledge within professional processes of the kind we describe below.

Two further issues should concern us when we consider the extent to which disciplined knowledge forms part of a profession's knowledge base. One use of disciplines is to provide a critical perspective when judging the validity of a profession's generalizations and practical principles (Hirst, 1985). Another use is when concepts and ideas from disciplines are drawn upon directly during deliberations about practical situations and actions. As suggested above, the use of such theoretical knowledge may not always be in the application mode stressed by the technical rationality model, but in the interpretative mode where it is more difficult to detect. Moreover, just because busy professionals do not use a particular idea, does not imply that they should not: that remains to be argued. It is also likely that a profession's awareness of possibly relevant research in a related discipline will be limited.

Virtually all discipline-based knowledge and most of the generalizations and practical principles of the profession will be publicly available, codified knowledge. So will the kind of facts which appear in reference books. However, not all propositional knowledge is public. Personal knowledge contains propositions; and public theories and principles may give rise to personal interpretations. Finally, there is collegial knowledge, such as case material, which may not have been published but nevertheless has been organized, recorded and treated as true by people other than the author.

Impressions, Personal Knowledge and the Interpretation of Experience

All people acquire knowledge through experiences the purposes of which have little overt connection with learning, through social interaction and trying to get things done. Such knowledge covers people and situations encountered, communications received and events and activities experienced through participation or observation. While some of this knowledge is sufficiently processed to be classified as propositional knowledge or process knowledge, much will remain at the level of simple impressions. Nevertheless, impressions gained from experience contribute to professional action in ways that are still only partially understood.

To pursue this problem further, I wish to examine the range of phenomena associated with two ideas in general circulation: those of 'personal knowledge' and 'experiential learning'. Since I will be traversing such a philosophical minefield without the appropriate qualifications I shall take as my guide Schutz's classic text *The Phenomenology of the Social World*. Schutz (1967), following Husserl, provides theories to explain how experience is apprehended and made meaningful; how configurations of meaning are constructed at higher levels; and how these become 'taken-for-granted' schemes of experience constituting the patterns of interpretation which provide order in our lives.

Each of us is embedded in a continuous flow of experience throughout our lives. Discrete experiences are distinguished from this flow and become meaningful when they are accorded attention and reflected upon. The 'act of attention' brings experiences, which would otherwise simply be lived through, into the area of conscious thought; where treatment may vary from actual comprehending to merely noting or hardly noticing. Such attention may be given on a number of occasions, each conferring a different meaning on the experience according to the meaning-context of the moment.

However, these basic experiences become subsumed within a higher level 'object' of attention when separate acts of attention are gathered together into a higher synthesis. We remember a table rather than a long series of occasions when it was encountered. Hence, higher levels of meaning can be built up layer upon layer; and higher meaning-configurations themselves become objects of attention if they can be apprehended as single entities. For example, a friend or colleague is apprehended as a person in the first instance, not as a selection of the encounters which contributed to our knowledge of that person. But if we need to think more deeply about the nature of that person, we can return to lower levels of aggregation or penetrate beyond those levels to particular incidents. As Schutz suggests, 'the reflective glance will penetrate more or less deeply into lived experience depending on its point of view'. The particular level of meaning which presents itself as not in need of further analysis is defined by Schutz as the 'taken for granted'; and what is taken for granted depends on the pragmatic purpose of the reflective glance.

The ordinary person perceives the world as ordered. This order seems natural and can be seen both as a synthesis of past experience and as knowledge of what to expect in the future. Schutz calls these patterns of order the 'schemes of our experience', including both experiences of the external world and inner experiences of the activity of our mind and will. These 'schemes of experience' are normally taken for granted. We do not question them unless a special problem arises and even then we are unlikely to probe very deeply. They also provide the framework through which new experience is interpreted and in this way order the future as well as the past. But also, to varying degrees according to the intention of the person concerned, schemes will adjust and develop in the light of new information and new schemes may be constructed to handle new types of experience. Such development is readily apparent during childhood, when receiving effective education and in the early formative years of a professional career.

Returning to our earlier concern with types of knowledge, three important questions need to be addressed.

1. To what extent does the ordinary person's stock of knowledge constitute propositional knowledge?
2. What, if any, is the difference between the personal knowledge whose construction we have just been discussing and the largely codified propositional knowledge taught in universities?
3. What are the implications for professional education?

Question 1 was pre-empted by my decision to group types of knowledge into three rather than two major categories. This was intended to stress that, at least at the lower levels of personal knowledge, that which has been accorded little attention (and therefore only partially subsumed into higher configurations of meaning) cannot be regarded as either propositional knowledge or process knowledge. I referred to it earlier as prepropositional, but even that would be making unwarranted assumptions. The term 'impressions' describes it well.

A more difficult problem arises, however, when we consider higher-order knowledge in the form of schemes of experience. Such knowledge undoubtedly includes propositions, but can it be fully expressed in propositional form? Personally, I think not; and I recall an epigram (source unknown) from the debate in the early 1970s between proponents of qualitative and quantitative methods of inquiry. To the well-known claim: 'If you can't count it, it doesn't count.' The qualitative reply was: 'If you can count it, it isn't it.'

If you do describe a scheme purely in terms of propositions, you have probably left something out; and it could be something quite important. This view of the limited scope of propositional knowledge is not only supported by scholars like Schön but also by those concerned with the arts. Even the field of artificial intelligence appears to be experiencing a paradigm shift in this direction, following recent failures to convert many areas of human expertise to wholly propositional form.

Question 2 recognizes that the educational experiences of graduates will have incorporated years of continuous encounters with propositional knowledge in its codified, public forms. So it can be safely assumed that a professional person's stock of knowledge will owe a great deal to the contributions of such knowledge. However, this will not be all. As stated at the beginning of this section, there are many experiences from which people learn without there being any intended educational purpose and without any codified, propositional knowledge being drawn to their attention. People naturally develop some constructs, perspectives and frames of reference which are esssentially personal, even if they have been influenced by public concepts and ideas circulating in their community. Another proviso is that even schemes which are consciously and directly attributable to codified propositional knowledge become at least partially personalized through the process of being used. The personal meaning of a public idea is influenced both by the personal cognitive framework in which it is set (what propositions it is linked to) and by the history of its personal use (which also influences the meaning-contexts in which it is seen to belong).

Question 3 addresses the implications of this analysis for professional education. These are greatest for those whose work involves regular contact with clients. First, aspiring professionals already possess a great deal of relevant knowledge as a result of growing up in a particular culture; but that knowledge needs to be brought under critical control by developing greater awareness of how it is used and re-examining taken-for-granted assumptions. They also possess a lot of impressions which can contribute to their professional knowledge base, but still need to be further organized and processed. Second, they will continue to learn experientially throughout their professional lives, for example in getting to know other people; but they will need to be more aware of how they operate and to be able to supplement such knowledge with more deliberately gathered information. Third, they need to recognize that other people learn experientially as well. In spite of its fallibility, they must learn to use experience rather than disregard it (see Chapter 5).

Finally, I wish to use the foregoing analysis to provide a definition of experiential learning to which I can refer in later sections. To avoid the truism that all learning is experiential, at least in some sense, I propose to restrict the term 'experiential learning' to situations where experience is initially apprehended at the level of impressions, thus requiring a further period of reflective thinking before it is either assimilated into existing schemes of experience or induces those schemes to change in order to accommodate it. Most models of experiential learning assume that this further reflection will happen, but that will depend on the disposition of the learner. Hence our ability to discuss the extent to which somebody has learned from experience. One reason why learning might remain initially at the level of impressions may be that there is often no specific learning intent; another is that the flow of experience and need for simultaneous action is so rapid that little further attention can be devoted to reflection until some later occasion.

Process Knowledge

When people are asked to describe what professionals do or to examine the nature of professional action, the result will be a list of processes. Indeed, the quality of professional performance largely depends on the manner in which such processes are conducted. All professional processes make considerable use of propositional knowledge; and this will be a recurrent theme in this section. But nevertheless Ryle's (1949) distinction between 'knowing that' and 'knowing how' remains. In this context 'process knowledge' can be defined as knowing how to conduct the various processes that contribute to professional action. This includes knowing how to access and make good use of propositional knowledge.

There also exists a body of propositional knowledge about processes. People write books about them, especially in the area of management. But the purpose of these books is usually to provide guidance. If they attempt to provide blueprints for higher-level processes, their validity is immediately disputed. Indeed it would be interesting to pursue the question of how it might be possible to determine whether such propositions were true. Our task here, however, is simply to note that the way people conduct professional processes can be only partially described by such propositions. 'Knowing how' cannot be reduced to 'knowing that'.

In order to illustrate the initial importance of process knowledge for professional action, I have selected five kinds of process for further discussion. These are:

* acquiring information;
* skilled behaviour;
* deliberative processes, e.g., planning and decision-making;
* giving information; and
* metaprocesses for directing and controlling one's own behaviour.

These five are interdependent; so also, I suspect, would be any additions to this list. My purposes during the following analyses of these types of process will be threefold:

1. to indicate how process knowledge contributes to professional action;
2. to prepare the ground for considering how and where process knowledge might be best learned;
3. to provide a basis for considering the merits of competency-based approaches to professional education.

Acquiring information

Processes for acquiring information involve the use of recognized methods of inquiry. However, not all professionals are thoroughly trained in all the methods they use. The reason, I believe, is that methods like interviewing and observation are often regarded as just common sense: so exposure to the practice of senior professionals is more than sufficient training. Perhaps this explains why a significant minority of professionals does not communicate well with clients?

Professional training will not remove the experiential element from information acquisition, nor is it necessarily desirable that it should. People still make tacit use of schemes of experience derived from their past; and will also acquire information simply by being present on a relevant occasion: such information often complements that which is obtained by more rational approaches. Even when reading a book one may learn many things other than those one originally had in mind. During a formal interview, one may pursue a planned list of questions and still learn as much from the unplanned aspects of the encounter. On the other hand, it is equally important to ask appropriate questions and to recognize relevant information when one comes across it.

An effective and efficient approach to the acquisition of information requires at least four types of knowledge:

- an existing knowledge-base in the area concerned;
- some kind of conceptual framework to guide one's inquiry;
- skills in collecting information; and
- skills in interpreting information.

This could be characterized as a combination of appropriate propositional knowledge and the ability to select and implement appropriate methods of inquiry. Some methods such as interviewing, listening and observation are used in most professions, while others such as certain scientific tests are highly specialized in particular professions, for example, psychiatric interviewing, listening for a foetal heartbeat, observing a microorganism under magnification. Although propositional knowledge is vitally important in all these examples, none of these methods of inquiry can be learned from propositional knowledge alone. The knowing how is as important as the knowing that.

As suggested above, interpretation is a particularly important aspect of information acquisition; and it is useful to distinguish between three separate modes:

- instant interpretation, as in recognizing a person;
- rapid interpretation, as in monitoring one's progress in the middle of an interview; and
- deliberative interpretation, when there is time for thought and discussion, and even for returning to collect more information.

The mode adopted is affected by the expertise of the interpreter as well as the nature of the task. The expert translator, for example, will interpret a written foreign language text in the rapid mode unless it is an especially difficult passage: whereas the novice may have to deliberate for some considerable time. There is also a shift from the deliberative mode towards rapid interpretation when people gain expertise in examining complex visual information, e.g., an aerial photograph, an electron micrograph, an X-ray image, an architect's drawing, an infrared spectrum.

When there are products to examine, deliberation is the obvious approach for the novice. But when the evidence appears during real-time incidents in a busy or crowded environment such as a casualty department or a classroom, there may be little time for deliberation. A live encounter passes in a flash. What is remembered will depend on the ability of the perceiver to notice and select the right information rapidly at the time of the encounter. There is no opportunity to start learning to interpret such incidents in 'slow motion'. Reflection has to take place after the event and may not be helpful without an experienced tutor who has observed the same incident and noted the significant evidence.

Pattern recognition may also involve making comparisons over time. Experienced professionals learn to detect changes in a familiar person or situation. This is particularly important in nursing where intuitive detection of change in a patient's condition often precedes more dramatic events or alerts nurses to the need for other sources of information (Benner, 1984). This capability appears to be experientially developed, though there may be a significant role for tutors in accelerating the learning process. It clearly depends on continuity of contact with the client with obvious implications for how nursing care is organized. Similar situations probably arise in other professions, for example, social work, environmental protection, military intelligence.

Different issues emerge when people combine evidence from a number of incidents and sources. For example, let us consider how a teacher acquires information about individual pupils in his or her class. Although teachers receive some information from records and comments from other teachers, their knowledge of individual pupils is based mainly on direct encounters in the classroom. These encounters are predominantly with the class as a group, but nevertheless a series of incidents involving individuals in whole-class, small-group or one-to-one settings is likely to be stored in memory, rather like a series of film clips. Insofar as a teacher has made notes, these are likely to serve as *aides-mémoire* rather than independent sources of information. How is the information then used? Under conditions of rapid interpretation, teachers will respond to situations on the basis of their current images of the pupils; though these images may have themselves been formed by rapid assimilation of evidence with little time for reflection. Under conditions of deliberative interpretation, the most accessible evidence is likely to be carefully considered; but even that may be a sample of remembered encounters selected for their ready accessibility rather than their representativeness.

Pyschological research on the information-gathering aspect of human decision-making has shown that a number of errors regularly occur, from which professionals are certainly not exempt (Nisbett and Ross, 1980). When retrieval from memory is a critical factor, incidents involving a person are more likely to be recalled if they are more recent and/or more salient: quiet unobtrusive people may not be remembered at all. Also sufficient allowance may not be made when a highly atypical sample of incidents provides the basis of the memory record. For example, a senior manager will rarely see junior employees at their ordinary work, a teacher in charge of discipline may only see pupils when they are in trouble, a clergyman sees parishioners in their Sunday best, and so on.

Misunderstanding is also likely to ensue from the strong tendency endemic in all of us to interpret events in accordance with our prior expectations. Thus earlier incidents may affect how later incidents are perceived. Worse still, informal second-hand reports or rumours may affect how the first direct encounters with a person are interpreted. People tend to see what they expect to see. Professional education needs to ensure that students are both fully aware of these pitfalls and able to review existing evidence and to collect new evidence in ways that avoid them.

Another information-gathering process of particular importance in social and community work, but not to be neglected in other professions, is networking. Effective performance can depend on having developed a wide range of contacts and sources of information, keeping it current and having the right relationship to be able to acquire authentic information in a hurry.

Finally there is a series of information-gathering processes associated with academic study and the extraction of information from documentary sources. These range from general library skills and study skills to the use of specialized references or techniques of textual analysis. The typology of Parker and Rubin (1966) is particulary helpful in this context.

1. Processes which expose the student to a particular body of knowledge: formulating questions, reading, observing, listening, collecting evidence, discovering principles.

2. Processes which allow the student to extract meaning from the body of knowledge: analyzing, experimenting, reorganizing, consolidating, integrating.
3. Processes which enable the learner to affix significance to the knowledge: inferring generalizations, reconstructing, relating to other situations, testing for usability. (Parker and Rubin, 1966)

These go well beyond the acquisition of information to the extraction of meaning and to the cognitive processing of propositional knowledge, thus moving into my 'deliberative processes' category which is further discussed below.

Skilled behaviour

The term 'skill' is given a wide range of meanings, all carrying a positive connotation of competence. The most appropriate dictionary definition is probably 'practical knowledge combined with ability'. I shall use what I believe to be its core meaning in discussions about knowledge and competence, and define 'skilled behaviour' as a complex sequence of actions which has become so routinized through practice and experience that it is performed almost automatically. For example, much of what a teacher does is skilled behaviour. This is largely acquired through practice with feedback, mainly feedback from the effect of one's actions on classes and individuals. Feedback and advice from tutors or more experienced teachers is variable in quantity and quality, according to the system of initial training and the attitude of teacher colleagues to student or beginning teachers. Teachers' early experiences are characterized by the gradual routinization of their teaching and this is necessary for them to be able to cope with what would otherwise be a highly stressful situation with a continuing 'information overload'. This routinization is accompanied by a diminution of self-consciousness and a focusing of perceptual awareness on particular phenomena. Hence, knowledge of how to teach becomes tacit knowledge, something which is not easily explained to others or even to oneself.

Many similar examples can be found in other professions, particularly in the area of interpersonal skills and communication skills. However, unlike some commonly cited examples such as swimming or riding a bicycle, professional skills tend to involve a significant amount of rapid decision-making. For example, Jackson (1968) estimated that a primary teacher might make a thousand decisions a day. These decisions do not involve the deliberative processes discussed below, but are interactive decisions made on the spur of the moment in response to rapid readings of the situation and the overall purpose of the action. Such decisions have to be largely intuitive, so the person concerned will find it quite difficult to provide a quick explanation. This creates a dilemma that characterizes large areas of professional work. The development of routines is a natural process, essential for coping with the job and responsible for increased efficiency; but the combination of tacit knowledge and intuitive decision-making makes them difficult to monitor and to keep under critical control. As a result, routines tend to become progressively disfunctional over time: not only do they fail to adjust to new circumstances but 'shortcuts' gradually intrude, some of which only help professionals to cope with pressure at the expense of helping their clients.

Apart from these minor modifications, routinized actions are particularly difficult to change. Consider, for example, my analysis of the problems facing attempts at educational reform:

> For teachers to change their classroom practice in any radical way involves both modifying their classroom persona and embarking on a learning task of enormous magnitude. Changing one's routines involves a great deal of unlearning before one can begin to reconstruct new routines; and the experience is like going back to being a novice again with all the difficulties of coping and maintaining classroom order but little of the tolerance and sympathy which is normally accorded to beginners. Even the intuitive decision-making is disrupted because one's 'navigation lights', those semi-conscious cues which alert teachers to the need to change the pace or the activity or to attend to certain pupils, are extinguished when the pattern of practice is modified. The experience of disorientation and alienation is profound; and unless teachers are given considerable psychological and practical support over a long period, they will revert to their old familiar practice. (Eraut, 1992)

Deliberative processes

Deliberative processes such as planning, problem-solving, analysing, evaluating and decision-making lie at the heart of professional work. These processes cannot be accomplished by using procedural knowledge alone or by following a manual. They require unique combinations of propositional knowledge, situational knowledge and professional judgment. In most situations, there will not be a single correct answer, nor a guaranteed road to success; and even when there is a unique solution it will have to be recognized as such by discriminations which cannot be programmed in advance. More typically there will be:

- some uncertainty about outcomes;
- guidance from theory which is only partially helpful;
- relevant but often insufficient contextual knowledge;
- pressure on the time available for deliberation;
- a strong tendency to follow accustomed patterns of thinking; and
- an opportunity, perhaps a requirement to consult or involve other people.

These processes require two main types of information: knowledge of the context/situation/problem, and conceptions of practical courses of action/ decision options. In each case, there is a need for both information and analysis. What does this mean in practice? We have already discussed the wide range of means by which such information can be acquired; and alluded to the phenomena of pattern recognition and rapid interpretation during the process of collection. Here, we consider the more cognitively demanding activities of deliberative interpretation and analysis, for which professionals need to be able to draw upon a wide repertoire of potentially relevant theories and ideas. Also important for understanding the situation is knowledge of the theories, perceptions and priorities of clients, co-professionals and other interested parties. While some may be explicitly stated, others may be hidden, implicit and difficult to detect. Thus one of the most challenging and creative aspects of the information-gathering process is the elucidation of different people's definitions of the situation.

The other information-gathering task is equally demanding, the formulation of a range of decision options or alternative courses of action. This depends both on knowledge of existing practice and on the ability to invent or search for alternatives. Such knowledge of practice is mainly propositional knowledge acquired during training, but in need of regular updating thereafter. The research on change shows that busy people outside academia and the most highly specialized practices rely mainly on personal contact for such information rather than courses or professional literature. This may not be desirable but has to be taken into account. One problem for the professional is the difficulty of evaluating new ideas on the basis of limited information. All too often reports refer to work in contexts different from one's own and are written by advocates and enthusiasts. Thus the skills of acquiring and evaluating information about new ideas and new forms of practice are probably more important than the retention in memory of an increasingly obsolescent block of propositional knowledge.

If we confine our attention for the moment to processes like problem-solving and decision-making, much of the literature tends to suggest a rational linear model, in which a prior information-gathering stage is succeeded by deductive logical argument until a solution/decision is reached. In practice, this rarely occurs. Research on medical problem-solving, for example, shows that hypotheses are generated early in the diagnostic process and from limited available data (Elstein *et al.*, 1978). Further information is then collected to confirm or refute these hypotheses. Although described as intuitive, the process is essentially cognitive; but it allows pattern recognition and other experiential insight to contribute at the first stage. In less scientific areas, the need for continuing interaction between information input and possible courses of action is even greater. The information cannot be easily summarized and can usually be interpreted in a number of ways. There is also a need for invention and insight when considering possible actions, so new ideas have to be generated, developed and worked out. The process is best considered as deliberative rather than deductive, with an interactive consideration of interpretations of the situation together with possible actions continuing until a professional judgment is reached about the optimal course of action.

Such deliberation requires a combination of divergent and convergent thinking which many find difficult to handle, especially when working in a team. Some find it difficult to focus sufficiently to be good analysts or are too impatient to think things through, while others feel uncomfortable with any departure from routine patterns of thinking. The need for adopting several contrasting perspectives is also increasingly recognized; and this is one of the arguments for teamwork.

Giving information

Giving information to clients is a major part of the role of many professionals, and one in which it is frequently suggested that their performance could be improved. First, there is the obvious need to use intelligible vocabulary, which relates to attitude as much as competence because some professions use eso-teric vocabulary to preserve their status and to give the impression of greater knowledge than they possess. Secondly, there is the need to ascertain what information is most needed by the client and to relate it to the client's goals and level of understanding. This may require a wider consultation and more attentive listening than clients are sometimes accorded. A study by Tuckett *et al.* (1985) of doctor–patient communication in general practice found that in 'as many as one in every two consultations patients could not recall all the key points . . . , could not make correct sense of them, or were not committed to them' (pp. 167–8).

> Because doctors did not know the details of what patients were think-ing, the information they did give could not relate, in any precise or considered way, to the ideas patients themselves possessed. In short, there was little dialogue and little sharing of ideas. In consequence, doctors could have no way of knowing whether the information they offered was being understood 'correctly' or not. Equally, patients could have no way of knowing whether their understanding of what doctors said was 'correct'. (Tuckett *et al.*, 1985, p. 205)

There is clearly a need both to listen with care and to translate informa-tion into a form which the client can understand. While these are clearly interpersonal processes, they draw on propositional knowledge in a variety of ways. Such knowledge is probably most developed in teaching, because teachers need both to understand children's conceptions and ways of thinking and to develop a repertoire of possible representations of every aspect of their subject (Sigrun Gudmundsdottir, 1989; McNamara, 1991). However, it is equally important in medicine. The consultation process described above would be significantly improved if doctors were familiar with common client concerns and unarticulated questions; and if they also had developed a wider repertoire of explanations and ways of communicating advice.

Oral communication is often planned, at least in skeletal form, but its transaction resembles skilful behaviour guided by rapid, intuitive decisions. Whereas the main advantage of written communication is that it can be treated as a deliberative process. There is an opportunity to think things through and revise early drafts. Whether this is taken will depend upon priorities. Formal reports will be composed with great care, while correspondence with individual clients is often routinized. The temptation is to assume that, as long as the content is correct, the mode of its communication is relatively unimportant. Yet, in addition to a basic linguistic competence and lack of ambiguity, the style and the choice of words can significantly affect how a document or letter is received and understood. Good written communication requires both time and skill.

In professions such as law, accounting and surveying, the detailed drafting of documents is of critical significance, an essential competency for even newly qualified professionals. However, there is still a need to ensure that such documents are properly understood by clients and other interested parties. Often they need translation on paper by judicious use of commentaries or alternative modes of representation, in addition to the accustomed but often inadequate oral presentation. The 'teaching role' is important in most professions, yet rarely included in training.

Metaprocesses

The term 'metaprocess' is used to describe the thinking involved in directing one's own behaviour and controlling one's engagement in the other processes discussed above. We described their nature and discussed the development of this kind of capability in Chapter 5 under the heading of 'Control Knowledge'. Controlling one's own behaviour involves the evaluation of what one is doing and thinking, the continuing redefinition of priorities, and the critical adjustment of cognitive frameworks and assumptions. Its central features are self-knowledge and self-management, so it includes the organization of oneself and one's time, the selection of activities, the management of one's learning and thinking and the general maintenance of a metaevaluative framework for judging the import and significance of one's actions. During rapid interaction self-direction is necessarily intuitive, drawing on previous experience with little deliberation. But when there is time for deliberation, it involves the overall control of one's thinking, the informal scheduling of the deliberation, its conceptualization as a problem and as a process, and ongoing evaluation of its progress.

The value of this control process was highlighted by Argyris and Schön (1976) who demonstrated that for many professionals there is a significant gap between their espoused theories (their justifications for what they do and their explicit reasons for it) and their theories in use, those often implicit theories that actually determine their behaviour. This gap between account and action is a natural consequence of people's perceptual frameworks being determined by what they want or expect to see, and by people reporting back to them what they think they want to hear. The solution Argyris and Schön recommend is to give priority not so much to objectives — for then one reads situations purely in terms of one's own preplanned ideas of how they ought to develop — as to getting good quality feedback. Unless one is prepared to receive, indeed actively seek, feedback — which may be adverse or distressing — one will continue to misread situations and to deceive oneself that one's own actions are the best in the circumstances. This process of obtaining feedback on one's practice corresponds to what others have called 'action research' (Elliott, 1991). However it is not only obtaining good feedback that matters but making good use of it by being open to new interpretations which challenge one's assumptions.

The Challenge to Professional Education

The traditional dual-qualification system, combining a degree with a period of subsequent professional practice, fails to address many of the most difficult problems I have identified. The syllabus for the higher-education component is based on propositional knowledge and discipline-based methods of inquiry within a strictly academic frame of reference, thus largely ignoring the problem of developing and using such knowledge in professional contexts. The professional requirement is defined in terms of satisfactory completion of a minimum period of practice in an approved work-setting, including a minimum number and range of professional tasks, often supplemented by further examinations, written and/or oral, and evidence in the form of reports and logbooks. There may be little attempt to analyse the processes involved, to develop professional thinking, to clarify learning goals and to provide the appropriate kind of support. The prevailing assumption is that the professionals who run the system know what competence is and do not need to spell it out. They have little difficulty in recognizing incompetence, which is all that is really necessary. Neglecting such important aspects of professional education considerably reduces its quality and its effectiveness.

More serious still are the implications of my analysis for post-qualification education. Careful examination of the processes discussed above will show (1) that they characterize the actions of experienced professionals possibly more than those of novices (2) that they demand thinking skills of a high order in addition to skilled behaviour developed through practice and (3) that, even for experts, professional performance involves learning and there is always more to be learned. The support of a system of continuing professional education after qualification is essential for sustaining and improving the quality of professional work; and much of it will have to be based in or around the workplace. In this context, the precise stage at which professionals are deemed to have qualified will depend on what they are expected to do, that is on the organization of professional work. The appropriate question is 'qualified to do what?' and the appropriate answer cannot be 'qualified to do everything in the profession'.

For me, this mapping of the professional knowledge base provides sufficient grounds for a major rethink of current practice. The professions, however, will see it differently. They live in the world of *realpolitik*. And respond to political rather than academic pressures. But there also the professions are being challenged on several different fronts. It is important, therefore, to discuss the nature of those challenges before putting forward my conclusions.

The first challenge comes from Europe. Traditions across Europe are very different, professions being more highly trained in some countries and in others rather less. Mutual recognition of qualifications is expected, so that idiosyncratic systems will need to be convincingly justified or else modified. Government pressure will be towards the less expensive options, unless there is very convincing evidence that they cannot deliver competent practitioners. So claims about each profession's knowledge base will be subjected to increasing scrutiny. There will also be pressure for closely related British professional bodies to merge. On a longer time-scale, there could even be some convergence between the higher-education systems of different countries.

Second, there is the challenge posed by changes in financial practice in both private and public sectors. Many professional groups find themselves organized into cost centres which have to justify themselves according to financial criteria in addition to providing services to clients. Apart from giving the financial aspect greater prominence in professional decision-making, this is causing groups to consider different ways of organizing professional work. One result is likely to be the greater use of people with intermediate qualifications, for example technicians, paraprofessionals or auxilliaries. There might even be some further differentiation within the professional group. Almost certainly there will be tighter job specifications.

Third, there has been growing public concern about professional competence, monopoly and accountability. The reputations of professions in this age of mass media are increasingly dependent on their weakest members; can the public be guaranteed that even the least capable can provide a satisfactory service? Without public confidence in all their members, how can their monopolies in providing certain services be justified? Would not competition bring the price down and widen consumer choice? This challenge, in particular, may force the pace in the development of continuing education; and it will become increasingly difficult for professions to sustain the policy that qualification is 'for life'.

Accountability systems are often inaccessible and opaque, while self-regulation looks increasingly like self-serving. Which individual or organization is responsible when things go wrong? Who is answerable to the public for the policies and priorities of the profession as a whole? While many of these questions concern the organization of the profession, they also focus around the profession's interface with the public, for which most professional practitioners have had little 'professional' preparation.

Fourth, there is the challenge coming from the growing system of National Vocational Qualifications (Burke, 1991), which is beginning to impinge on the professions. The National Council for Vocational Qualifications (NCVQ) has a mandate to cover the professions as well but is proceeding cautiously while it has other priorities. Attention is now moving to the upper levels, and several professional bodies are already engaged in discussions and pilot projects. The NVQ system will bring radical changes, because it has adopted a competence-based system of accreditation using assessments based on performance at work (Fennell, 1991; Jessup, 1991). So its adoption would correct the current overemphasis on propositional knowledge and give more attention to the processes which determine the quality of professional action. However, some of its other features might need modification before implementation at the professional level.

One suggestion would be to consider using a wider range of approaches to the analysis of professional work. The current system of functional analysis breaks the job down into functional units, and the units into elements, each of which has to be separately assessed to cover a range of situations according to a list of performance criteria. The result is a very long document and an enormous assessment programme, even for qualifications at a subprofessional level. This is a natural consequence of focusing on behaviour alone. In contrast, an emphasis on professional processes of the kind discussed earlier would give a more economical structure to the qualifications, as well as providing close links to the modes of learning and the use of propositional knowledge. It would also attend to the thinking which underpins a professional's capacity to perform in a wide range of contexts and situations.

Another issue is the binary nature of the competence concept. A person is either competent or not competent, and no gradations such as 'just competent' or 'highly competent' are recognized, at least not for accreditation purposes. This implies that the only way to progress is to become competent in something new, when it might be more appropriate simply to do the same thing better. Capabilities associated with the processes I have identified as being essential to the quality of professional work can be continually developed throughout one's life. Thus I am more in sympathy with the five-stage model put forward by Dreyfus and Dreyfus (1986): novice, advanced beginner, competent, proficient, expert. Even this model, however, neglects the impact of social and technical change on what counts as a good professional performance. That apart, it provides a useful basis for extending our discussion into the post-qualification period as well. The question then arises as to the point of development at which various levels of qualification should be awarded; and whether this might vary from one element of assessment to another. People might need to be proficient rather than competent in some elements, while remaining at only the advanced-beginner stage in others. Spelling out the minimum essential requirements for qualification is essential, but beyond that a profile of achievement which acknowledged the need for further development would be less misleading and much more useful.

Finally, the NVQ system highlights the problem of reaching a compromise between three conflicting approaches to determining a profession's knowledge base:

1. To ascertain the *profession's preferred view* of its own knowledge base — this is rarely unanimous, likely to be based mainly on existing or recently developed training schemes and closely linked to the profession's search for autonomy and status.
2. To examine *professional knowledge currently in use* — this raises questions about the wide range of work-contexts and whether to focus on experts or ordinary members of the profession.
3. To predict the knowledge base needed for *the profession's future role* in society — a difficult and controversial task, yet arguably better than settling for planned obsolescence.

There will be a degree of overlap between the outcomes of these three approaches, but still some significant differences of emphasis. NCVQ has chosen to focus on the second approach, using committees led by employers to resolve differences arising from the range of work-contexts. This is a sensible decision but the danger of neglecting the third approach altogether will increase as the level of qualification rises. All these issues arising from the onset of the NVQ system are more fully discussed in Part 2.

Reconstructing Professional Education

This chapter has argued that three central questions need to be addressed by every profession:

1. What is our professional knowledge base?
2. What is best learned in higher education, what is best learned in professional practice and what is best learned through an integrated course involving both contexts?
3. What has to be learned before qualification, and what is best postponed until after qualification?

The first has been my central theme, while the second and third have been discussed only briefly. Now this concluding section brings all three questions together in order to formulate the principles on which, I believe, the reconstruction of professional education and training ought to be based. The foregoing analysis of professional knowledge and my discussion of knowledge use in earlier chapters both demonstrate that professional work of any complexity requires the *concurrent use* of several different kinds of knowledge in an *integrated, purposeful manner*. Yet this is difficult to achieve without significant interaction between formal teaching and professional practice, and specific attention to developing the appropriate modes of thinking.

Process knowledge must be given a high priority in both academic and practice settings but without neglecting the contribution of propositional knowledge to the process. This is not always best done by introducing propositional knowledge as and when it is required, because this destroys its coherence, leads to an uncritical, half-understood acceptance of ideas, and avoids practice in the appropriate selection of relevant knowledge from the repertoire. On the other hand, it is now well established that knowledge which does not get used in practice is rapidly consigned to cold storage. From a student perspective we have to recognize that, although knowledge may be included in the curriculum because somebody else has deemed it relevant to professional practice, it does not become part of professional knowledge unless and until it has been used for a professional purpose. Thus a piece of biological knowledge does not become professional knowledge for a nurse until it has been used as part of a nursing process. The solution is not to reject theory courses but to introduce a general curriculum principle into professional education, that if the time-gap between the introduction of theoretical knowledge and its first use in professional practice is too large, that knowledge is being introduced at the wrong point in the sequence.

This takes into account empirical evidence from several professions that knowledge not perceived as professionally relevant is accorded low status by students, memorized if needed for examinations but rapidly forgotten thereafter; and provides a strong argument against the common practice of front-loading discipline-based knowledge in professional education programmes. Two responses are possible, either to insert practical work closer to the point where the topic is introduced, or to postpone the introduction of the topic until a relevant context for using it has become available.

We also argued in earlier chapters that using propositional knowledge in practical situations requires considerable intellectual effort, and learning how to use concepts and ideas is usually a more difficult cognitive task than simply comprehending them and reproducing them. In curriculum terms, this implies that as much time and effort should be allocated to enabling and supporting the use of propositional knowledge as is currently devoted to its acquisition. The time required to learn how to use propositional knowledge in professional contexts is considerable; so there is a potential conflict between time allocated to the acquisition of such knowledge and the time required to learn how to use it. This suggests rigorous pruning of the quantity of propositional knowledge in order to improve its quality. Alongside this is the need to postpone some areas of content until after initial qualification, when the learner will be better prepared to use it. Hence, we need to consider a qualification system rather than a single qualification.

What further principles can we extract from this discussion?

- First, a significant part of the initial qualification must be performance-based: otherwise professional accountability will be a sham.
- Second, initial blocks of propositional knowledge should be kept as short as possible, unless there are many opportunities to use that knowledge in practice-related processes.
- Third, process knowledge of all kinds should be accorded central importance.
- Fourth, there should be a clearly articulated approach to professional learning and development, linked to a system of initial and advanced further qualifications.

It should be noted that I am not recommending that the whole of the qualification be performance-based: that would be impractical and possibly undesirable. But I am rejecting the obvious compromise of a dual qualification system which separates professional practice and the development of performance capabilities from the teaching of propositional knowledge, claimed to be relevant to current or future practice. Such a system cannot properly develop process knowledge of central importance to the profession and its future. Moreover, it is based on a false epistemology which assumes a clearcut distinction between theory and practice. This leaves the question of how much of the qualification should be performance-based and what should be the nature of that part which is not. We shall return to such questions in Chapter 10.

There are encouraging signs that the curriculum principles outlined above are beginning to be recognized, if not followed, in the premier professions of medicine and law. A recent series of review articles on medical education in the *British Medical Journal* has been republished in book form (Lowry, 1993); and the General Medical Council (1993) has issued its strongest recommendations yet in favour of radical reform. Both reports advocate an integrated approach to the training of doctors which interweaves theory courses with clinical experience, and emphasizes a problem-solving approach rather than the banking of ill-digested and soon-forgotten information. An interesting feature in medicine is the growing recognition accorded to the rationales and achievements of a group of 'new generation' medical schools, most notably McMaster, Newcastle (Australia) and Maastricht, which have been following these principles for ten to twenty years.

Changes in legal education are much more recent, at least in Britain. The introduction, following a range of experiments, of practice-training courses for barristers in 1989 and solicitors in 1993, and compulsory continuing education for solicitors qualified since 1965 are causing people to rethink what is being taught apart from textbook knowledge and what is appropriate at each stage of training.

In common with other occupational groupings, legal training is therefore changing, tending towards a continuing system of education which involves learning by experience and from experience. In this sense, tomorrow's lawyers will be better trained to deal with life as a lawyer rather than simply being trained in law-book law. (Sherr, 1992, p. 172)

Note

1. This chapter is an expanded version of the chapter 'Developing the Knowledge Base: A Process Perspective on Professional Education' which first appeared in *Learning to Effect* edited by Ronald Barnett, 1993 (Society for Research in Higher Education/Open University Press).

Chapter 7

Theories of Professional Expertise

Chapter 6 was largely devoted to an analysis of professional processes and the relative contributions of propositional knowledge and learning from practical experience to developing the quality of professional performance. Our discussion then moved to a consideration of professional competence and to different approaches to defining and assessing the kind of performance expected from qualified professionals. We strongly argued, however, that definitions of competence should be set in the broader context of lifelong professional learning and that it was meaningful, indeed necessary, to consider progression beyond competence to proficiency and/or expertise. Hence, before proceeding to discuss conceptions of competence in Part 2, it is useful to examine the nature of proficiency and expertise.

This chapter reviews the range of theories of expertise to be found in the literature and discusses their scope and validity. In particular, it notes how different theories of expertise emphasize different professional processes and asks whether some theories presented as conflicting may not better be treated as complementary. It begins with the Dreyfus model of progression from novice to expert, which was introduced at the end of the last chapter, then moves on to consider theories of clinical decision-making by physicians. These are more strongly linked to research evidence, yet encompass both intuitive models based on memory and analytic models based on probabilities and reasoning. The full range, including mixed models, is mapped out by Hammond's Cognitive Continuum Theory which links the mode of cognition induced to the characteristics of the process of task. Attention then turns to Schön's widely quoted 'reflective practitioner' model, whose insights and ambiguities are examined in some detail. Finally we review those aspects of professional expertise which have been neglected by the theories discussed in the rest of this chapter, giving special attention to the role of deliberation, to interaction with clients and to work within a team or large organization.

The Dreyfus Model of Skill Acquisition

The Dreyfus brothers' model of skill acquisition has attracted considerable interest in professional education. Hubert is a philosopher and Stuart an industrial engineer working in computing and operational research. The title of

Table 7.1: Summary of Dreyfus Model of Skills Acquisition

Level 1 Novice
- Rigid adherence to taught rules or plans
- Little situational perception
- No discretionary judgment

Level 2 Advanced Beginner
- Guidelines for action based on attributes or aspects (aspects are global characteristics of situations recognizable only after some prior experience)
- Situational perception still limited
- All attributes and aspects are treated separately and given equal importance

Level 3 Competent
- Coping with crowdedness
- Now sees actions at least partially in terms of longer-term goals
- Conscious deliberate planning
- Standardized and routinized procedures

Level 4 Proficient
- See situations holistically rather than in terms of aspects
- See what is most important in a situation
- Perceives deviations from the normal pattern
- Decision-making less laboured
- Uses maxims for guidance, whose meaning varies according to the situation

Level 5 Expert
- No longer relies on rules, guidelines or maxims
- Intuitive grasp of situations based on deep tacit understanding
- Analytic approaches used only in novel situation or when problems occur
- Vision of what is possible

their book *Mind Over Machine, the Power of Human Intuition and Expertise in the Era of the Computer* (1986) reveals that their theory first developed as an attack on the claims made by experts in artificial intelligence, before becoming a more broadly based theory of expertise. Moreover, they see their model as defending the contemporary experiential approach to philosophy against the rationalist tradition of analytic reasoning and the formulation of rules, and as supporting 'Merleau-Ponty's claim that, perception and understanding are based in our capacity for picking up not rules, but flexible styles of behaviour' (p. 5). Their use of the term 'picking up' stands in marked contrast to the behaviourists' emphasis on direct instruction, behavioural modelling and coaching (the McBer version is described in Chapter 8). So also does their endorsement of the existentialist view that:

> Human understanding was a skill akin to knowing how to find one's way about in the world, rather than knowing a lot of facts and rules for relating them. Our basic understanding was thus a *knowing how* rather than a *knowing that*. (Dreyfus and Dreyfus, 1986, p. 4)

Although the Dreyfus describe their model as depicting five stages of skill acquisition (see Table 7.1), the emphasis is on perception and decision-making rather than routinized action. Thus they define skill as an integrative overarching approach to professional action, which incorporates both routines and the decisions to use them, while still maintaining that the term 'skilled behaviour' connotes semi-automatic rather than deliberative processes. They cite two groups of examples: those taken from the application of rational methods such as decision analysis, mathematical modelling and 'intelligent' computer systems which are used to demonstrate the inadequacy of those methods; and those judged as authentic representations of expertise which are taken from the areas of chess, car-driving, plane-flying, senior management and daily life. However, the most comprehensive account of the applications of the Dreyfus model to professional work is provided by Benner (1984) who used it to analyse evidence collected from critical incident interviews with a sample of ninety-three nurses. Significantly she did not choose examples only to explain and justify the model, but also to describe the nature of nursing expertise as a whole. Thus she applied the model to each of thirty-one competencies, classified into the following seven domains:

- the helping role;
- the teaching-coaching function;
- the diagnostic and patient-monitoring function;
- effective management of rapidly changing situations;
- administering and monitoring therapeutic interventions and regimens;
- monitoring and ensuring the quality of health care practices; and
- organizations and work-role competencies.

The main features of the Dreyfus model are depicted in Table 7.1. As befits its philosophical underpinning, the emphasis is almost entirely on learning from experience with only occasional references to theoretical learning or the development of fluency on standard tasks. The pathway to competence is characterized mainly by the ability to recognize features of practical situations and to discriminate between them, to carry out routine procedures under pressure and to plan ahead. Competence is the climax of rule-guided learning and discovering how to cope in crowded, pressurised contexts. Whereas proficiency marks the onset of quite a different approach to the job: normal behaviour is not just routinized but semi-automatic; situations are apprehended more deeply and the abnormal is quickly spotted and given attention. Thus progress beyond competence depends on a more holistic approach to situational understanding.

Usually the proficient performer will be deeply involved in his task and will be experiencing it from some specific perspective because of recent events. Because of the performer's perspective, certain features of the situation will stand out as salient and others will recede into the background and be ignored. As events modify the salient features, plans, expectations, and even the relative salience of features will gradually change. No detached choice or deliberation occurs. It just happens, apparently because the proficient performer has experienced similar situations in the past and memories of them trigger plans similar to those that worked in the past and anticipations of events similar to those that occurred. (Dreyfus and Dreyfus, 1986, p. 28)

Progression from proficiency to expertise finally happens when the decision-making as well as the situational understanding becomes intuitive rather than analytic; and thus requires significantly more experience. The Dreyfuses describe the distinction as follows:

The proficient performer, while intuitively organising and understanding his task, will still find himself thinking analytically about what to do. Elements that present themselves as important, thanks to the performer's experience, will be assessed and combined by rule to produce decisions about how best to manipulate the environment. The spell of involvement in the world of the skill will thus be temporarily broken. (*ibid.*, p. 29)

An expert generally knows what to do based on mature and practiced understanding . . . An expert's skill has become so much a part of him that he need be no more aware of it than he is of his own body . . . the expert business manager, surgeon, nurse, lawyer, or teacher is totally engaged in skillful performance. *When things are proceeding normally, experts don't solve problems and don't make decisions; they do what normally works.* (*ibid.*, pp. 30–1)

Thus most expert performance is ongoing and non-reflective. The Dreyfuses do acknowledge that experts will deliberate before acting on some occasions, either because the outcomes are particularly critical or because they feel uneasy with their first choice of action. But this deliberation is described as being not so much problem-solving as critical reflection on their own intuition.

Before proceeding to critique this model, we should note that the Dreyfus definition of competence is based on how people approach their work, not on whether they should be judged as qualified to do it. Indeed Benner suggests that competence is typically acquired by a nurse who has been on the job in a same or similar situation for two or three years, so that regular procedures have become standardized and routinized.

The competent nurse lacks the speed and flexibility of the proficient nurse but does have a feeling of mastery and the ability to cope with and manage the many contingencies of clinical nursing. The conscious, deliberate planning that is characteristic of this skill level helps achieve efficiency and organisation. (Benner, 1984, p. 27)

One could describe the situation as one where the nurse has become proficient at the level of the individual task but is not yet proficient in the integrated performance of the whole role. That integration, Benner estimates, is likely to take another three to five years in the same kind of situation. We shall return to the question of situational specificity in a later section.

The strength of the Dreyfus model lies in the case it makes for tacit knowledge and intuition as critical features of professional expertise in 'unstructured problem areas'. The Dreyfuses also provide a devastating critique of what they call 'calculative rationality', the world of mathematical modelling, decision analysis and computerized simulations. However, they tend to regard their own model as the only alternative, devoting much of their argumentation to the attack on calculative rationality with very little attention to other options. This is clearly demonstrated by their ambiguous treatment of deliberative processes:

> This Hamlet model of decision-making — the detached, deliberative, and sometimes agonising selection among alternatives — is the only one recognised in much of the academic literature on the psychology of choice. While that type of carefully thought-out behaviour certainly sometimes occurs, frequently for learners of new skills and occasionally for even the most skillful, an unbiased examination of our everyday behaviour shows it to be the exception rather than the rule. (Dreyfus and Dreyfus, 1986, p. 28)

Not only does this ignore the work of the *gestalt* psychologists and other empirical studies of professional judgment but it makes questionable assumptions about everyday behaviour. Deliberation may not be a daily occurrence but it is certainly not rare, nor is it based on mathematical models. Moreover, many professionals are continually complaining about the lack of thinking time.

This ambivalence is continued in a later section about deliberation in management:

> Experienced intuitive managers do not attempt to understand familiar problems and opportunities in purely analytic terms using calculative rationality, but realise that detached deliberation *about the validity of intuitions* will improve decision-making. Common as it is, little has been written about that conscious deliberative buttressing of nonconscious intuitive understanding, probably because detached deliberation is often incorrectly seen as an *alternative* to intuition. (*ibid.*, pp. 163–4)

Here, their obsession with attacking mathematical models is revealed in the use of the term 'calculative rationality' and the weakness of their argument disguised by including the word 'purely'. Analysis is being associated with quantitative methods and the logic of computer programming while the ana-lytic skills of a historian, which might be much more relevant, are conven-iently disregarded. Their statement about using deliberative methods to check the validity of intuitions is important, but represents just one way in which to combine intuition with deliberation. Another is when prior experience, apprehended intuitively, suggests which lines of deliberative inquiry are most worth pursuing. Yet a third is when after a period of analysis and discussion, the problem is mulled over until one particular option seems to provide the best fit: here it is intuition which follows deliberation and analysis, rather than the other way round. There are also many situations in which several people need to be consulted and their differing intuitions fed into group deliberations.

My other concern with the model is its neglect of the metaprocesses involved in controlling one's own behaviour, especially the self-evaluation dimension of professional work. The only image we are given of the process of learning from experience is that of the gradual accumulation of memories of cases. The problem of how this huge volume of information is selected, organized and retrieved is not addressed. Important aspects of a case may not have been retained, theories are likely to have been developed of dubious validity which then become self-confirming. In short the process of learning from experience has been idealized and psychological research in the fallibility of human judgment ignored.

In conclusion, therefore, we can note that the Dreyfus model provides an analysis of skilled behaviour under conditions of rapid interpretation and decision-making, in which the logically distinct processes of acquiring infor-mation, following routines and making decisions are fully integrated. It de-picts not so much the simple skill of riding a bicycle but the more complex process of riding a bicycle through heavy traffic. It accounts for the greater complexity of professional work and the long time needed to develop profi-ciency and expertise. Its description of the role of tacit knowledge is consist-ent with professionals' self-accounts and with other research we review later in the chapter. But it leaves two important questions unanswered: How seri-ous is its neglect of the problem of expert fallibility? — and — What propor-tion of professional work does it cover? My own view is that it constantly underestimates the former and overestimates the latter.

Theories of Clinical Decision-making

Medicine is probably the most thoroughly researched of the professions, with clinical expertise being most strongly linked to the process of diagnosing an illness and deciding how to treat and manage it. Whether this process is more appropriately described as skilful behaviour or deliberative action is a matter of some contention. The Dreyfuses regard it as skilful behaviour because their model emphasizes intuition rather than reasoning as the major characteristic of expertise. But they offer no explanation of how learning from experience, the central feature of their model, occurs in practice. Cognitive scientists working in the field of medical education have attempted to address this important question empirically as well as conceptually; and have reached conclusions that are not so far removed from the Dreyfus model, a somewhat ironic outcome since it was the criticism of cognitive science which originally stimulated the Dreyfuses to develop their model.

The traditional assumption has been that diagnosis is based on two distinctive kinds of knowledge: propositional knowledge about diseases and their symptoms and a generalizable skill of clinical reasoning. In this context it should not perhaps be forgotten that the first attempt to legislate the requirements for qualified physicians, the decree of Frederick II in c.1241, specified a first degree in logic before embarking on the study of medicine. However, research into the differences between novice and expert physicians has revealed little significant difference between them on tests of deductive reasoning: there is even a slight decline when people become recognized experts. The conclusion to be drawn is not that doctors do not reason, but that they are already sufficiently competent at it at the time of qualification. Tests of propositional knowledge then showed that propositional knowledge about diseases, symptoms and treatments reaches a plateau at the time of acquiring a specialist qualification (knowledge, that is, which comes within the domain covered by the qualification). Recently qualified specialists have as good an information base as most experts. This led to the hypothesis that it was not propositional knowledge in itself which characterized expertise, but having it better organized and more readily available for use. Certainly there was plenty of evidence that experts made decisions more rapidly. But just how do experts organize their accumulated clinical knowledge, and in what form does it become available for use?

The traditional textbook approach to the organization of clinical knowledge involves developing classification systems rather like those used by botanists and zoologists. But this raises questions about which principles of classification are appropriate. Most diseases have multiple symptoms and many symptoms can come from several diseases. The patient may have more than one disease at the same time. More fundamental distinctions based on pathophysiological causes of disease depend on these causes having already been established beyond reasonable doubt. The greatest problem, however, is that while any cause-based classification system that is well indexed can retrieve information relevant to the confirmation of a diagnosis or the treatment of a disease, it cannot logically assist with recognizing that disease in the first phase.

During the mid 1970s cognitive scientists began to put forward alternative ideas for the representation of knowledge in memory, using what Boreham (1988) calls a 'template model'. Instead of diseases being stored in memory like a filing system, indexed according to their critical attributes, it was suggested that they are stored in the form of schemata or stereotypes against which data patterns for new patients could be compared until a suitable match was found. Although this accounts in a more satisfactory way for evidence that expertise is built up from many years of relevant experience, it does not in itself explain how the template represents knowledge of a disease, nor how matching data against a large store of disease templates can be achieved so quickly. A librarian, for example, would still opt for a category system, in spite of its many disadvantages.

Minsky's 'frame-system' theory (1977) was an early and extremely influential revision of this template model. Minsky characterized a 'frame' as 'a data-structure for representing a stereotyped situation', to which several kinds of information could be attached, both a pattern which could be recognized and matched to new data sets and a connection box with links to other frames or appropriate behavioural responses:

> A *frame* is a data-structure for representing a stereotyped situation like being in a certain kind of living room or going to a child's birthday party. Attached to each frame are several kinds of information. Some of this information is about how to use the frame. Some is about what one can expect to happen next. Some is about what to do if these expectations are not confirmed.

> We can think of a frame as a network of nodes and relations. The 'top levels' of a frame are fixed, and represent things that are always true about the supposed situation. The lower levels have many *terminals* — 'slots' that must be filled by specific instances or data. Each terminal can specify conditions its assignments must meet. (The assignments themselves are usually smaller 'subframes'.) Simple conditions are specified by *markers* that might require a terminal assignment to be a person, an object of sufficient value, or a pointer to a subframe of a certain type. More complex conditions can specify relations among the things assigned to several terminals. (Minsky, 1977, p. 355)

Boreham (1988) describes how Swanson (1978) applied Minsky's theory to cardiologists, using the term 'disease frame' to represent the diagnostic expectations of an expert in a form which could be built into a computer programme to provide other less experienced cardiologists with assistance in diagnosis. This theory of expertise depends on two assumptions: that a disease frame can provide a sufficient representation of relevant information to be useful and reliable in diagnostic process; and that through professional practice the diagnostician is able to build up a larger and more differentiated store of frames.

> . . . over the years, the expert sees cases not quite fitting the expectations of existing frames, and creates new ones which encode the differences, refining his initial knowledge in the light of experience. (Swanson, cited in Boreham, p. 99)

This quotation raises a question, however, about the relationship between levels of representation, suggesting that these might be a set of several linked frames for representing a disease rather than a single disease frame. The underlying problem is that assessing a frame will be easier if there are less matches to be made, at least initially; and this would form a single disease frame. But representing a disease will be more accurate if there is scope for handling a range of situational variations; and this would favour a set of linked disease frames. These criteria can be reconciled by recourse to images of frames and subframes, or Minsky's notion of higher levels for pattern recognition and lower levels for connecting to further information. But such speculation has little empirical support, apart from well documented evidence that expert physicians do in practice succeed in interpreting these two different requirements.

A more fundamental criticism, perhaps, is Boreham's argument that frame-system theory ignores the effect on the diagnostic process of the personal character of the physician. Our account in Chapter 6 emphasized the very personal nature of conceptual frameworks developed through experience. Not only does the personality and prior experience of physicians affect the way in which they acquire and interpret information but each encounters a unique series of cases during the process of constructing and further developing their frame systems. This perspective is still compatible with the notion of representation by frames, but not with the concept of a standard frame which can represent a body of expertise rather than that of a single expert. Minsky had to assume that standard frames were possible in order to develop computerized models, but we are under no such compunction.

Two further questions which need to be addressed by this and other models concern the nature of both the diagnostic process and the learning process. Frame-system theory allows the possibility of a staged process in which the matching of data to a frame or subframe triggers the next diagnostic stage, but when and why does such staging occur? It may be enforced by the situation if diagnostic tests take time or symptoms require time to mature. But is it ever necessary to reduce the cognitive overload? Then secondly, there is the problem of how the frame system is developed and refined by experience. To what extent is this a process of conscious reflection or can it be accomplished, as the Dreyfuses suggest by intuitive adjustment alone?

A more sophisticated approach which both encompasses and broadens frame theory is the four-stage model of developing clinical expertise put forward by Schmidt, Norman and Boshuizen (1990). They argue that 'memory is the overriding source of differences in diagnostic performance between medical students and physicians having different amounts of experience'; and that the functioning of memory is dependent on the knowledge structures used to represent the information being stored. The gradual progress from novice to expert can be depicted by four developmental stages, each characterized by the emergence of a distinct type of knowledge structure. However these representations do not decay or become inert in the course of developing expertise but rather remain available for future use when the situation requires their activation. (*ibid.*, p. 613)

The first two stages of the model are reached during training. Stage 1 involves the development of richly elaborated causal networks which medical students can use to explain the causes or consequences of diseases in terms of underlying pathophysiological processes. This knowledge is largely derived from lectures and books, and accounts of cases are very lengthy. Stage 2 then involves the transformation of these elaborated networks into abridged networks using high-level causal models, with information about signs and symptoms being 'subsumed under diagnostic labels' rather than spelt out in detail. This is exemplified by two contrasting protocols for the same case: that from a fourth-year student contained over 250 words and forty separate propositions, while a sixth-year student summarizes it more accurately with only thirty-four words and six propositions. The latter had developed the capacity both to select only the most critical information and to use higher-level concepts to handle clusters of interrelated detail. Although this change is attributed to the student being exposed to real patients, there are other possible explanations. This particular change involves a transition from an academic environment which stresses the elaborate presentation of knowledge to a clinical environment which stresses rapid decision-making and action, similar to that described in Chapter 2 when discussing knowledge use by school teachers. It may also be compared to the increase in conceptual sophistication expected of graduate students as they begin to understand the central theories and paradigms of their disciplines.

Stage 3 is more obviously dependent on accumulated experience of working with patients, but takes much longer to reach. Its principle feature is the emergence of a particular kind of template called an 'illness script' (Feltovich and Barrows, 1984). Constructing such scripts involves organizing one's knowledge about an illness to conform to the pattern depicted in Figure 7.1, which uses temporal more than causal relations to order information in a format that resembles a story rather than an argument:

> An important feature of an illness script is its serial structure: items that make up the script appear in a specific order. This order closely matches the way in which physicians inform other physicians about their patients' conditions; as such, one could say that illness scripts obey certain conventions regarding an optimal story structure in medicine. (Feltovich and Barrows, 1984, p. 615)

Schmidt *et al.* summarize evidence in favour of the gradual development by physicians of this script mode of representation. Less experienced physicians can recall information more effectively when it is presented in the order of a script, but more experienced physicians do this for themselves and gain

```
┌─────────────────────────────────────────────────────────────────────────────┐
│                                                                               │
│  Illness script                                                               │
│                                                                               │
│     Enabling conditions →    Predisposing factors, boundary conditions,       │
│                              hereditary factors etc.                          │
│     Predisposing factors →   Compromised host factors, travel, drugs, etc.    │
│     Boundary conditions →    Age, sex, etc.                                    │
│                                                                               │
│     Fault →                  Invasion of tissue by pathogenic organism,       │
│                              inadequate nutrient supply, inability of tissue   │
│                              to survive, etc.                                  │
│                                                                               │
│     Consequences →           Complaints, signs, symptoms                      │
│     Complaints →             Etc.                                             │
│     Signs →                  Etc.                                             │
│     Symptoms  →              Etc.                                             │
│                                                                               │
└─────────────────────────────────────────────────────────────────────────────┘
```

Figure 7.1: A Generic Illness Script

no special benefit from having it done for them in advance. Their notion of script derives from Schank and Abelson (1977) who saw scripts as 'a specialisation of the frame idea', but there is also a wider research literature on the use of narrative structures to convey knowledge. Another significant finding was that expert physicians made greater use of information in the 'enabling conditions' category than less experienced colleagues, suggesting that the construction and use of this type of knowledge requires greater experience.

Confirming Boreham's critique of frame theory and our own account of learning from experience in Chapter 6, Schmidt *et al.* describe the illness scripts developed by physicians as highly idiosyncratic, depending both on the character of the physician and the particular examples of the disease that he or she encounters:

> . . . based on his or her unique experience with a certain disease, each physician develops rich, idiosyncratic scripts for that disease, which may or may not resemble the scripts of other physicians or the textbook. This may explain why some doctors have difficulty diagnosing some diseases where others immediately recognise the essential patterns. It may also explain why extensive exposure to many different cases may be the crucial factor in developing expertise. (Schmidt *et al.*, p. 617)

The fourth stage of development involves yet another type of knowledge structure, the use by experienced physicians of memories of previous patients. Significantly, and one could argue in perfect counterbalance with illness scripts, these case memories are retained as individual entities rather than merged into the prototypical form espoused by Cantor *et al.* (1980) and Bordage and Zachs (1984). Again Schmidt *et al.* cite evidence that such memories play a significant part in diagnosis by experts; but they do not offer any explanation as to why this particular mode of knowledge representation should develop at a later stage than illness scripts. However the following passage does suggest that the organizational conventions established by illness scripts may be needed before recollections of prior patients can become a reliable and accessible form of knowledge.

> The different representations we have described coexist in the mind of the physician. In other words, the ways in which a disease expresses itself in human beings are represented both as 'generalised experience' in the form of illness scripts for the disease, pathophysiologic descriptions, and so forth, and as an elaborate set of lively recollections of specific patients who suffered from that disease. These representational formats have a synergistic effect. The recollections of prior patients, indexed by the relevant illness scripts, are stored in episodic memory, which makes them very easily accessible. (*ibid.*, p. 617)

Although the earlier modes of representation get used much less as later modes become available, Schmidt *et al.* emphasize the essential complementarity of all four modes. Moreover they hasten to add that:

> . . . we are not implying that experts work at some 'deeper' level of processing but rather that expertise is associated with the availability of knowledge representations in various forms, derived from both experience and formal education. (*ibid.*, p. 618)

Like other researchers they note the relative absence of basic science information in clinicians' protocols, thus ruling out the frequently proposed theory that such knowledge forms the basis of expertise. However they do not examine the extent to which scientific knowledge is embedded into practice in ways that disguise its underpinning contribution. There is clearly a danger in assuming that, because experts do not appear to possess or use scientific knowledge more than those who are recently qualified, such knowledge is unimportant. Different kinds of research would be needed to investigate that question.

The Schmidt theory successfully explains the frequently confirmed research finding that expertise in medicine is domain-specific. A physician with acknowledged expertise in one speciality will perform at no better than average level in another. But it goes beyond this now accepted conclusion in suggesting that the expertise of different scientists in the same domain will differ according to their accumulated store of illness scripts and individual cases. Earlier Elstein *et al.* (1978) had shown that in most cases the intuitive phase of diagnosis leads to hypotheses which still have to be confirmed or modified, in others it helps to narrow the range of possibilities so that subsequent diagnosis becomes a more achievable problem-solving task. Hence Schmidt *et al.* were able to conclude that:

(1) there are at least two separable levels or stages — a rapid, non-analytical dimension, which is used in the majority of problems, and a slower, analytic approach, applied to a minority of problems that present difficulties; (2) neither is to be preferred, since both may lead to a solution; (3) it is not now possible to predict which kinds of problems will cause difficulty for an individual, since difficulties arise from individual experience. (*ibid.*, pp. 619–20)

Although Schmidt *et al.* describe their theory as 'a stage theory of clinical reasoning' it focuses entirely on the process of diagnosis. Rather different models of reasoning appear when the treatment or management of illness are under review. Boreham (1989) analyses the expertise needed for making decisions about the optimum dose of the drug *phenytoin sodium* in the management of epilepsy. Too small a dosage fails to prevent seizures but too large a dosage is toxic. The problem for the physician is first to achieve, and then to maintain, the optimum concentration of drug in blood serum for each individual patient. The situation is accurately represented by a mathematical equation, but this contains two constants the value of which depends on the individual patient. So the equation can only be used after two measurements of serum concentration have been made, separated by a significant time interval. The physician's response to a new patient has to involve either (1) an initial 'loading' dose to significantly increase the concentration followed by 'maintenance' doses with a level adjustment as more information becomes available, or (2) withdrawing the drug until toxic effects have dissipated and it is safe to restart with (1). By interviewing an expert about three different cases, Boreham was able to establish that his dosage decisions were based on a set of fifteen If-Then rules which covered all possible circumstances. The most difficult group of decisions concerned the first dose to prescribe for patients currently having seizures, for which he measured the current concentration of serum then applied the following 'rule of thumb':

> . . . if serum concentration is less than 7 mg/l, an increase of 100 mg a day is safe. Between 7 and 10 mg/l, an increase of 50 mg a day is safe. Over 10 mg/l, one would want to edge up in 25 mg increments. (Boreham, 1989, p. 192)

which Boreham represented as three If-Then statements as follows (p. 172):

If   (10 mg/l < serum concentration)
Then   (add 25 mg to present daily dose *and* reassess after several weeks)

If   (7 mg/l < serum concentration < 10 mg/l)
Then   (add 50 mg to present daily dose *and* reassess after several weeks)

If   (serum concentration < 7 mg/l)
Then   (add 100 mg to present daily dose *and* reassess after several weeks)

This decision system was evolved from professional experience over several years. It was consistent with, but could not be derived from, the equation; and it was completely successful in predicting current doses for a series of simulated cases. However, the expert did not claim to follow these rules rigidly; and a second expert, while generally regarding the decisions for the simulated cases as correct, suggested that they were occasionally suboptimal. One suggested modification was intended to improve the safety margin in a case where (1) previous evidence of toxicity at a certain level provided enough information to use the equation to calculate the optimum dose instead of having to rely on rules of thumb, and (2) the low body weight of the patient also suggested a more cautious approach. This is an example of a 'normal' decision being modified both by recourse to theory and by making good use of additional contextual information. The other adjustment recommended by the second expert also required an appreciation of the underlying mathematical model: the first new dose in a toxicity case was administered a little earlier to take into account the lapse of time before it would come into effect and the time which had already lapsed since the 'current' concentration had actually been measured.

Boreham's study also covered an aspect of clinical decision-making neglected by Dreyfus and only briefly discussed by Schmidt, the interactive and progressive nature of decision-making. The process of collecting information about a case is rarely instant and may be extremely protracted. Apart from the need, as in Boreham's study, to wait and see what happens next and to monitor the effects of any treatment, diagnosis can involve decisions about what information to collect and in what order, which require judgments balancing the time and expense of getting some particular kind of information against its anticipated contribution to the diagnosis. Such decisions lend themselves to evolving personal rule systems, which experts can then modify for cases they perceive as abnormal. But changes in scientific knowledge or investigative technology can make rules out of date, as well as generating a significant period of uncertainty while people find out how best to take advantage of them. The quality of judgments about collecting information and the capacity to change established patterns in the light of advances in science and technology could both be considered as aspects of process expertise in diagnosis. So also might the process of interacting with one's patients, an issue to which we shall shortly return.

Medicine is a field where decisions have to be made under conditions of considerable uncertainty. So physicians have to deal with probabilities whether or not they choose to express them in figures. At least three kinds of probability are highly relevant:

- the probability that a test for a particular condition will give the right result, a false positive or a false negative;
- the probability that a given treatment will lead to a particular outcome; and

- the probabilities associated with risks of complications, infections, mortality.

Where only one of these probabilities is relevant and there is a single, simple decision, the decision situation is easy to conceptualize. But when there is a chain of decisions and several sets of probabilities to consider, the problem is difficult to conceptualize and intuitive decision-making unlikely to be a good option. The technique of decision analysis was developed to bring some clarity of thinking to such situations and to work with multiple probabilities in a disciplined manner. Like most professions, there are those who are perceived as enthusiasts for quantitative methods and those who avoid them whenever possible. Given the very qualitative flavour of the discussion so far it is time to examine these more quantitative aspects of expertise.

Let us begin with a case quoted by Lilford (1992) of a woman with an early cancer of the reproductive tract. A small tumour was removed by an excisional biopsy which enabled the pathologist to estimate a 2 per cent probability of residual tumour. This risk could be halved by further surgery which has a mortality rate of 0.5 per cent. The technique involves exploring all possible outcomes then calculating their respective probabilities. This suggests that further surgery will improve her chances of survival, but the analysis is only there to provide a guide. Three other factors have to be considered: the reliability of the probability estimates used in the calculation; the likelihood of further contextual information about the woman suggesting an adjustment in one or more of the probability figures; and her preferences for the possible outcomes. In this case a woman who wishes to continue to have children might wish to take a slightly higher risk of mortality in order to retain her fertility.

Lilford gives considerable emphasis to the role of decision analysis in facilitating consultations with clients; and argues more generally that the technique exposes assumptions for discussion which should not be allowed to remain hidden. For example, he points out that it is quite common to suggest that amniocentesis should be recommended to pregnant women when the risk of their child having Down's Syndrome is greater than the risk of miscarriage caused by the procedure. But, although this advice sounds plausible, it implicitly assumes that the woman places equal value on both a Down's birth and foetal loss, which could be true for only a small percentage of women. There are a range of treatments and outcomes to be considered when making a decision. The physician's role is to explain the choice to his or her patient using the best available estimates of outcome probabilities. The relative desirability of the possible outcomes is a matter for the patient, who may need assistance in recognizing the implications for his or her future quality of life. This model suggests three distinctive areas of expertise

1. The physician has to be able to draw up a decision analysis using up-to-date information about possible treatments and outcomes, their

respective probabilities and the reliability of the figures. This latter requires a critical reading of research.

2. Research may also provide some information about how probabilities may vary according to context and patient. This together with the physician's ability to collect and interpret relevant information about context and patient will enable him or her to make appropriate adjustments to the probabilities.

3. The physician has to be able to interact with patients in order to best prepare and advise them, without unduly influencing their choice. Even in this situation, however, there may be some empirical evidence that is relevant.

Decision analysis uses the term 'utility' to indicate the weight to be attached to an outcome which reflects a client's preference and in some cases researchers have attempted the difficult task of establishing the range of values commonly associated to certain outcomes. Where the evidence is accompanied by information about people's arguments and feelings, it provides a useful background to discussions with individuals (and often counteracts physicians' first intuitive assumption about utilities).

The danger inherent in analytic approaches is overestimating the significance of the typical case which conforms with published estimates of probabilities and utilities, and underestimating the variation between patients. It can also be more time-intensive than many medical institutions are prepared to allow. However, there are other reasons why many physicians shy away from it. They may not feel competent in the mathematical handling of multiple probabilities; or they may feel their autonomy threatened by any suggestion that their unaided diagnosis of individual patients might need external guidance, especially when that guidance 'appears' to devalue the significance of individual cases. Intuitive approaches, on the other hand, tend to get reported in a manner that assumes that they always result in the right decision. The expert-oriented theories of the Dreyfuses and Schmidt *et al.*, start from the assumption that how clinical decisions *are made* by experts is also how clinical decisions *ought to be made*.

The limitations of a purely intuitive approach have been reviewed by Elstein and Bordage (1979), using Elstein *et al.*,'s earlier (1978) research as a starting point.

> . . . physicians engaged in diagnostic clinical reasoning commonly employ the strategy of generating and testing hypothetical solutions to the problem. A small set of hypotheses is generated very early in the clinical encounter, based on a very limited amount of data compared to what will eventually be collected. Often the chief complaint or the data obtained in the first few minutes of interaction with the patient

are sufficient to establish this small set of working hypotheses. The clinician can then ask: 'What findings would be observed if a particular hypothesis were true?' and the collection of data can be tailored to answer this question.

This reasoning process transforms the ill-defined, open-ended problem 'What is wrong with the patient?' into a series of better-defined problems: 'Could the abdominal pain be caused by acute appendicitis? or a twisted ovarian cyst? or pelvic inflammatory disease? or ectopic pregnancy?' This set of alternatives makes matters more manageable. By constructing a set of hypothesised end points, it becomes possible for the clinician to work backwards from the diagnostic criteria of each hypothesis to the work-up to be conducted. The search for data is simplified because only certain points will be addressed. (Elstein and Bordage, 1979)

The empirical evidence strongly confirms the intuitive nature of 'hypothesis generation', but does not suggest that it is error free. The heavy dependence on memory suggests that it is the most salient hypotheses which are most likely to be identified (see Chapter 6) and not necessarily the most probable. The research suggests that the most prevalent cause of incorrect diagnosis was a 'failure to generate and consider the relevant diagnostic hypothesis'. Experienced clinicians try to counteract this problem by deliberately constructing alternatives to those immediately suggested by the problem, a process which also draws on experience but clearly differs from the pattern recognition method of the template model.

The process of moving from a small set of hypotheses to a diagnosis involves both acquiring new data and interpreting the data already collected, often a major information processing task. Elstein and Bordage note that experienced physicians simplify this task by interpreting cues on a three-point scale: 'as tending to *confirm* or *disconfirm* a hypothesis or as *non-contributory*'. Then finally all this data has somehow to be interpreted and integrated in the clinician's head. Not surprisingly, a number of problems arise at this stage. The most common error is to treat non-contributory evidence as confirming a hypothesis; and there is also a strong tendency to re-emphasize negative findings. Other problems can arise from the tendency to give equal weighting to all the confirming or disconfirming issues, when some may be much more reliable and significant than others. This is less likely during later work-up when routines are likely to have been established that start with the most reliable ones, unless of course those particular tests involve time delays or are highly expensive. In general, the interpretation of data tends to be biased in support of early 'favoured' hypotheses. This conclusion warns us against the adoption of the totally intuitive approach described by Dreyfus, though not against the use of intuition *per se*. We shall return to this issue shortly when we discuss the role of reflection.

Hammond's Cognitive Continuum Theory

Our review of clinical decision-making has yielded models of expertise that are relevant outside the field of medicine; and drawn attention to empirical evidence that is rarely available for other professions. In particular, it has highlighted the role necessarily played by intuitive thinking, together with its advantages and limitations. The need for long periods of practical experience in order to develop and refine professional expertise has been explained in terms of theories about the role of memory in supporting intuitive thinking. The important role of more analytic approaches such as decision analysis and logical argument has also been discussed, raising important questions about the appropriate balance between intuitive and analytical approaches and the best ways in which they can be combined. Hamm (1988) points out that this last problem involves two important factors: the nature of the task, and the nature of the practitioner's expertise. Hence the initial questions to be answered are:

1. What kinds of thinking, analytic or intuitive (or a mixture) should be used in various types of situation?
2. How does the practitioner discover or decide which mode of cognition to use?
3. How can the appropriate kind of thinking be performed as well as possible? (Hamm, 1988, pp. 80–1)

These questions are addressed by Hammond's Cognitive Continuum Theory (1980) which defines analytic and intuitive thinking as poles of a continuum, arguing that most thinking is neither purely intuitive nor purely analytical. A variety of 'quasi-rational' modes of cognition lies somewhere in between. At the fast and ill-structured end of the continuum these quasi-rational modes include peer-aided judgment and system-aided judgment (decision analysis) while at the slow and well-structured end of the continuum are modes of inquiry involving surveys or quasi-experiments. It is interesting to note that on the time-scale in which clinicians work, decision analysis is perceived as the most analytic mode whereas for an engineer or a manager it would be perceived as closer to the intuitive end of the spectrum. However, even for them it would require information from previous analytically conceived research to supply the necessary evidence of probabilities.

Elstein's work, discussed earlier, drew attention to the 'mixed mode' of inquiry in which intuitive and analytical approaches are combined in a problem-solving approach to diagnosis. Similar results were obtained by Boreham (1987) from a study of expert management consultants. His account is worth quoting at some length as it epitomizes what many now regard as one of the most fruitful approaches to problem-solving.

> The subjects' expertise was quite obviously strongly dependent on their intuitive abilities to operate on mental models of what they

implicitly recognised in the problem givens. Their initial problem spaces included constraints (not part of the problem givens, but recalled from the subjects' memory of similar situations) which drastically reduced the amount of the problem domain which needed to be searched for the causal factor. This was unmistakably the result of a pattern recognition process similar to those postulated in the knowledge-based theory outlined earlier.

However, the problem was not actually solved just by activating these templates. Despite the substantial prior experience of these consultants, and the fact that the problem was one which they had 'seen a lot of' in industry, the solution was not actually contained in the schemata which were activated. The intuitive processes were used only to generate a problem space which isolated the crucial aspects of the problem and guided subsequent search.

In order to model the consultants' problem-solving behaviour accurately, it was necessary to represent the process of diagnosis as an alteration between knowledge-driven operations on a mental model of the situation, and sensory-driven operations on the problem givens. Insights gained in the former type of episode narrowed down to the cause of the problem remarkably quickly, but the management consultants still felt the need for local search to verify that what they suspected was actually the case, and to delineate the nature of the problem exactly. (Boreham, 1987, p. 94)

Boreham's evidence also showed very clearly that the local-search stage involved the use of inferential procedures which conformed to models of logical deduction rather than pattern recognition. The subjects' reasoning followed the classical laws governing inferences from categorical propositions. He also found that performance by post-experience students of management science was improved by practice in the formal operations involved in hypothesis-testing.

The second part of Hammond's theory is a 'task continuum' to differentiate those features of a task which should determine the most appropriate mode of cognition to use. Thus:

In Cognitive Continuum Theory, tasks are considered to occupy a position on a task continuum, ranging from analysis-inducing to intuition-inducing, indicated by task features that influence the model of cognition that the thinker will adopt. These features include the complexity of the task, the ambiguity of the content of the task, and the form of task presentation. (Hammond, 1980)

For example, the greater the number of pertinent cues and the higher the extent of their overlap or redundancy, the more likely there will be an intuitive response. The availability of a complex organizing principle is likely to encourage analysis. Pictorial forms of presenting information induce intuition and quantitative forms induce analysis. Decomposition into subtasks will also aid analysis, but lack of time causes people to adopt a faster, more intuitive approach.

Hammond's central argument is that people's reasoning is more effective when the mode of thinking they adopt corresponds to these critical features of the task. But to many professionals this advice must seem a little idealistic. The time factor alone forces people into a more rapid, intuitive mode of cognition; and as routines get developed, many would rather keep it that way. While some professionals are disposed to take time over their decisions and tasks, others clearly prefer not to linger. The current emphasis on professional productivity severely limits that choice.

The Theories of Donald Schön

The Reflective Practitioner (Schön, 1983) has been probably the most quoted book on professional expertise during the last ten years. Its success derives from many factors: the reputation of the author, the receptiveness of readers to those particular views at that particular time, the range of examples, the eloquence and persuasiveness of its argument have all contributed to its impact. It combines a devastating critique of the dominant 'technical rationality' model of professional knowledge based on positivist epistemology with a celebration of the artistry of professional practitioners who have avoided being seduced by it or simply found it inapplicable to their normal work. Its publication coincided with a period of growing disillusion with the role of science and social science in our society; and was directed at a North American academe in which positivism still retained a hegemony which it never quite acquired in Europe. Schön's critique is based on two complementary arguments. First, there are severe limitations to what can be achieved by a purely positivist approach in the complexities of the real world, as it is only capable of tackling simple or simplified problems. Second, the technical rationality model fails to take proper account of how professionals work in practice in order to achieve their desired goals. Technical rationality is inadequate both as a prescription for, and as a description of, professional practice. Schön's eloquent exposition of these arguments articulated what many professionals at that time were aware of but had neither clearly understood nor felt able to discuss.

Schön then introduces the rationale for his own alternative theory of professional knowledge in the following terms:

> If the model of Technical Rationality is incomplete, in that it fails to account for practical competence in 'divergent' situations, so much the worse for the model. Let us search, instead, for an epistemology of practice implicit in the artistic, intuitive processes which some

practitioners do bring to situations of uncertainty, instability, uniqueness, and value conflict. (Schön, 1983, p. 49)

Few commentators have noted the extent to which Schön's book is constructed from this perspective. Schön is not primarily concerned with describing the general, unproblematic aspects of professional work but with searching out examples of professional work which demonstrate artistry and thereby most clearly refute the technical rationality model. Hence he is principally concerned with developing an epistemology of professional creativity rather than a complete epistemology of everyday professional practice. The evidence he cites consists almost entirely of critical cases or incidents which illustrate professional creativity in design, problem-solving or problem-setting; and he places considerable emphasis on professionals' intuitive capacity to reconceptualize a situation or reframe a problem. There is no comparable search for counterexamples.

Schön's defensible thesis can be summarized as follows:

- There is a significant number of episodes or incidents in the work of professionals when they find themselves engaged in ill-defined situations and tackling complex problems which require a creative approach, both in their conceptualization and framing and in the search for a solution.
- When engaged in this kind of work, professionals are drawing on their own practical experience in a highly intuitive manner, and at the same time reflecting on what they are doing. The process is the opposite in almost every respect to that suggested by the technical rationality model.
- The distinctive feature of this alternative model, however, is not its reliance on intuitive problem-setting or problem-solving — Schön shares this with many others, most notably the *Gestalt* psychologists — but Schön's view that this is embedded in a process which he describes as 'reflection-in-action'.

The immediate questions this raises are: What precisely does Schön mean by reflection-in-action and is it an adequate representation of the creative processes he seeks to describe? Finding answers is not easy because Schön proceeds mainly by example and metaphor rather than sustained argument. He also tends to stray away from his own definitions and evidence into making statements which are difficult to defend. Nevertheless I shall attempt to convey the essence of his theory as I perceive it, knowing that others may want to dispute my interpretation. I shall place greater reliance on his second book *Educating the Reflective Practitioner* (1987) because by then Schön would have discussed and debated his theory in numerous places and fine-tuned his own interpretation and representation of its key ideas.

Schön begins by acknowledging that 'the workaday life of the professional depends on tacit knowledge-in-action'. This corresponds closely to what I described in Chapter 6 as 'skilled behaviour'

> The knowing-in-action is tacit, spontaneously delivered without conscious deliberation; and it works, yielding intended outcomes so long as the situation falls within the boundaries of what we have learned to treat as normal. (Schön, 1987, p. 28)

Reflection is triggered by the recognition that in some respects the situation is not normal and therefore in need of special attention. The trigger may be an unexpected action or outcome, or just an intuitive feeling of unease that something is not quite right (this last kind of trigger was frequently reported in Benner's (1984) study of expert nurses). Thus what may have begun as a routine situation comes to be perceived as problematic. Schön then describes three salient features of reflection-in-action:

1. Reflection is at least in some measure conscious, although it need not occur in the medium of words. We consider both the unexpected event and the knowing-in-action that led up to it, asking ourselves, as it were, 'What is this?' and, at the same time, 'How have I been thinking about it?' Our thought turns back on the surprising phenomenon and, at the same time, back on itself.
2. Reflection-in-action has a critical function, questioning the assumptional structure of knowing-in-action. We think critically about the thinking that got us into this fix or this opportunity; and we may, in the process, restructure strategies of action, understandings of phenomena, or ways of framing problems.
3. Reflection gives rise to on-the-spot experiment. We think up and try out new actions intended to explore the newly observed phenomena, test our tentative understandings of them, or affirm the moves we have invented to change things for the better . . . What distinguishes reflection-in-action from other kinds of reflection is its immediate significance for action. (*ibid.*, pp. 28–9)

These features represent the past, present, and future aspects of the reflective process. The first can be considered as a rapid alert in which the cue to reflect pulls the practitioner out of the 'automatic pilot' mode of skilful behaviour. The third derives from the action-based nature of the situation. Action has to be taken and thinking has to be directed towards deciding what that action should be. The term 'on-the-spot experiment' is a somewhat flamboyant way of pointing out that, once the situation has been recognized as abnormal, alerted professionals will carefully monitor their actions until normality is resumed. The second present-oriented feature is more problematic and merits further discussion.

Several critics have argued that Schön fails to sufficiently clarify what is entailed in the reflective process itself. My own view is that he does not have a simple coherent view of reflection but a set of overlapping attributes; and that he selects whichever subset of attributes best suits the situation under discussion. There is insufficient discrimination between the rather different forms of reflection depicted in his many examples; and this overgeneralization causes confusion and weakens his theoretical interpretations. While Schön's theory is significantly less rational than Hammond's Cognitive Continuum, it would still benefit from careful consideration of how patterns of reflection vary according to profession, situation and circumstance.

One important variable which Schön effectively ignores is that of 'time'. When time is extremely short, decisions have to be rapid and the scope for reflection is extremely limited. In these circumstances, reflection is best seen as a metacognitive process in which the practitioner is alerted to a problem, rapidly reads the situation, decides what to do and proceeds in a state of continuing alertness. This resembles those situations involving rapid interpretation of information and decision-making in the midst of action which were described in Chapter 6. A familiar example would be the action of formulating questions during an unstructured interview in response to what the respondent reveals, whilst at the same time listening and noting what is is being said. Similarly, a teacher might need to respond rapidly in a classroom to a pupil's question or a disruptive action. If, however, we adjust this situation to one where the teacher is walking round a classroom of children quietly working on their own, the reflective process appears a little different. There is time for the teacher to look around, to contemplate in silence, and to decide whether or not to intervene. The period of reflection will still be fairly short, but it is already beginning to resemble a time-out of action. Extending the period for reflection still further is likely to result in the reflection assuming a more deliberative character, with time to consciously explore a range of possible options or even to consult with other people. This seems more in accord with Schön's description of reflection as a critical process in (2) above, admitting the likelihood of an analytic as well as an intuitive dimension; but less in accord with the notion of reflection being *in* the action.

Other problems are raised by Schön's favourite example, which occupies one long chapter in his first book and over four chapters in his second. The set is an architect's studio but the scene is not one of normal ongoing design but a twenty-minute tutorial in which a master designer coaches a student engaged in the design of a school. The master looks at her drawings, listens to her account of her problems, then quickly reframes the problems in his own terms and begins to demonstrate the working out of a design solution. This involves him in all of the following

- sketching ideas to explore the reframed problem;
- articulating the rationale for the reframing and explaining his ongoing design thinking as he sketches;

- explaining at a more abstract level the general principles of design which underpin his approach; and
- praising and reinterpreting some of the student's ideas, while also introducing some new ideas of his own.

Thus he is modelling a piece of design, articulating a theory of design, giving the student feedback on her work and giving her the stimulus to overcome a period of 'being stuck'. Schön makes it quite clear that he regards the 'action' as being the design process rather than the teaching process. Here, and in several other examples, he uses a coaching scene as a convenient means of prompting verbal description and discussion of what might otherwise be unexplained professional action; but pays no regard to the concomitant lack of authenticity and the probability that professional action will be different under such artificial circumstances. Presumably the design process is normally a relatively silent deliberative process combining thinking, sketching and accurate drawing over a long period of time. Yet Schön treats it as an archetypal example of reflection-in-action, without actually stating which parts or aspects of the master designer's behaviour are reflective and which are not. There appear to be three possibilities:

1. All his talk is reflective: this would suggest that reflection is just a synonym for thinking, and not a technical term to describe a particular kind of thinking.
2. Only his most strategic talk is reflective: the designer is in action when engaged in accurate drawing or detailed routine planning, but only reflective when he is thinking about the design as a whole. This accords with Schön's continuing emphasis on the framing and reframing of problems but seems a rather dubious distinction epistemologically.
3. Reflection is essentially a metacognitive process, the thinking about thinking which informs decisions about what to do next and what to think next, e.g., abandon Option X and try Option Y instead, stop working on Z and explore its effect on the rest of the design.

Although Schön examines the twenty-minute conversation from several perspectives, he never makes it clear which of these possible meanings of reflection he wishes to adopt: indeed one can find passages of his commentary in which each of the three appears to be his theory of reflection in use.

Schön's use of the term 'reflection-on-action' is less problematic. It refers to the process of making sense of an action after it has occurred and possibly learning something from the experience which extends one's knowledge base. It may affect future action but cannot affect the action being reflected upon because that has already passed. Though this appears to be logically distinct from 'reflection-in-action', the distinction may still need interpretation in many practical situations. The principal source of difficulty is when a task continues over several episodes. Is this to be interpreted as one action divided into several phases, or as a series of several actions in succession? What might be considered reflection-in-action under the former interpretation becomes reflection-on-action under the latter interpretation. To return to our dramatic metaphor, is the action a scene, an act or a whole play? Or is it reflection-in-action while the actors are on stage and reflection-on-action when they are not? From the actor's viewpoint, is it only what Goffmann (1959) calls 'front-stage' action which counts as action, or does 'backstage' action count as well?

If we return once more to the question of time-scale, we can see that rapid reflection-in-action is a very different kind of process from the reflection-on-action which authors from Dewey to Kolb have associated with learning from experience. But slow, deliberative, reflection does not seem any different whether it is described as *in* action or *on* action. Munby and Russell (1989) appear to endorse the less deliberative form of reflection in their essay review of Schön's two books:

> Several years of research activity in which we have attempted to apply and better understand the term 'reflection-in-action' have led us to realize that this phrase so central to Schön's argument is easily mis-read if we focus on reflection rather than on action. 'Reflection' typically suggests thinking about action, but the crucial phrase, on our reading is 'in-action'. The reflection that Schön is calling attention to is *in the action*, not in associated thinking about action. (Munby and Russell, 1989, p. 73)

However, later they also begin to despair of getting much further:

> There is a clear description of what we might wish reflective practice to be like. Yet it is not quite clear what Schön's cases are cases of, and this point requires elaboration. The cases themselves seem to provide an account of the surface characteristics of reflection-in-action and the coaching that nurtures it. Yet there is virtually *no elaboration of the psychological realities* of reflection-in-action, in ways that would enable us to use the case studied as examples of what happens when reflection-in-action begins, as examples of what causes it to begin, and as examples of what the precise conditions are that would assure us that it is occurring . . . His work is not sufficiently analytical and articulated to enable us to follow the connections that must be made between elements of experience and elements of cognition so that we may see how reflection-in-action might be understood to occur. (*ibid.*, p. 74)

The difficulty is exacerbated by Schön's inconsistencies. When expounding his theory he stresses the distinction between reflection-in-action and reflection-on-action, but when selecting and discussing his examples he fails to sustain it. Indeed, the only criterion which he consistently applies to his selection of examples is that reframing of the problem takes place. Many of his long examples fail to provide any evidence that reflection-in-action is occurring; and in several examples, including all those from science, engineering and management, reflection-on-action appears to have been at least as likely a cause of reframing as reflection-in-action. In some cases the master-professionals have set up processes for participants to sort out a problem rather than attempt to solve it themselves: a sensible strategy no doubt but Schön describes them as setting up the conditions for reflection-in-action, implying that participative problem-solving and reflection-in-action are the same thing.

Schön also describes a few examples of unsuccessful action; but in each case, although suggesting that the problem was caused by a failure to reflect, his real analysis appears to be based on his earlier theory (Argyris and Schön, 1974) about single-loop learning and double-loop learning. As explained in Chapter 5, they argued that feedback during objectives-driven behaviour was only single-loop learning because it was framed by pre-existing expectations. It failed to yield evidence of other people's views of the situation which might lead to double-loop learning and modification of the practitioners' implicit theories about how best to achieve their goals. Reading Schön's account of the tutorial in the architect's studio, I could not help but wonder whether the master designer was not a single-loop teacher even if he may have been a double-loop designer. Certainly Schön seems to take for granted the transfer of expertise in professional practice into expertise in coaching students or interns without supporting evidence and sometimes in the face of indications to the contrary.

One important consequence of Schön's books has been the proliferation of a wide variety of professional education programmes claiming to be based on his theory. This partly results from the natural range of interpretations which results from putting any theory into use: but this natural variation has been exacerbated by the ambiguities and inconsistencies in Schön's theory. Hence a recent review of the compendium of North American practice in 'Reflective Teacher Education' in the aftermath of Schön, concludes:

> Each of the seven programs has unique assumptions and organizing principles, some working with little more than a common-sense definition of reflection that seems to come naturally to all teacher educators. The six critiques similarly convey unique senses of 'reflection'. This collection will certainly stimulate productive thinking about issues and tensions within teacher education, but there is no shared sense of 'reflection' to give direction to future developments. (Munby and Russell, 1993, p. 431)

To rescue Schön's original contribution from this morass, I believe it is necessary to take the term 'reflection' out of his theory, because it has caused nothing but confusion. I find it more helpful to view all of Schön's work on

Speed

Analysis	Instant recognition	Rapid interpretation	Deliberative analysis
Decision	Instant response	Rapid decisions	Deliberative decisions
Action	Routinized unreflective action	Action monitored by reflection	Action following a period of deliberation

Figure 7.2: The Link Between Speed and Mode of Cognition

professional knowledge, including his earlier work with Argyris, as a theory of metacognition. As I suggested earlier, Schön's notion of rapid reflection-in-action provides an original and useful theory of metacognition during skilled behaviour. His ideas about reframing and reflective conversations with the situation might also be construed as contributing to a theory of metacognition during deliberative processes. This makes a clear distinction between delibera-tion and reflective metacognition of that deliberation.

The Relationships Between Expertise and Deliberation

The central importance of time and speed in professional work has already been stressed in our reviews of Hammond and Schön. Figure 7.2 summarizes our position so far. The top row depicts the distinction made in Chapter 6 between the instant, rapid and deliberative modes of analysing a case or situ-ation. The middle row carries this distinction forward in order to represent the different types of decision-making discussed in the first half of this chap-ter. The bottom row takes into account the discussion of Schön in the pre-vious section.

Giving more attention to the time dimension suggests that we need to re-examine our earlier classification of planning, problem-solving and decision-making as deliberative processes. Daily talk among many professionals suggests that deliberation may be more the exception than the rule. As they are con-fronted with waiting clients, loaded in-trays and calls for efficiency gains, plans get 'cobbled together' in a hurry, decisions are made 'on the hoof' and symptoms are treated instead of attending to the problems they disclose.

The practicalities of professional work and the respective contributions of rapid and deliberative processes are usefully illuminated by the notion of a 'performance period' (Eraut, 1989, 1990). The analysis of a performance is concerned with everything done by the performer during a specified period of time, particularly with such aspects as reading the situation, deciding what to do, changing one's plan, responding to unforeseen events, allocating time and managing the transition to other periods. The precise definition of each period is at the discretion of the analyst. It might, for example, be a distinct part of the day, e.g., from lunch-break to tea-break; or it might extend from the initiation to the completion of some major transaction or task. What is important, however, is that all the tasks or transactions performed during the period are included, even if they have no connection with each other beyond their claims on the performer's attention. Without this requirement, a major feature of some occupations would be excluded, namely the handling of competing demands. Thus focusing on a performance period provides a much needed contrast to the normal tendency to consider expertise solely in the context of individual problems, cases or tasks.

The generic model of a performance period depicted in Figure 7.3 is characterized by a context, a beginning and an ending, by conditions (which may change during the course of the period) and by a developing situation. Plans may pre-exist on paper or in the practitioner's mind, they may be developed or modified during an initiation period; or the practitioner may simply decide to handle the situation in a routine way or even to improvise. In every case, however, there has to be a correct reading of the situation so that appropriate action can be taken — quality input as well as quality output. One advantage of focusing on a performance period is that this is an ongoing process. Instead of a static model in which all decisions and plans are made at the beginning, it suggests a dynamic model in which a constantly changing environment provides a changing input which leads to the constant modification of plans. Nor is it only the external environment which changes of its own accord. The performer is an actor who affects that environment, not always in totally predictable ways. So another role of input is to provide feedback on the effect of one's own performance. This applies whether one is making something and sensing it change, or talking to someone, listening to their reply and observing their reaction. The model also emphasizes that practitioners need not only be competent at professional tasks but able to complete them on time. Otherwise the conclusion will be curtailed by a sudden departure which leaves a legacy of scribbled notes, unrecorded decisions and unfinished business.

This analysis suggests that deliberation is unlikely to occur in the workplace unless the professional(s) concerned build deliberation time into their performance periods at the beginning, in the middle or (more riskily) at the end. Deliberation time outside the workplace may be equally difficult to find: the tyranny of the briefcase prioritizes the urgent over the important, private life makes its entirely proper demands and tiredness may reduce the likelihood of any deliberation being productive. Hence the deliberative use of expertise will depend on both the skilful management of working time and the disposition to make time for deliberation.

Why then did I state in Chapter 6 that deliberative processes lie at the

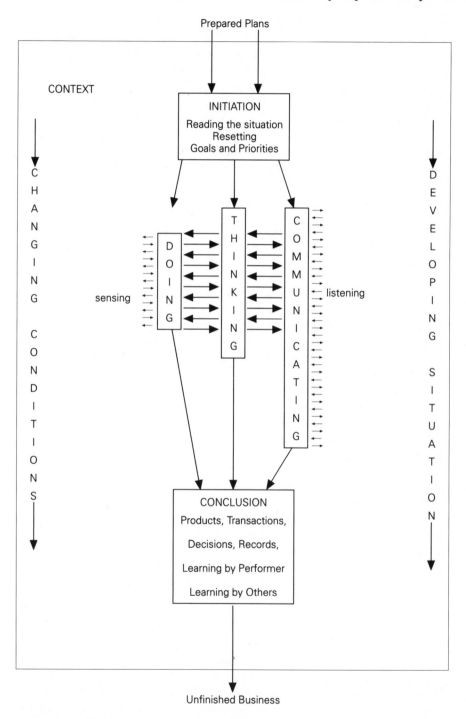

Figure 7.3: Activities During a Performance Period

heart of professional work? First, there are groups of professionals whose work does not consist of a long series of individual cases and/or small tasks. An architect or engineer, for example, might be working on a single project for two or three years. Their performance periods will consist of a long uninterrupted series of sessions on the same task; they will have plenty of scope for reflecting on what they are doing and discussing and deliberating over their general approach to the problem: indeed they are likely to waste time rather than save time if they fail to stop and think. Their work will still involve intuitive as well as analytic thinking, but their learning from experience will not be confined to the intuitive accumulation of memorized cases and patterns. They will also learn from their investigations, from their analysis of options, from small experiments, from consultations and from conscious evaluation of their ongoing work. While much of this learning will be project-specific, some of it will also add to the knowledge-base they carry forward to future projects. The extent to which this longer-term learning occurs will depend both on the intellectual milieu of their work context and on their own personal disposition.

Second, many professionals receive work that contains mainly routine cases or well-defined problems that can be handled without a great deal of deliberation unless something unexpected occurs. Schön described this in terms of proceeding normally until some cue triggers reflection-in-action. What Schön did not discuss was the extent to which such cues are liable to be missed or disregarded by a practitioner under pressure. But alongside the straightforward cases will be others that are more problematic, the 'ill-defined problems' to which we referred earlier. There appears to be little argument that such cases require deliberation, but finding time to handle them properly is easier in some contexts than others. In Law it will depend on the client's ability to cover the cost. In a large business, an important problem might be tackled by setting up a special team or having a consultant. In many organizations, the more routine tasks and cases are allocated to technicians or newly qualified professionals, so that the more experienced professionals combine a supervisory role with a regular flow of more difficult and challenging problems. In teaching, spending extra time with a single problem student will be very obviously at the expense of time devoted to others; and will therefore be limited unless special organizational arrangements can be made. We need to note, however, that it is the ability to cope with difficult, ill-defined problems rather than only routine matters which is often adjudged to be the essence of professional expertise.

This issue was highlighted by the Construction Industry Standing Conference (CISC) when it judged that the qualifications it was developing paid insufficient attention to the nature of professional work. The response was to add a unit entitled 'Provide solutions to and advice on complex, indeterminate problems within an ethical framework' which is reproduced in Tables 7.2, 7.3 and 7.4. This provides an excellent illustration of the range of expertise required in many professions and the critical importance of analysis, consultation,

Table 7.2: Exchange Information and Provide Advice on Matters of Technical Concern (Element F226.1)

Performance Criteria:

(a) Terms of Reference and expectations of contracting parties are identified, clearly stated and confirmed in writing.

(b) Information is acquired to a level of detail suitable for its purpose in a context of openness, dialogue, questioning and sensitivity to feedback.

(c) Information and advice are given in a format which is complete, accurately summarised and focused on critical subject matter.

(d) Information and advice are given in a manner which is in accordance with the ability, knowledge and disposition of the recipients.

(e) In instances where recipients are having difficulties in understanding instructions or specifications, language and terminology is suitable adapted and modified to increase the likelihood of understanding whilst retaining the critical points and purpose of the information.

(f) Recommendations presented to contracting parties are clear, accurate and valid, realistically estimating the implications of considered alternatives and containing the best available advice within the constraints of the information and resources available.

(g) Recommendations contain clear descriptions of information sources consulted, analytical techniques applied, and criteria used for evaluation and justifiable conclusions.

Source: CISC, 'Provide Solutions to and Advice on Complex, Indeterminate Problems Within an Ethical Framework', Unit Title F226.

deliberation and judgment. We shall return specifically to the ethical dimension in Chapter 11.

Another aspect of expertise involving deliberation is what is often called 'strategic thinking'. Even more than problem-solving, this requires an ability to conceptualize and to look at an organization, a policy or a programme of work from several different perspectives. The significance of various quantitative trends has to be assessed, various strands of forward thinking have to be balanced against one another and integrated. Judgment is at a premium. This kind of expertise is needed not only by managers but also by senior professionals whose advice is essential to forward thinking about the organization and policy framework within which professional work is conducted. Another strong emphasis in strategic thinking, to which we will return in Chapter 11, concerns the future of professional services and the relationship between organizations employing professionals, individual professionals and their clients. What will be the future role of the various professions in our society? Addressing these questions requires judgment and the ability to consult with interested parties outside the profession.

A fourth aspect of professional expertise that is closely linked to deliberation is team work and consultation. Where groups of people are involved in problem-solving, planning or policy-making, with full participation the process is necessarily deliberative for much of the time. This brings both advantages and disadvantages. The main advantages are that it enables expertise to be shared as different perspectives are brought to bear, that it forces people to stop and think and be challenged and that the stimulus of productive groups

Table 7.3: Identify, Re-frame and Generate Solutions to Complex, Indeterminate Problems (Element F226.2)

Performance Criteria:

(a) Problematic conditions are identified, their implications are realistically estimated and clearly presented to relevant parties.

(b) Available and identified information and data are checked for accuracy and completeness.

(c) Significant gaps in the coverage and accuracy of information are identified and additional relevant and accurate information is sought and assessed.

(d) Appropriate tests are selected, accurately specified, commissioned and implemented to gather data which is not directly accessible.

(e) Test results are analysed and interpreted using a valid and reliable method and conclusions are drawn which are justifiable in the light of the data and the known reliability for the analysis method.

(f) In cases which are outside the practitioner's technical competence, appropriate specialists are promptly consulted and provided with clear and accurate information.

(g) The probable factors out of which problematic conditions arose are plausibly identified, coherently formulated, and appropriately recorded.

(h) The perceptions of a problem are interpreted, translated, represented and reframed to such a level of detail that elements amenable to known solutions and procedures can be identified, and the solutions applied.

(i) The analysis of available data contains continuing reflection on precedent, similarities between previous cases and the current situation, the outcomes required, known limitations, anticipated limitations and constraints and criteria for evaluation.

(j) Aids and techniques are applied which inform and increase the reliability of decisions and judgements.

(k) Optional solutions and procedures, in which the probability of resolution is balanced against disruption and risk, are identified and justified on the basis of declared criteria and reasoned argument.

(l) Solutions are proposed with sufficient controls, including collection of valid and reliable data, to minimise additional disruptions to systems.

Source: as Table 7.2.

often enhances individual creativity. The main disadvantages are that it frequently lengthens the time taken, thus increasing the cost of the process; and that it introduces interfering agendas such as the micropolitics of the group. In this context one should note that the handling of groups itself constitutes a form of expertise, as described for example in books like Schein's *Process Consultation* (1988) and Friend and Hickling's *Planning Under Pressure* (1987). Moreover, this expertise is not widely distributed among professionals, making many of them less effective and in some situations even incompetent; because they cannot use their expertise without obstructing or upsetting other people.

More easily neglected in some professions is the need for consultations with clients to be conducted in a deliberative mode. We mentioned this earlier when discussing the use of decision analysis in medicine and the need to ascertain how clients regard the utilities of various decision options. In situations of any complexity, it is virtually impossible to establish any logical connection between decision options and long-term outcomes for clients without moving into a deliberative mode. Indeed it is difficult to see how a

Table 7.4: Contribute to the Protection of Individual and Community Interests (Element F226.3)

Performance Criteria:

(a) Formal and informal contracts and agreements for advisory and problem-solving services conform to legal requirements and recognised good practice.

(b) Offers and contracts which are illegal and which may generate conflicts of interest are declined.

(c) Relevant and appropriate values, principles, goals and expectations are clearly articulated and unequivocally stated in the development and communication of technical strategies.

(d) Sources of knowledge of current practice with reference to technical information and opinion are critically investigated.

(e) Judgements and advice are sound and justifiable, based solely on valid, reliable criteria including the interests of the contracting party within the constraints of statute law, recognised good practice and current information.

(f) The needs of contracting parties are balanced against resource constraints and the needs of others directly and indirectly affected within the community.

(g) Clear and unequivocal personal responsibility is taken for personal decisions.

(h) Appropriate systems are established to protect the interests of and to compensate contracting parties in instances where advice results in loss or damage to the contracting party.

(i) Funds and benefits derived therefrom held on behalf of contracting parties are kept separate from the personal and organisational funds of the practitioner.

(j) Information obtained from parties with which the practitioner has an advisory relationship is made available only to those who have a statutory right to receive it.

(k) Interaction is conducted in a style and manner which maintains the independence of the practitioner and maximises goodwill and trust with contracting parties.

Source: as Table 7.2.

professional could be client-centred in anything other than a token sense without some period of deliberation. We shall return to this issue in Chapter 11.

Then, finally, there is the problem discussed several times in earlier chapters of the fallibility of routinized behaviour and purely intuitive decision-making. Too many theories of professional expertise tend to treat experts as infallible, in spite of much evidence to the contrary. Not only do professionals succumb to many of the common weaknesses which psychologists have shown to be regular features of human judgment; but some allow aspects of their expertise to decay and become a little less relevant or even out of date. Thus there is a need for professionals to retain critical control over the more intuitive parts of their expertise by regular reflection, self-evaluation and a disposition to learn from colleagues. This implies from time to time treating apparently routine cases as problematic and making time to deliberate and consult. It is partly a matter of lifelong learning and partly a wise understanding of one's own fallibility.

Let us now return once more to the meaning of the word 'reflection'. *The Shorter Oxford Dictionary* gives two distinct meanings to reflection as a thought process, both dating back to the seventeenth century if not earlier[1]

1. The action of turning (back) or fixing the thoughts on some subject: meditation, deep or serious consideration.

2. The mode, operation or faculty by which the mind has knowledge of itself and its operations, or by which it deals with the ideas received from sensation and perception.

The first of these meanings treats reflection as a form of deliberation, while the second treats it as a form of metacognition. Both are important contributors to professional expertise. We have already discussed the metacognitive meaning of reflection in our review of Schön, and it also featured significantly in Chapter 6 where we referred to Schutz's notion of the 'reflective glance' challenging the taken-for-granted level of meaning. Here we shall briefly examine what is involved in the deliberative meaning of reflection.

The key to reflection as a deliberative process lies in the phrases 'turning back', 'fixing thoughts' and 'deep and serious consideration'. The focus is on interpreting and understanding cases or situations by reflecting on what one knows about them. This knowledge may include both impressions which have hitherto not been reflected upon and any available personal and/or public knowledge deemed relevant. Two aspects of such reflection are noted by Dewey (1933). The first describes reflection as a process for bringing personal knowledge under critical control:

> Active, persistent, and careful consideration of any belief or supposed form of knowledge in the light of the grounds that support it and the further conclusions to which it tends constitute reflective thought. (Dewey, 1933, p. 9)

We discussed the importance of bringing routine behaviour and intuitive thinking under some kind of critical control in the earlier chapters. It is a central part of a professional's responsibility for the continuing development and ongoing evaluation of their personal knowledge base, which we will discuss further in Chapter 11. Our argument is that failure to engage in such reflection on a regular basis is irresponsible.

Dewey's second aspect is that picked up by Schön:

> The function of reflective thought is, therefore, to transform a situation in which there is experienced obscurity, doubt, conflict, disturbance of some sort, into a situation that is clear, coherent, settled, harmonious . . . (*ibid.*, p. 100)

This view appears somewhat overoptimistic from a post-modernist perspective, but nevertheless points to qualities such as 'conceptualization' and 'situational understanding' which are highlighted in many accounts of professional expertise. It also resembles the process we described in Chapter 4 and elsewhere as 'theorizing'.

To conclude this chapter, perhaps we should note the revolution in thinking about professional expertise. Thirty years ago, professional expertise tended to be identified with propositional knowledge and a high theoretical content, regardless of whether such knowledge ever got used in practice. Whereas most of the theories of expertise discussed in this chapter appear to have assumed that expertise is based mainly on experience with further development of theoretical knowledge having almost ceased soon after qualification. Why has the pendulum swung so far in the other direction? Several explanations come to mind. One is the strong anti-intellectualization of the 1980s exacerbated by the exaggerated claims of the immediate post-war era. Another is the failure to properly recognize theory in use, a point strongly emphasized by Argyris and Schön (1974). A third, I could argue is the failure to recognize how theory gets used in practice, that it rarely gets just taken off the shelf and applied without undergoing some transformation. The process of interpreting and personalizing theory and integrating it into conceptual frameworks that are themselves partly inconsistent and partly tacit is as yet only minimally understood. The first part of this book has been an attempt to take our understanding a little further.

Note

1. Other dictionary meanings are those of 'a thought or idea occupying the mind' and 'a thought expressed in words', but neither refers to reflection as a process.

Part 2

Professional Competence and Qualifications

Part 1 has revealed the inherent complexity of professional thought and action. Professional processes, which are not extremely rapid, usually involve an integrated mixture of types of knowledge and modes of cognition that is difficult to unravel. This reflects the complexity of the cases, problems and situations which many professionals have to handle. The development of professional knowledge depends on a continuing capacity and disposition to learn from the experience of such cases, as well as the ever-growing corpus of public codified knowledge. Nevertheless, by social convention and common consent there are points on this continuum of professional learning at which individual professionals become qualified in a formal, publicly-recognized manner. Qualification is in every sense a *rite de passage*, which affects people's status in society, a landmark in the process of professional socialization.

The public expects that a qualified professional will be competent in the discharge of normal professional tasks and duties. To suggest, therefore, that professional qualifications should be designed to indicate that aspiring professionals have completed their initial training and are now competent appears to be simply stating the obvious. However, such statements also carry other connotations. First, to make such a statement is to imply that that is not what happens in practice: not all professional qualifications certify competence; and by innuendo this 'malpractice' is common. Second, there is a hint that competence in practical matters must be preserved against the encroachments of the intellectuals. The use of the word 'competence' is not value-neutral.

Historically, it is interesting to note the gradual transition in English-speaking countries from a situation where competence was a concept developed by the professions to justify the introduction of qualifying examinations to one where competence became a concept used by government to justify control over licensing arrangements and/or public expenditure. In the first case the professions were concerned with maintaining their status and reputation by excluding unqualified practitioners, in the second government was seeking to limit professional autonomy in order to safeguard the interests of the public. Naturally, the definition of what in practice was meant by 'competence' reflected the political purpose it was intended to serve.

Definitions of competence, however, may be designed for one purpose and in practice serve quite a different purpose. Certainly, they entail assumptions about the nature of professional knowledge which remain unexamined or get relegated to the periphery of political vision; and they result in side-effects unanticipated by their proponents. It is no accident, therefore, that much of the discussion about competence in the literature appears to bypass the kind of discussion about professional knowledge which we conducted in Part 1. I have tried, however, to bring the issue of knowledge back into the discussion on those occasions where it is most relevant.

Chapter 8 seeks to describe the range of definitions of competence found in the literature, to put them in their historical context and to examine their underpinning assumptions. Beginning with its historical association with professional examinations, it moves on to consider how claims about the scope of a professional's competence have been settled or disputed. The alternative everyday meaning of 'competent' as 'tolerably good but less than expert' is introduced and with it the tension between the formal priority given to initial qualification and the informal awareness that professional learning has only just begun at that stage of a person's career. It is suggested that in practice, competence may be defined by the work allocated to newly qualified professionals rather than by paper-based examinations or standards.

Previous research into competence has followed three main traditions. Competency-based training and education has relied on very detailed specifications of competent behaviour in the tradition of behaviourist psychology but also combining the analytic techniques of psychologists with observations of, and consultations with, practitioners. Mastery learning approaches were supported and there was a limited role for theory. Generic approaches to competence differed in almost every respect. They used psychometric techniques to identify overarching qualities linked to excellent job performance, focused more on mid-career professionals than trainers and more on selection than training. Nevertheless they had a strong influence on programmes of training and development, especially in management. A third approach based on cognitive constructs of competence is less reported in the professional education literature because it has been referenced more to academic settings. The distinction made by linguists, however, between competence (being able to speak in a certain way) and performance (actually speaking in that way) can hardly be considered irrelevant to the world of work. Some approaches to competence appear to equate what a person can do with what they are observed to do in a performance context; and that can be very misleading. The cognitive approach also raises difficult and disturbing questions about the relationship between depth of understanding and long-term performance.

The chapter then concludes by clarifying the distinction sometimes made between competence (macro) and competencies (micro); and noting a developmental model linking competency development to continuing on-the-job learning and career progression.

Chapter 9 describes the development of a national system of vocational qualifications in the UK during the last five years, which is competency-based and has a government remit to extend eventually into the area of professional qualifications. The principal features of the model are discussed with careful examination of the underpinning assumptions. Its most notable characteristic, perhaps, is its attempt to integrate a broad concept of job competence and the generic nature of a national occupational qualification, which has to cover a wide range of employment settings, with the high degree of specificity associated with competency-based training systems and performance criteria. The laudable principles that (1) access to qualifications should not be limited by access to any particular form of training, and (2) every element of the qualification should have performance evidence in its assessment, have led to great weight being placed on a complex system of predominantly work-based assessment. Hence the main criticisms of the system have centred round the complexity, practicality and reliability of the assessment system, the appropriateness of the qualifications for the range of jobs they cover and the assumption that underpinning knowledge will be covered by standards based primarily on observed behaviour. Several examples of standards developed within the new NVQ/SVQ framework are included to illustrate how it operates.

Chapter 10 reports the results of the author's research into how professions in the UK currently assess the professional competence of their new entrants, and discusses the extent to which their practice is similar to, or different from, the NVQ/SVQ system. The research found that there was a wide range of assessment methods in use, and that every profession included a strong component of performance evidence. However, unlike the NVQ/SVQ system (in theory if not always in practice), the professions sought to assess professional knowledge and thinking in non-performance contexts. We call this kind of evidence 'capability evidence' and argue that it constitutes an important component of professional competence. It sometimes overlaps with performance evidence but also complements it by demonstrating how candidates think with and use their knowledge in work-related projects and reports. This use of the term 'capability' is closely analogous to the concept of competence used in linguistics (the cognitive approach described in Chapter 8); but the argument is that for purposes of professional certification it should complement performance evidence and replace evidence of propositional knowledge elicited in purely academic settings. Thus capability evidence both suits the professions and is generally compatible with the concept of a competency-based qualification.

Other issues raised in Chapter 10 are the problems of quality assurance, standards and progression. Quality assurance in professional qualifications could certainly be improved by developing assessment criteria and verification procedures, but the training and networking of a community of assessors is also important. Public standards of competence should be expected of every profession in today's accountable world, but they need not be as detailed as those currently favoured by the NVQ/SVQ system and new ways of representing standards need to be developed which show their interconnectedness and make it easier for people to comprehend them. However, there is no inherent problem in incorporating an ethical dimension, one of the main concerns expressed by the professions. Finally, it is argued that there is no need to adopt models of competence which appear to deny the possibility of further improvements in the quality of work after qualification. Competence should be viewed as an appropriate cut-off point on a learning continuum, not as a state of mastery. This alone does justice to the complexity of professional thought and action.

Chapter 8

Concepts of Competence and their Implications

Historical Antecedents

Carr-Saunders and Wilson (1933) argue that the revival of professional training in the nineteenth century began with the formation of study societies
where people doing the same kind of work facing the same problems began
to get together for social discourse and the mutual exchange of ideas. One
pressing concern was the public status accorded to their occupation, which
they perceived as continuously undermined by those who used the same title
(architect, engineer etc.) without the requisite capability. Thus members of
these study associations saw themselves as skilled practitioners whose future
status and livelihood was threatened by the public's failure to distinguish
those who were 'competent' from those who were not. This led to the introduction of qualifying examinations to give some degree of assurance to the
public about the competence of members of the associations. However, the
transition was usually quite lengthy because, while it was acceptable to subject
new members to such hurdles, it was less acceptable for existing members, a
problem which recurs on a minor scale wherever qualifications are upgraded.
Similar considerations led to the development of codes of conduct to give
assurance of honest as well as competent service.

Although they devoted a special section of their pioneering book on the
professions to 'Professional Training and the Testing of Professional Competence', Carr-Saunders and Wilson made no attempt to define the term 'competence'. While their rationale of public assurance suggests a performance-based
distinction between qualified and unqualified practitioners, the use of qualifying examinations suggests a distinction based on examinable knowledge.
However, what seems to us like inconsistency may not have appeared so to
Carr-Saunders and Wilson, for whom the terms 'competent' and 'properly
qualified' may have had almost identical meanings. Their attention was focused on the transition from a concept of 'professional' based only on social
status to one based also on being properly qualified. Thus they described the
position in law and medicine in the eighteenth century as follows:

> . . . the Royal College of Physicians and the Inns of Court had ceased
> to interest themselves in training, and the tests imposed upon entrants

were of no value; in the case of the former they were little more than tests of social accomplishments. The surgeons and apothecaries, however, so far from allowing their system of training and testing to decay, were devoting themselves to its improvement. Since these professions were not 'fit for gentlemen', social accomplishments played no part and technical competence was demanded. (Carr-Saunders and Wilson, 1933, p. 309)

adding in a footnote that:

When attorneys and solicitors began to associate about 1739 it is perhaps significant that they called their society the Society of *Gentlemen* Practisers in the Courts of Law and Equity. (*ibid.*, p. 302)

Their view of competence can be deduced from their description of the chief distinguishing feature of the professions in one place as 'special competence, acquired as a result of intellectual training' and in another as 'specialized intellectual techniques, acquired as the result of prolonged training'. Their frequent reference to examinations as tests of competence suggests a view of professional competence as a specialized intellectual capability rather than a practical skill. One might surmise therefore that the 'gentlemen' of 1933 were prepared to accept intellectual capability as a criterion for professional status but still regarded practical skills as belonging to the realm of 'trade', possibly necessary but certainly not distinctive nor worthy of conversation. Hence the apparent gap between being 'properly qualified' and being 'able to perform' went unrecognized.

The Scope of Competence

Another, closely related, distinction concerns the scope of a competence claim. Sometimes this is very general and means just a little more than being properly qualified, especially in professions where the unqualified are not permitted to practice. For example, when employers claim to have competent staff, they imply that they would not be employing people who were not generally competent as well as properly qualified. When clients or service users describe a professional as competent, they usually mean that they have had some satisfactory service from that person, and that they have heard nothing detrimental on the grapevine. So the everyday use of the term 'competent' carries some performance-referencing, although it may be neither extensive nor specific. It tends to be treated as a characteristic of the person rather than a statement about the range of their competence.

Specific competence claims, however are usually intended to convey information about what a competent person can do without implying that he or she is competent beyond the area specifically mentioned. For example, if someone described a solicitor as competent in handling divorce cases, the listener would assume that he or she regularly undertook this kind of work and probably that the speaker knew some satisfied clients. They would make no assumption about the solicitor's competence in handling other legal issues apart from the general presumption that a qualified solicitor would at least know something about most commonly encountered aspects of the law and would refer to another if it was outside their area of expertise. In this particular case, the listener might also deduce that the solicitor was someone to whom they could talk fairly easily, i.e., that they also had some generic competence (see below).

In professions (or specialisms within professions) where work is relatively homogeneous, there will be little confusion between statements of general and specific competence because the one can be reliably inferred from the other. But in professions or specialisms where the work is relatively heterogeneous and one professional may handle a completely different set of situations from that of another, general statements become rather dangerous. The client or prospective employer will need a profile of specific competences which clearly demonstrates those aspects of the job in which each professional is competent. However, this nice tidy picture ignores the fact that in many occupations the nature of professional work is changing quite rapidly, not only as a result of technical change but also as a result of social change and institutional change. Constant redefinitions of the role of the public sector in Britain and several other countries have probably had an even greater influence than technical change, though some of it has certainly been facilitated by the advent of information technology.

Returning once more to a historical perspective, we can see quite clearly that the scope of a professional's claim to competence has always been a contested issue. Indeed the impetus behind the formation of professional associations usually derived from the perceived need of a relevant group to occupy and defend for its exclusive use a particular area of competence territory. Politically, their interest lay in claiming that all their members and only their members were competent within that territory. Moreover, they had to choose a territory that enabled them to have a membership of sufficient size and significance to be both viable and powerful. Only then could they assert sufficient control over entry to the profession and establish a distinctive market position by preventing others from encroaching. Overambition could lead to lack of credibility or incessant border disputes. However, for the reasons stated above, the nature of their territory was changing over time and constantly in need of redevelopment, while new unoccupied territories also began to emerge in their vicinity. Both redevelopment and expansion continually presented professional groups with new problems and opportunities. In each case they needed to develop new expertise, to find sufficient members who were redevelopment or exploration-minded, and to use their power and influence to keep or establish ownership.

Professional associations in fields such as medicine, psychology and chemistry cope with their more diversified membership by creating specialist sections; but this does not solve all the problems. For example, newer sections will naturally want the basic entry qualification to reflect their existence, while longer established groups oppose and even resent making changes which introduce material into the basic qualification of which they themselves have limited knowledge; because such changes threaten their own claims to competence. Historically, failure to adapt has often led to schisms. Today, the costs of running associations and lobbying for, or coping with, change are tending to lead towards mergers or cooperating groups of professions.

Looked at from the outside, one can observe situations where new areas of work can be picked up by more than one professional group, the result being determined not only by the relevance of their current expertise but also by their political influence and the entrepreneurial talent of their members. The move into management accounting by the former Institute of Cost and Works Accountants, which has now become the Chartered Institute of Management Accountants, is a prime example (Armstrong, 1993). Another consequence is that new areas of competence get defined in ways which best suit the existing expertise of the colonizing profession. This is not necessarily a deliberate strategy, as people naturally define problems in ways determined by their background knowledge and experience. In some occupational sectors, such as construction, international comparisons reveal quite different allocations of work among professions due to the different traditions and evolutionary patterns of professional groups. Not only does this affect the identities of the professions concerned, but also the way in which problems get defined. The conclusion to be drawn from this historical sortie is that, whether overtly acknowledged or not, questions about the competence profiles of professions and their members are political as well as technical.

Competence as a Stage in the Professional Development of Expertise

At this point it is useful to introduce yet another meaning of the word 'competent', expressed in *The Oxford English Dictionary* as '. . . sufficient in amount, quality, or degree'. According to circumstances this can have the positive meaning of 'getting the job done' or the negative meaning of 'adequate but less than excellent'. Thus one might be pleased to have any 'competent' lawyer for a relatively routine task, but be more discriminating for a particularly difficult and important brief.

An ambitious company would not employ an architect to design its new headquarters building who was described only as 'competent', and a rich woman might look for rather more than competence in her tax adviser. Where there is a need for extra quality or expertise the description 'competent' is tantamount to damning with faint praise; but for routine tasks competence might be preferred to excellence if it resulted in quicker and cheaper service.

This difference in connotation stems from whether the judgment is being made on a binary scale, where a person is judged to be either competent or not competent, or on a graduated scale where 'competent' is a position on a continuum from 'novice' to 'expert'. Occasionally, somebody has in mind a graduated scale of task difficulty, e.g., playing a piano accompaniment, and asks 'what is her level of competence?' However, this can be interpreted not as an attempt to create different grades of competence but rather as meaning 'at what levels of task does she remain or cease to be competent?'. The 'Peter principle' stated that people were generally competent but then got promoted until they reached the level at which they became incompetent.

Pearson (1984) expressed this meaning of competence very clearly when he stated that:

> If we can think of a continuum ranging from just knowing how to do something at the one end to knowing how to do something very well at the other, knowing how to do something competently would fall somewhere along this continuum. (Pearson, 1984, p. 32)

The preceding discussion has highlighted the fact that a professional person's competence has at least two dimensions, scope and quality. The scope dimension concerns what a person is competent in, the range of roles, tasks and situations for which their competence is established or may be reliably inferred. The quality dimension concerns judgments about the quality of that work on a continuum from being a novice, who is not yet competent in that particular task, to being an expert acknowledged by colleagues as having progressed well beyond the level of competence. For many tasks, neither broad scope nor special expertise is expected; and if such tasks are in frequent demand or particularly important, they will form part of the agreed core of the appropriate professional qualification. For some tasks and roles, however, quality is of considerable significance, and there will be limited interest in a professional profile which gives no indication of quality in these areas. Progression in quality then becomes a major issue in defining qualifications. Returning to the brief analysis of the learning professional in Chapter 1 we may suggest that throughout a professional career, professionals will be changing the scope of their competence, through becoming more specialist, through moving into newly developing areas of professional work, or through taking on management or educational roles; and they will also be continuously developing the quality of their work in a number of areas, beyond the level of competence to one of proficiency or expertise. Thus the problem facing professional associations can be viewed in terms of how to map a system of professional qualifications onto a group of learning professionals who are continually expanding the scope of their competence and developing the quality of their work.

The current expectation of professional qualifications is based on a general judgment of competence which divides learning professionals into two groups, those who are properly qualified and those who are not. But for those who want more specific information about a person's competence this division will seem somewhat arbitrary; as it is extremely unlikely that any student will have progressed to the same level of competence right across the range of roles and tasks included in the qualification. Moreover it can be difficult to base a qualification even on agreed standards of minimum competence because, whatever the scope for planning teaching in educational settings, there will always be constraints on learning opportunities in work settings. In particular, organizations will be reluctant to entrust certain tasks to students or even to newly qualified professionals. Although students may have knowledge and skills relevant to these tasks at the point of qualification, they may not have had sufficient experience to be even minimally competent, especially if minimal competence is defined in terms of requiring only minimal supervision.

Learning opportunities for work-based learning are crucially dependent on the way in which work is organized and allocated; and that in turn is dependent on prevailing assumptions about the competence of the people involved. Such people could include students at various stages of training, newly qualified professionals and members of other occupational groups; and expectations of their competence will be greatly influenced by tradition. This makes it difficult to introduce significant changes in qualifications which depend on new learning opportunities at work being made available. But it also confers important benefits when it encourages trainees, examiners and employers to develop shared assumptions about what to expect from a newly qualified professional. In practice, what is accepted as competent in one area may be less than what is expected in another, so that 'competent' can come to mean anything from ready-to-start work-based learning to being highly reliable and proficient. Moreover, in some occupations, e.g., schoolteaching, qualified workers may be expected to perform their core role with virtually no supervision, while in others e.g., architecture, they are expected to work in teams comprising several senior professionals and are only delegated routine tasks. They may contribute to more problematic tasks but will not be given responsibility for them until they have considerably more experience.

Concepts of Competence in Post-war Research and Development

So far we have uncovered a range of everyday meanings for the term competence and discussed their application to, and implications for, the professions. Research since World War II has not created new meanings but given operational significance to those in everyday use; and in some cases the more systematic application of certain concepts of competence has revealed issues that might otherwise have been neglected. Norris (1991) distinguishes three main research traditions during that period: a behaviourist tradition focused around the slogan of competency-based training, whose influence in the professions has hitherto been mainly confined to North America; a generic competence tradition based mainly in management education, which has also been quite widely used in Britain; and a cognitive competence tradition, most clearly articulated in linguistics but also present in research into higher education. The further development of research into competence under the aegis of the UK Employment Department and similar work in Australia will be discussed in the following chapters.

In reviewing these research traditions, certain common questions need to be asked. First, as Short (1984) has argued, competence is not a descriptive concept but a normative concept. Before a person can be judged as a competent teacher or manager, there needs to be agreement on a particular view of what it is to be a teacher or a manager, what will be the scope of any statement of competence, what criteria will be used and what will be regarded as sufficient evidence. In examining research into competence, we need to ask not only how competence is defined in general, but how it is defined in particular situations, i.e., how these normative agreements are constructed.

Competency-based Training and Education

The post-war behaviourist tradition has focused more on training than on qualifications with a number of practical consequences. While popular training programmes have been widely disseminated, there has been more emphasis on common processes for developing training programmes in local contexts than on common products. This suits both the North American tradition of controlling (or not controlling) qualifications at state level and the behaviourist goal of tightly coupling training to specifications of need so detailed as to limit the possibility of generic programmes. The earliest American examples of competency-based training (CBT) relied on task analysis based on structured observation to derive their specifications of competency and were often oblivious to the normative judgments made during this process. By neglecting the social and political dimensions of the construction of competence and treating the process as a purely technical matter, they made themselves highly vulnerable to criticism and developed products which revealed all too clearly the narrow perspectives of their designers. It should be noted, however, that behaviourist approaches have no monopoly of 'poor' designs, the transparency of their system of specification just makes them easier to criticize.

Some of the strengths and weaknesses of the behaviourist tradition can be better appreciated in more recent adaptions. So I have chosen for closer scrutiny a very readable and easily accessible account by two Australians. McMahon and Carter's impudent title *The Great Training Robbery* (1990) reflects the opinion, commonly expressed by behaviourists, that all other forms of training have been poorly designed and ineffective; but unlike many accounts it gives considerable attention to the normative aspects of defining competencies, drawing heavily on previous work in Canada (DACUM, 1983). They advocate a two-stage process for deriving specific competencies, 'job analysis' followed by 'skills analysis':

> A job analysis is an investigation into the current job (what is?) and the future job (what ought to be?). A job analysis breaks the job down into a series of activities and analyses the relationship between each of the activities in the job. These activities are in turn broken down to duties and tasks (and sub-tasks where appropriate). Because of the changing nature of work it is imperative a job analysis should look at existing duties — tasks — sub-tasks (descriptive) and future duties — tasks — sub-tasks (normative). A job analysis . . . can be used as base information for job design and the reorganisation of work patterns as well as being used in the Award Restructuring context. (McMahon and Carter, 1990, p. 40)
>
> A skills analysis . . . is a second level analysis which is concerned with identifying the key competencies required to perform the duties and tasks identified through the first level (job) analysis described earlier. A skills analysis is about describing what skills an employee needs to acquire to be competent in a particular job. (*ibid.*, p. 49)

The prime use of these competencies is to guide the design of training, but it is not the only use.

The normative aspect of the process is stressed throughout. First they stress the need to link competencies to:

- the goals and strategies of an enterprise;
- current jobs, future jobs and the job redesign implications of technology and process changes; and
- award restructuring (where appropriate) or the unions' agenda for training.

Second, they advocate a consultative process between all stakeholders, including likely trainers, and maximum use of group processes involving employees who actually do the jobs (not just their supervisors). Other techniques of analysis may also be used, e.g., general questionnaires, structured interviews and task analysis by observation, but these should feed into the employee groups, which will need properly trained and briefed facilitators. Both these features would appeal to professional organizations concerned about competences taking proper account of technical and social change and the central role of their members in determining the kind of expertise needed to do the job. However, in spite of the reference to award restructuring, the process is mainly organization-specific, thus avoiding the problem facing the professions of devising generic qualifications appropriate for a highly differentiated set of specific work contexts.

The profession given the greatest attention by behavioural approaches was school teaching. A strong North American movement in the 1970s pressed for competency-based teacher education (CBTE) and competency testing in schools as part of a new 'back to basics' movement. Considerable emphasis was placed on individualized 'mastery-learning' approaches to the delivery of teacher-education programmes, which required specific behavioural objectives. These in turn were to be derived from competencies specifying the role requirements of teachers. Thus Houston (1985) describes the process of designing a CBTE programme at the University of Houston in the following terms:

> 16 competency statements were hammered out by faculty. The prospective teacher (a) diagnoses the learner's emotional, social, physical, and intellectual needs; (b) identifies and/or specifies instructional goals and objectives based on learner needs; (c) designs instruction appropriate to goals and objectives; (d) implements instruction that is consistent with plan; and (e) designs and implements evaluation procedures which focus on learner achievement and instructional effectiveness. Other competences were related to cultural awareness, demonstration of a repertoire of instructional skills, classroom communication, adequate knowledge of subject matter, and analysis of one's own professional effectiveness . . .
>
> Each competency is stated briefly (as in the first five, listed above), then described more fully as a paragraph, then expanded as instructional objectives which are in turn rearranged and integrated. The statement of 16 competencies is a logical process of program requirements; the hundreds of instructional objectives are grouped psychologically for developmental and instructional purposes. (Houston, 1985, p. 903)

The methods used to guide the selection of competencies and formulation of more detailed objectives were:

- task analysis (twenty teachers maintained logs for six weeks);
- perceptions of College of Education faculty, school pupils, and teachers; and
- the conceptual model based on work at Michigan State University and the various models of teaching delineated by Joyce and Weil as the basis for using appropriate teaching strategies.

Houston describes professional perception as the most common approach and hints at complex techniques for combining and reconciling multiple views on the behaviours believed to characterize effective teachers. Conceptual models also played an important role in the design of CBTE programmes, especially in providing some coherence to long lists of separate requirements. Other approaches include task analysis, reference to research literature on effective practice, needs of pupils, needs of society and the local community, and simple reformulation of existing programmes in new terminology. Typically, CBTE programmes were justified in terms of the face validity of their competence statements (normative judgment) and the instructional effectiveness of mastery learning (ostensibly an empirical argument but one which had little research evidence to confirm it). Programmes were not uniform across the country and often benefited from the good will generated by their initial consultations with local stakeholders.

Two main criticisms of CBTE are of special relevance to our discussion: its representation of the teaching process, and the practicality and validity of its assessment. Houston summarizes the representation problem as follows:

> The specification of competencies was criticised because such lists atomised the teaching process. Teachers do not teach using independent competencies, but in context and using in an integrated fashion a number of skills and knowledges. The value of dissecting general competence into a number of specific and autonomous objectives was questioned. Further, limiting objectives to those leading to observable action or results appeared to stifle the development of professionals whose personal characteristics might lead to a wide range of successful teaching practices. (*ibid.*, p. 902)

and quotes Elam's (1972) early but still relevant judgment that

> The overriding problem before which the others pale to insignificance is that of the adequacy of measurement instruments and procedures. (Elam, 1972, p. 21)

The main difficulties were the sheer number of objectives to be assessed, with consequent lack of proper attention to each; and the lack of any valid theoretical construct for combining or prioritizing assessment evidence.

Similar competency-based programmes were developed in other professions (law, medicine, nursing) during the 1970s (Grant *et al.*, 1979) but not to the same extent as in teacher education where the influence of state legislatures was much stronger.

Generic Approaches to Competence

Research into generic approaches to competence presents a complete contrast to the competency-based training described above. Whereas CBT is designed to ensure that all workers are sufficiently competent to do what is required of them, generic competences are concerned with what enables them to do it; and this includes what are sometimes called 'personal qualities'. The main thrust of research into generic competences has been to distinguish between average and excellent workers, primarily for selection and appraisal purposes. Most research in this area has been conducted in the area of management, where there has always been great concern about selecting and preparing the right people for the top jobs. There has been some research into personal qualities needed in various professions, but this has had far less impact and has avoided using the word 'competence' in its theoretical underpinning.

The pioneering research into management competences was undertaken by the American psychologist, David McClelland, and his associated company, McBer. They developed lists of eight to fifteen competences, which were claimed to differentiate average and superior managers; and their research was based on refining these lists for various groups of managers, together with the research techniques for measuring these competences and validating their competency model. The most frequently cited of these lists is probably that of Boyatzis (1982) who analysed an aggregate sample of over 2000 managers in forty-one different jobs in twelve organizations. Of twenty-one characteristics initially hypothesized on the basis of consultative meeting and previous research, he found that twelve differentiated superior from average managers:

- Concern with impact
- Diagnostic use of concepts
- Efficiency orientation
- Proactivity
- Conceptualization
- Self-confidence
- Use of oral presentations
- Managing group processes
- Use of socialized power
- Perceptual objectivity
- Self-control*
- Stamina and adaptability*

All but the last two (asterisked) were perceived as skills rather than traits. Other researchers notably Schroder (1989) have developed similar lists, as have several individual companies.

As with other approaches, it is important to emphasize how the lists of management competences were constructed. The following summary of the McBer approach is derived from the accounts of Boyatzis (1982) and Spencer (1983).

Stage 1
Identifying two criterion samples whose performance is agreed to be (a) superior or (b) average by both supervisor and peer ratings.
Stage 2
A normative approach to characterizing good performers. Quite independently of Stage 1, panels of job incumbents are asked first to brainstorm a list of characteristics which they think might distinguish superior performers, then to refine the combined list from all panels by rating each item for criticality and for discriminating power.

Stage 3

A behavioural approach to characterizing good performers. Members of the two criterion samples were given individual 'Behavioural Event Interviews' in which they were asked to describe six critical incidents, three when they felt effective in the job and three when they felt ineffective. The interview evidence is then subjected to a compare and contrast thematic analysis to identify characteristics which differentiate managers in the two groups.

Stage 4

The lists of hypothesized characteristics from Stages 2 and 3 are combined and a coding system developed and refined to enable judges to reliably rate interview transcripts according to these criteria. Blind ratings of the two samples are then used to determine which of those characteristics have discriminating power.

Stage 5

The list of characteristics which discriminate, organized into meaningful clusters, is described as a 'competency model' and cross-validated on a second sample.

The methodology is designed to produce a set of generic competences valid across different kinds of management job, so competences specific to a particular product or service are eliminated. Much of the work has been done in individual organizations — their uniqueness is stressed — but this has built on previously conducted research and resulted in relatively minor variations. Dulewicz (1989) estimates that the proportion is usually about 70 per cent generic and 30 per cent organization-specific. It should be noted, however, that organization-specific research of this kind is likely to have a very considerable impact on the organization concerned: developing an agreed competency model across an organization is likely to improve coherence and in-house management development whatever model is finally adopted.

Another important by-product of the generic competency approach has been the growth of management-assessment centres. These are independent organizations which use a range of off-the-job techniques such as tests and simulations to assess the competence of managers and predict their future potential. They are widely used but by no means universally accepted.

Critics of the McBer methodology have noted a certain circularity in the validation process with similar kinds of judgment being made at each stage. But this is inevitable whenever normative judgments are involved; and the evidence from behavioural-event interviews is very different from that in performance ratings. The whole process is necessarily subject to subtle nuances of language (Hirsh and Bevan, 1991) and suffers from conflating varied interpretations of certain key words; so it would be useful to have a sociological as well as psychological account of how generic competences have been constructed. The strength of the approach may lie at least as much in the face validity of its competency models as in their technical research-based underpinning. Boyatzis, for example, found that use of the model only improved the rating of managers as poor, average or good from 33 per cent (the random success rate) to 51 per cent.

Another frequent criticism is that the approach assumes a single type of 'good' manager. Schroder, for example, has found that managers usually have only three high-performance competences as strengths, confirming the view that it is more appropriate to think in terms of omni-competent teams rather than individuals. Others argue that only some of the generic competences will be valued in any particular organizational culture, and warn against using the competences of today to select the managers of tomorrow.

One very practical issue, still unresolved by research, is whether these generic competences are learnt, inherited or both (Furnham, 1990). Are good managers born, developed or trained? Spencer (1983) argues that an effective approach has been developed by McBer for teaching most of the competences on these generic lists. The method originally developed by McClelland for teaching achievement motivation involves:

- teaching people the behavioural coding system developed for the competency in Stage 4 above;
- practice in using the system to assess their own and others' behaviour;
- skill practice off-the-job through case studies or in simulated job settings; and
- further practice with feedback on-the-job itself.

This training approach is surprisingly similar to that used in some of the more sophisticated competency-based training. Whatever its merits it involves a significant investment in time and resources for each individual competency, and one might not expect to find it outside large, ambitious, forward-looking organizations. For others, the focus of generic competences is more likely to be on selection and performance appraisal rather than training.

An interesting offshoot of this work on management competences has been its adaptation by the US Council for Adult and Experiential Learning (CAEL) in association with McBer and Co to the problem of selecting mature students for entry to higher education in ways which take account of their potential to succeed in college rather than performance on conventional precollege academic programmes. Using similar methods, they derived a set of eleven 'capabilities' (note the change in terminology) and a coding system for assessing these capabilities through behavioural event interviews. Otter's (1989) study indicated that it would need considerable adaptation for the British context, but the list of capabilities is nevertheless worth examining.

- Initiative
- Persistence *
- Creativity
- Planning Skill

- Leadership *
- Influence skills *
- Self-confidence *
- Interpersonal diagnosis

- Critical thinking
- Restraint *

- Responsiveness

The asterisked entries resemble very closely comparable entries in the Boyatzis list for senior managers; and most of them also appear in lists of qualities described as 'personal effectiveness'. Once more the terminology carries high-face validity, but the reappearance of the same terms in such radically different contexts suggests that their operational definitions as opposed to semantic labels may also vary considerably. Using the same word does not mean making the same judgment; so the question of how generic are these so-called generic competences requires thorough investigation. The evidence is far from conclusive.

Somewhat similar models of competence have been developed for medicine, using a wide range of methods. These are described by Norman (1985) whose methodological review led to the following set of categories

1. **Clinical skills**
   The ability to acquire clinical information by talking with and examining patients, and interpreting the significance of the information obtained.
2. **Knowledge and understanding**
   The ability to remember relevant knowledge about clinical conditions in order to provide effective and efficient care for patients.
3. **Interpersonal attributes**
   The expression of those aspects of a physician's personal and professional character that are observable in interactions with patients.
4. **Problem-solving and clinical judgment**
   The application of relevant knowledge, clinical skills, and interpersonal attributes to the diagnosis, investigation and management of the clinical problems of a given patient.
5. **Technical skills**
   The ability to use special procedures and techniques in the investigation and management of patients.

These were based primarily on observation and conceptual analysis of encounters between physicians and patients.

Other researchers, who were test and measurement specialists, used psychometric analysis to establish critical factors in the competence of physicians. Thus a recent review by Maatsch (1990) was able to present a model of general clinical competence in emergency medicine which he claimed to be the best predictor of job performance. This comprised three overlapping, highly correlated constructs (see Figure 8.1): medical knowledge, clinical problem-solving and a general competence factor.

However he also admits that predictions of the average quality of care provided to a large sample of patients are moderate at best. As the medical

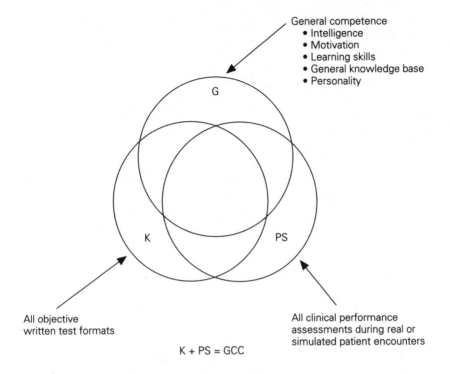

General competence
- Intelligence
- Motivation
- Learning skills
- General knowledge base
- Personality

G

K

PS

All objective
written test formats

All clinical performance
assessments during real or
simulated patient encounters

K + PS = GCC

Figure 8.1:   General Clinical Competence (Cognitive Domain)

career progresses, the knowledge and clinical problem-solving factors become
even more highly correlated, reflecting increased integration of all kinds of
knowledge.

Cognitive Constructs of Competence

Research into both CBT and generic competences sought to validate competence in terms of performance, CBT at a highly specific level and generic
competences at a more abstract level. However, research in cognitive psychology has frequently sought to distinguish competence from performance. Noam
Chomsky's theory of linguistics (1968) argued that, because humans are constantly generating new sentences and distinctive new utterances, they possess
'linguistic competence' in the form of deep structural patterning rather than an
amalgam of behaviourally acquired speech acts. Hence the ability of humans
to express and understand new thoughts within the framework of an old
language. Linguistic performance, however, requires more than linguistic
competence; because there is a range of culturally specific conventions about
the 'correctness' or 'incorrectness' of statements which still accords with the
basic rules of language. The type of performance required in school language

examinations requires more than linguistic competence, and poor performance in such examinations does not indicate lack of basic linguistic competence.

Similar distinctions were made in the psychology of child development by Flavell and Wohlwill (1969) and in cross-cultural psychology by Scribner and Cole (1981), leading to attempts by researchers to find performance settings which reveal more of a person's underlying linguistic and cognitive competence than those traditionally used by either educators or psychologists. Messick (1984) summarized this view of competence as follows:

> Competence refers to what a person knows and can do under ideal circumstances, whereas performance refers to what is actually done under existing circumstances. Competence embraces the structure of knowledge and abilities, whereas performance subsumes as well the processes of accessing and utilising those structures and a host of affective, motivational, attentional and stylistic factors that influence the ultimate responses. Thus, a student's competence might not be validly revealed in either classroom performance or test performance because of personal or circumstantial factors that affect behaviour. (Messick, 1984)

Messick, like Chomsky, is making two important points about competence. The first is about the competence-performance gap and its implications for assessment methodology. The second is that 'competence embraces the structure of knowledge and abilities', which almost amounts to a definition.

This led Wood and Powers (1987) to describe a developmental model of competence in the following terms:

> Education entails not just the accretion of knowledge, but the constant structuring and restructuring of knowledge and cognitive skills. Successful adaptation to the circumstances encountered as one develops is more often accomplished through the co-ordination of abilities and appropriate knowledge, affect and behaviour patterns than through the capacity to utilise a single ability or reproduce a piece of information on demand. 'Competence', then, must be distinguished from the 'competencies' assessed in contemporary testing programmes. It rests on an integrated deep structure ('understanding') and on the *general* ability to co-ordinate appropriate internal cognitive, affective and other resources necessary for successful adaptation. A successful conceptualisation of competence would show how specific competencies are integrated at a higher level and would also accommodate changing patterns of salience among these skills and abilities at different ages and in different contexts. (Wood and Powers, 1987, p. 414)

Evidence in support of such a model comes mainly from research into learning in educational contexts. For example, higher-education research has found that students tend to adopt either surface-level or deep-level approaches to learning and that only the latter result in developing greater competence in the subject in the sense of an integrated conceptual framework and confidence in explaining and applying their knowledge (Marton and Säljö, 1984; Entwistle and Entwistle, 1991).

Competence and Competency

Finally, we should note a useful distinction in the American literature between the term 'competence', which is given a generic or holistic meaning and refers to a person's overall capacity, and the term 'competency', which refers to specific capabilities. However, even the word 'competency' can be used either in a direct performance-related sense: a competency . . . is an element of vocational competence . . . a performance capability needed by workers in a specified occupational area (Hermann and Kenyon, 1987, p. 1) or simply to describe any piece of knowledge or skill that might be construed as relevant. Short (1984) describes this as deriving from a conception of competence as 'the command of pertinent knowledge and/or skills,' the word 'command' being used to imply that the competent person not only possesses the requisite competencies but is also able to use them.

Australian work on competency standards for the professions (Gonzi *et al.*, 1993) has adopted a similar approach with somewhat greater clarity of definition. They first use the word 'competence' in a holistic sense, noting that:

> Performance is what is directly observable, whereas competence is not directly observable, rather it is inferred from performance. (Gonzi *et al.*, 1993, p. 6)

then continue as follows:

> The competence of professionals derives from their possessing a set of relevant attributes such as knowledge, skills and attitudes. These attributes which jointly underlie competence are often referred to as competencies. So a competency is a combination of attributes underlying some aspect of successful professional performance . . . [But] attributes of individuals do not in themselves constitute competence. Nor is competence the mere performance of a series of tasks. Rather, the notion of competence integrates attributes with performance. (*ibid.*, pp. 5–6)

What they describe as 'attributes' corresponds to what I have chosen to call 'capability', a concept which is more fully discussed in Chapter 10.

Elkin (1990) adds yet another perspective to this issue when he defines

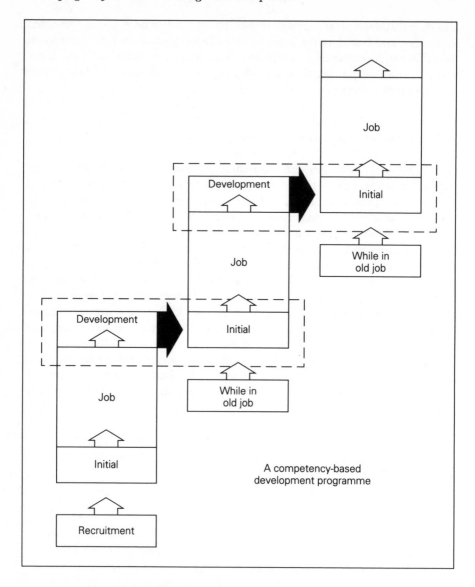

Figure 8.2: Elkin's Model of Competency Development

competencies of the kind used in competency-based training systems as 'micro-competencies' and competencies of the more generic kind used by McBer as 'macro-competencies'. For managers, he then suggests that

> the further up the occupational hierarchy in an organization the more important the underlying macro-competencies and the less important the micro-competencies. (Elkin, 1990, p. 23)

Similar trends may be found in those professions where senior professionals become either practice managers or project managers. For example, the competencies required by a senior architect or engineer will include both capability in project management and an ability to envision and sustain strategic oversight of a whole project while more junior professionals work only on the individual components.

Elkin also suggests that people develop many of their job competencies in post, that is after they have been appointed. These competencies allow long-term career employment in the job. But once this core competence has been achieved, individuals may aspire to further growth by gaining a set of developmental competencies. While not irrelevant to the current job, these developmental competencies may be an important, if not essential, factor in gaining promotion to a more senior post. Thus the Elkin model (Figure 8.2) incorporates two features which are normally omitted from simpler models of competence: a recognition that competence continues to develop on the job; and a model of career progression. We shall return to these features of competence at the end of Chapter 10.

Chapter 9

Competence in the NVQ/SVQ System

The Development of a National Framework

During the early 1980s government thinking in the UK moved gradually towards a competence-based model of education and training, though the final shape of this new policy did not become clear until late in the decade. The critical decisions were taken in 1986 when following a national Review of Vocational Qualifications and the White Paper 'Working Together — Education and Training' the government set up a National Council for Vocational Qualifications (NCVQ) with the following remit.

1. to secure standards of occupational competence and ensure that vocational qualifications are based on them;
2. to design and implement a new national framework for vocational qualifications;
3. to approve bodies making accredited awards;
4. to obtain comprehensive coverage of all occupational sectors;
5. to secure arrangements for quality assurance;
6. to set up effective liaison with bodies awarding vocational qualifications;
7. to establish a national data-base for vocational qualification;
8. to undertake, or arrange to be undertaken, research and development to discharge these functions;
9. to promote vocational education, training and qualifications. (NCVQ, 1986)

Close cooperation with the Employment Department and the Scottish Vocational Education Council (SCOTVEC) ensured compatibility between Scotland and the rest of the UK.

The new NCVQ was required to rationalize the existing system of vocational qualifications, and to ensure that the new National Vocational Qualifications (NVQs) were based on 'standards of occupational competence'. This involved both the political task of developing a qualifications framework and deciding who would be responsible for particular qualifications and the technical task of determining what kind of standards should be used to define occupational competence in practical terms and how such competence might be assessed. These tasks were pursued in tandem, but with greater mutual influence than is usually recognized. Underpinning both was the assumption, most clearly articulated in the 1988 White Paper 'Employment for the 1990s' that the process should be employer-led:

> Our training system must be founded on standards and recognised qualifications based on competence — the performance required of individuals to do their work successfully and satisfactorily.
> These standards must be identified by employers and they must be nationally recognised. Thus we need a system of employer-led organizations to identify and establish standards and secure recognition of them, sector by sector, or occupational group by occupational group.

These organizations were called 'lead bodies' and their role was perceived by the Employment Department as

- overseeing the technical process of defining and elucidating competence-based standards;
- incorporating into this process (a) consultation with a representative sample of users (employers) and (b) pilot assessment using these standards; and
- marketing the standards as a focus for education and training and seeking their incorporation into NVQs. (Debling, 1989)

In practice some lead bodies are highly focused, e.g., forestry and hairdressing, while some cover an extremely wide range, e.g., business administration and health and social care. The former have been based on existing organizations, while the latter have involved the creation of complex consortia.

In February 1989, NCVQ was invited by the government to extend the framework to include qualifications at the 'professional' level, though on a voluntary basis. So Debling's careful description of the role of lead bodies in professional areas merits careful reading.

> As far as professional bodies are concerned, nobody has questioned the right of such bodies to define standards of competence for their members, for the 'professionals' that constitute their membership. Further, where such bodies, by law or practice, in effect provide a licence to practice, there is no question as to their continued responsibility. Also, where the membership is primarily self-employed it would seem that the professional body in essence forms the lead body (assuming that it does in fact ensure that its membership can provide the service expected of it by the customer). However, for some professional bodies, members are employed in diverse situations, perhaps in different sectors of industry, commerce and public service. Under

such conditions it would seem that the prime responsibility continues to lie with the employer-recognised organizations. (Debling, 1989, p. 82)

The role of experienced educators and trainers was deliberately shrunk. Lead bodies were invited to 'draw on the expertise lodged with individuals and groups in education and training, especially where such groups or individuals are held in high esteem because of the quality of what has gone before'; and many of them have 'included individuals from the further and higher education scene on committees and working parties'. Thus instead of joint committees of employers and professional educators planning qualifications for examination bodies such as the Business and Technician Education Council (BTEC) educators were limited to occasional involvement and examination bodies to preparing qualifications to meet already specified standards, if so requested by the relevant lead bodies.

The qualification framework itself is also employment defined, with the five levels being determined principally by the complexity of work activities and the level of responsibility (see NCVQ, 1991, p. 4). Wisely, the definitions of levels are not prescriptive.

Level 1
Competence in the performance of a range of varied work activities, most of which may be routine and predictable.
Level 2
Competence in a significant range of varied work activities, performed in a variety of contexts. Some of the activities are complex or non-routine, and there is some individual responsibility or autonomy. Collaboration with others, perhaps through membership of a work group or team, may often be a requirement.
Level 3
Competence in a broad range of varied work activities performed in a wide variety of contexts and most of which are complex and non-routine. There is considerable responsibility and autonomy, and control or guidance of others is often required.
Level 4
Competence in a broad range of complex, technical or professional work activities performed in a wide variety of contexts and with a substantial degree of personal responsibility and autonomy. Responsibility for the work of others and the allocation of resources is often present.
Level 5
Competence which involves the application of a significant range of fundamental principles and complex techniques across a wide and often unpredictable variety of contexts. Very substantial personal autonomy and often significant responsibility for the work of others and for the allocation of substantial resources feature strongly, as do personal

accountabilities for analysis and diagnosis, design, planning, execution and evaluation.

The proponents of this system will argue that it frees qualifications from being defined by the length of a training course. But it also risks a certain lack of comparability across occupational sectors; because the amount of training needed to reach Level 3 in one occupation could easily be twice as much as that needed in another. From a learning-needs perspective this presents no problem, but it conflicts with other societal norms. Not only do people generally expect qualifications at the same level to be equivalent, but their status partly depends upon it. Shorter training times could lead to reductions in salary, lower prestige and less competitive recruitment into the occupation. Moreover, government moves to pay for training according to qualifications output rather than teaching input will lead either to inequity or to nightmarishly complex funding arrangements unless there are simple equivalencies between qualifications.

Another consequence of this approach to defining the framework of qualifications is that the creation of a lead body has an enormous influence on the scope of its qualifications. It is usual for a lead body to begin its work by mapping its domain to discover the range of employing organizations and individual workers for which it has responsibility; and then to decide what qualifications it will seek to offer. But there are limits to how far it can accommodate the diversity of interests by developing separate qualifications for every subgroup. The lead body has to sustain a representation of the occupation that remains credible to employers, prospective entrants and the general public, and also has to operate within financial constraints. At a political level, greater size increases its external influence but decreases its chance of maintaining internal coherence. Thus the diversity of lead bodies has led to some qualifications serving tightly defined groups of people who work in similar kinds of organizations while others serve a much wider range of jobs and organizations, for which any common definition of competence is likely to be extremely difficult. The former will tend to adopt very specific definitions of competence and the latter rather general definitions.

Just as the series of political decisions required to define a new qualification framework had many technical implications, not all of which were anticipated, so also the technical process developed for specifying standards has an almost hidden political dimension. Most of the critical decisions were presaged in a 1985 technical paper by Jessup which sought to develop the policy implications of the 1981 White Paper 'A New Training Initiative: an Agenda for Action'. Jessup, who later became research director of the new NCVQ, argued that standards should be free-standing and widely accessible. Hence they had to be defined in terms of the performance of an individual without reference to the route by which they had learned. Assessment had to be uncoupled from training, so that only outcomes were judged. This would prevent access to qualifications from being limited by access to training and allow those who learned in other ways, e.g., work-based learning and/or distance learning, to get their competence accredited. This would also be facilitated if relatively small units of activity could be accredited within a modular structure, but still in relation to the overall goal of certifying competence in an occupation. Hence standards should also be criterion-referenced against the requirements of jobs. Apart from conferring flexibility and motivating learners, the accreditation of smaller units was seen as encouraging tighter specification of standards. Such specification was seen as pre-empting possible later problems in assessment by clear descriptions of each activity or task and accompanying performance criteria. Moreover, assessment should move towards comprehensive coverage rather than sampling. This whole pattern of thinking is closely aligned to that of the 'competency-based training movement' described in the previous chapter.

However, the need to develop qualifications for a whole occupation was pulling in the opposite direction, towards generality rather than specificity. At the technical level, the whole process developed by the Employment Department for developing competency-based occupational standards can be seen as an attempt to find the best possible compromise between the specificity requirements of a performance-referenced concept of competence and the generality requirements of a national qualification for a whole occupation. Competence-based training in its present form was designed for a single organization not a whole occupation; while the vocational qualifications superseded by NVQs were designed for a whole occupation but not performance-referenced. One important decision which improved on the CBT tradition was to broaden the concept of competence beyond the level of being able to perform a series of tasks to encompass the full set of expectations of a competent worker. This was achieved through adopting the 'Job Competence Model', developed by Mansfield and Mathews (1985) for a research project on work-based learning. The model has four components:

1. The specific technical aspects or tasks involved in the work role — activities with clearly discernible, tangible outcomes.
2. Contingency management — dealing with things that go wrong or with the unexpected.
3. Task management — handling the overarching management of the various technical and task components of the job, for example by setting priorities or allocating time.
4. The role/job environment — including both the physical environment with its health and safety implications and the interpersonal/ interactive environment made up of colleagues, customers and clients or the public.

Previously, most vocational qualifications had concentrated on the first component alone, with the possible addition of some communication skills.

Thus, competence was formally defined in Guidance Note 8 (Employment Department, 1991) as

> the ability to perform the activities within an occupation or function to the standards expected in employment. Competence is a wide concept which embodies the ability to transfer skills and knowledge to new situations within the occupational area. It encompasses organisation and planning of work, innovation and coping with non-routine activities. It includes those qualities of personal effectiveness that are required in the workplace to deal with co-workers, managers and customers. (Employment Department, 1991, p. 1)

The Detailed Specification of Competence

Each NVQ is described as 'a statement of competence' and comprises a set of 'units of competence', each of which is separately accreditable, just as envisaged in Jessup's earlier paper. These units can be further subdivided into 'elements of competence', and it is these elements which provide the basis for the standards. Guidance Note 8 defines elements and units as follows.

> An element of competence describes what can be done; an action, behaviour or outcome which a person should be able to demonstrate. Each element of competence has associated performance criteria which define the expected level of performance . . . A unit of competence will be made up of a number of elements of competence (with associated performance criteria) which together make sense to, and are valued by, employers so that they warrant separate accreditation. Vocational qualifications will normally be made up a number of related units which together will comprise a statement of competence relevant to an occupation. (*ibid.*, p. 1)

Although these definitions are presented in a bottom-up sequence, the process adopted by NCVQ for developing standards, though iterative in practice, was essentially top–down. There were two reasons for this. First, a bottom–up process would have made it very difficult to reach any agreement on a general statement of competence for a whole occupation. Second, the need for units to be intelligible and useful in the employment context led to them being defined in terms of distinguishable job functions. They could not be defined simply as convenient aggregations of separate tasks. Thus the process for developing standards had to begin with getting agreement on what these functions were, before analysing them down to their constituent elements. This process, which had somehow to reconcile conflicting demands for generality of application and specificity of standards definition, came to be called 'functional analysis'.

Functional analysis has been carried out almost entirely by small consultancy firms of recent origin comprising people with experience of vocational education and training and familiar with the NVQ system. It is presented as a method or technique but probably falls somewhere between being a craft and an art in Buchler's typology (see Figure 4.1). Though not entirely sequential, it is useful to conceptualize functional analysis as a three-stage process.

1. Deciding on functional units of competence.
2. Deciding on the elements of competence.
3. Adding performance criteria and other details to turn the elements into standards acceptable to NCVQ.

The first stage involves deciding on the key roles undertaken by competent workers at a particular level and, if necessary, dividing some of those roles into distinct functions. There are often many ways of doing this, so a good functional analysis will explore a range of options and consult widely in order to select the most suitable for the purpose of specifying occupational standards of competence. The main criteria to be satisfied by any given set of functional units are:

- that the set as a whole comprehensively covers the occupational domain;
- that individual units, as far as possible, do not overlap;
- that each unit indicates a job function which a competent worker can perform, so that its accreditation has practical value; and
- that each unit makes sense across the whole occupational domain and has value that is general rather than specific to only part of that domain.

The result of this first stage is a functional map which can be negotiated with a range of employers and other stakeholders. Large-scale consultation, however, may wait until the second stage has also been completed. A functional map for middle managers at NVQ Level 4 (MCI, 1991) is presented in Table 9.1.

At this stage lead bodies with complex occupational domains have to decide on their overall qualifications structure. For example, the lead body for health and social care set up a subgroup to handle child care and education, which then identified four qualifications at Level 2 and three qualifications at Level 3. However, these qualifications shared eight units out of ten at Level 2 and eleven units out of fifteen at Level 3. So calling them separate qualifications rather than options within a single qualification for each level was possibly a semantic nicety.

The second stage of analysis involves deciding on the elements. The analytic process is fairly similar but the criteria are slightly different. Even though elements of competence are not separately accredited, they still need to have face validity for those working in the occupation; and the need for

Table 9.1:   Key Roles of Middle Managers and their Associated Units of Competence

Manage operations	1.	Initiate and implement change and improvement in services, products and systems.
	2.	Monitor, maintain and improve service and product delivery.
Manage finance	3.	Monitor and control the use of resources.
	4.	Secure effective resource allocation for activities and projects.
Manage people	5.	Recruit and select personnel.
	6.	Develop teams, individuals and self to enhance performance.
	7.	Plan, allocate and evaluate work carried out by teams, individuals and self.
	8.	Create, maintain and enhance effective working relationship.
Manage information	9.	Seek evaluate and organize information for action.
	10.	Exchange information to solve problems and make decisions.

comprehensive cover and avoidance of overlap still applies. But there is an important new criterion to be satisfied: the elements form the basis of the standards against which competence will be judged, so they must be capable of independent assessment. The extent to which any particular element meets this criterion will become more apparent during the third stage of analysis. Hence some iterative recycling between stages is likely to be necessary.

Figure 9.1 shows the breakdown into elements of five of the nine units developed for management accountants. Unusually this incorporates an additional dimension, the distinction between operational management accountancy, control for management and strategic financial management. This could have provided another approach to the designation of units, but was presumably rejected because the resultant units would have been extremely large.

The official requirements for elements of competence, as stated in the criteria for NVQs, are that they should:

1. relate to what actually happens in work and not, for example, activities or skills which are only demonstrated on training programmes;
2. represent safe and healthy work practices;
3. be capable of demonstration and assessment;
4. describe the result of what is done not the procedures which may be used;
5. not contain evaluative statements — these belong in performance criteria;
6. be expressed in language which makes sense to the people who will use them and which is *unambiguous*;
7. be expressed in terms which apply across different tasks, jobs, equipment or organisational systems. (NCVQ, 1991, p. 3)

Units of Competence

Management Accountancy Key Roles

The key purposes of the professional management accountant are:

To design, operate and manage financial and economic information and other systems to enhance value, effectiveness and efficiency and to enable managers to achieve controlled change within organizations, and thereby realize stakeholder objectives.

Operational Management Accounting	*Control for Management*	*Strategic Financial Management*	
		A7 Plan the provision and promote the use of management-accounting services and systems	A Provide management accounting services and systems
A1 Maintain management-accounting services and systems	A4 Define the service requirements of users and initiate change		
A2 Implement change in management-accounting services and systems	A5 Promote and enhance the provision of services		
A3 Conform to professional standards in the delivery of services	A6 Define and develop information and communications systems		
		B6 Direct and motivate management accounting staff	B Manage management accounting staff
B1 Create and maintain effective working relationships	B4 Recruit and select management-accounting staff		
B2 Plan, allocate and evaluate work carried out by management accounting staff	B5 Develop management-accounting staff		
B3 Develop oneself professionally			
		C3 Formulate, implement and review financial policies and procedures	C Assure the quality of services and systems
C1 Conduct an internal audit	C2 Conduct an operational audit		
		D5 Build and integrate strategic financial plans	D Plan and provide finance
D1 Plan, monitor and influence movements in working capital	D4 Plan and arrange the financing of programmes and projects		
D2 Manage short-term finance			
D3 Establish an organisation's taxation obligations			
		E3 Advise managers on the effect of external factors on strategy	E Utilize intelligence from external sources
E1 Analyse and interpret external intelligence	E2 Advise managers of the effect of external factors on programmes and projects		

Figure 9.1: Breakdown of Management Accountancy Units

The seventh requirement draws attention to the problem facing developers of standards which are both broad in the scope of their content and cover a wide range of work contexts. In such circumstances it is difficult to devise a set of elements which neither excludes aspects of work considered important in some contexts nor includes aspects considered unimportant in other contexts. The former limits the coverage of the qualification, the latter not only increases its size but also limits access by making it difficult for candidates who do not work in appropriate settings to get the right opportunities for learning and for assessment. Compromises have to be made. Similar problems can arise when deciding how far to anticipate or reflect changes in technology or the organization of work. Not only may current practice be changing but it is likely to be changing at different rates in different organizations. Assessment to prescribed standards requires these judgments to be made at the point of standards definition rather than during the process of training, when the time gap will be less and better information available about local expectations.

The fourth requirement demonstrates the close affinity between the NCVQ model at the detailed level of standards specification and the behaviourist approach to education and training which has always stressed objectives and outcomes (Jessup, 1991). But it has also misinterpreted it, because being competent at a procedure *is* an outcome of training. Moreover inspection of NCVQ standards shows that nearly all the element titles describe activities and many refer to purposes or methods. Outcomes are only included in titles when there are clearly defined products; but they frequently get referred to in the performance criteria.

As Figure 9.1 illustrates, it is possible to present the units and elements of most qualifications on a couple of pages, no longer than a traditional syllabus and possibly more informative. It is the third stage of the functional analysis process which introduces the length and complexity for which these new-style competence-based standards have come to be renowned. When the system was first introduced, standards comprised only elements and performance criteria. These latter are defined as 'evaluative statements which define the acceptable level of performance required in employment' and should:

1. identify only the essential aspects of performance necessary for competence;
2. be expressed so that assessments of candidates' performance can be made against them;
3. form an unambiguous basis for the design of assessment systems and materials. (NCVQ, 1991, p. 3)

In the context of the committees and consultations which inform standards development, 'acceptance level' is likely to be defined in terms of the performance of a reliable worker who has been doing the job for at least several months and possibly two or three years, not in terms of the newly qualified. This may seem a good way to raise standards, but it could result either in standards being shortchanged in practice or in a longer time being required to get qualified.

The use of the word 'unambiguous' in both requirement 6 for elements and requirement 3 for performance criteria also merits attention. It is aspirational in the sense that language can never be wholly unambiguous. But does it mean unambiguous in a specific context or unambiguous in the sense of complete transfer of meaning across contexts regardless of local circumstances? Originally the range of contexts for which competence claims were to be regarded as valid was left unspecified; but by 1991 when the first clear set of criteria for NCVQ accreditation were published, a range statement was included as a required comparison for each element. Jessup (1991) suggests some common dimensions of range as being companies or organizations, equipment, materials, work conditions and pressures, customers or clients, products or services while warning that these are not the only sources of variation. His example of an element of competence from estate agency (Table 9.2) provides an excellent illustration of the range of applications within a single kind of work context, and also of performance criteria. But most estate agents do not have to cope with as much variation in work context as, for example, architects or community nurses. The practicability of being able to assess competence across a wide range of situations also has to be considered, which is why NCVQ has begun to require lead bodies to provide assessment guidance.

The Assessment of Competence for Accreditation as NVQs/SVQs

The central thrust of NCVQ policy on assessment can be summed up by two principles. The qualification and its assessment must be performance-based; and assessment should be uncoupled from training in order to promote access, recognition of prior learning and candidate choice of learning mode. Five of the ten assessment requirements closely follow the detailed NCVQ model of competence described in the previous section:

1. the method of assessment used in any circumstance is valid and reliable;
3. performance evidence should feature in the assessments for all elements of an NVQ;
4. performance must be demonstrated and assessed under conditions as close as possible to those under which it would normally be practised — preferably in the workplace;
7. the method of assessment should always enable eligible candidates to demonstrate competence, and place no unnecessary additional demands on them;

Table 9.2: Element of Competence from Estate Agency

Unit: Promote the sale of property available through the agency

Element:
Agree property requirements with applicant

Performance Criteria:

- applicants are acknowledged promptly and politely and treated in a manner which promotes goodwill;
- applicants are encouraged to ask questions and seek clarification;
- options and alternatives are offered to establish applicant's property requirements and reliability;
- likely availability of property meeting the applicant's requirements is described honestly;
- details agreed with applicant relating to type, price and preferred location of property are complete and recorded accurately and legibly;
- complete details relating to applicant's preferred method of communicating about newly available property is recorded accurately and legibly;
- complete details relating to applicant's current property position, timescale expectations and financial status are recorded accurately and legibly; and
- accurate and complete details (applicant requirements, method of communicating, completion timescale and financial status) are provided promptly to relevant staff in the agency.

Range of Applications to which the element applies:

- range of applicant expectations to include maintenance (ease or do it yourself), services available (nearby or remote), additional/alternative uses to present use, originality of features, quality of structure/fixtures/fittings;
- range of potential applicant situations to include first-time buyer, buyer part of a chain, buyer with property to sell but not yet on market, cash sale, job move;
- range of financial status to include mortgage needed, mortgage already organized, cash sale, bridging loan required;
- Range of financial situations to include low, medium and high earners; retired buyers; joint (equal) incomes; and
- range of market conditions to include both 'buyers' market' and 'sellers' market'.

---

10. a reliable system should be in place for recording evidence across the full range of circumstances in which the competence must be applied, as specified in the range statement. (NCVQ, 1991, p. 6)

Both 1 and 7 pose theoretical issues. Since it is units of competence which get accredited, it should be judgments about competence at unit level which have to be valid and reliable. Although it can be predicated that the use of certain methods in certain circumstances will not support valid and reliable judgments, the converse is more difficult to prove. Indeed the consensus among researchers is that the best approach is to use a combination of different methods rather than a single method of assessment. For similar reasons it is the whole approach which ought to be considered in requirement 7 rather than individual methods.

Requirements 3, 4 and 10 raise issues of practicality because 4 in particular implies observation at work and the demands of range and reliability suggest multiple observations. Under conditions of close supervision multiple observations will not be difficult to arrange, but the supervisor will require careful preparation and training if the assessment is to be reliable. Where there is little naturally occurring observation, the whole process of assessment can be not only intrusive but extremely expensive, especially when there are complex-range statements and many performance criteria. Although it is possible in theory to economize by combining several elements, the number of separate situations and criteria to be considered at once could defy the most brilliant of judges. We shall return to this problem in Chapter 10.

Three further assessment requirements concern flexible arrangements to increase access and accommodate a wide range of special needs and circumstances, a very welcome development. Then two of them address the problem of what to do when performance evidence is insufficient or not practical to collect:

5. if assessment in the workplace is not practicable, simulations, tests, projects or assignments may provide suitable evidence — but care must be taken to ensure that all elements and performance criteria have been covered, and that it is possible to predict that the competence assessed can be sustained in employment;
6. where performance evidence alone is limited and does not permit reliable inference of the possession of necessary knowledge and understanding, this must be separately assessed. (NCVQ, 1991, p. 6)

Though couched in the language of last resort, these requirements have been interpreted in practice as sanctioning more flexible arrangements. Evidence from outside the workplace is used to a considerable extent, but there must still be sufficient evidence that what is assessed can be sustained and used in employment. Indeed most of the technical discussion about assessment for NVQs has been about collecting appropriate mixes of evidence to enable valid and reliable judgments of competence (Gealey *et al.*, 1991).

The mention of 'knowledge and understanding' in requirement 6 can be more easily understood in the context of the NCVQ specifications on assessment guidance. Assessment guidance, although not part of the statement of competence, should also be provided by lead bodies for each element. In particular:

• where candidates may not be able to present sufficient evidence of competence through performance alone, it will often be necessary to collect evidence of their possession of the essential underpinning knowledge and understanding. Lead bodies should help awarding bodies and providers to interpret their requirements by indicating what knowledge and understanding is considered essential;
• where it may be impossible or uneconomic to assess performance across the whole of the range specified, the lead body should indicate

the minimum requirements for performance evidence. (NCVQ, 1991, p. 4)

It is perhaps strange to expect assessment guidance for each element when, as stated above, the most crucial judgments are made about units rather than elements. But the significant part of this brief is a 'backdoors' requirement for lead bodies to indicate what knowledge and understanding they consider to be essential. Given the insistence throughout several years of NVQ development on performance-based rather than knowledge-based qualifications, this sudden attention to knowledge and understanding is surprising. Hitherto the argument had always been that if knowledge was needed for competence it would automatically be embedded in performance: otherwise it was not really needed. Traditional qualifications were 'guilty' of including knowledge for its own sake, even when it never got used in employment. Not only was this wasteful but it increased the length of training and placed unjustifiable constraints on access. So what were the reasons for the change in perspective?

Although the inclusion of knowledge might be interpreted as a convenient concession to critics which did not detract from the central principle of performance-based competence, it was probably the emergent problems of assessing over a wide range of work situations which had the greater influence. Interest in knowledge naturally followed the introduction of range statements, when it was realized that knowledge evidence could improve the validity of judgments of competence based on a relatively narrow range of performance evidence. For example, oral questioning after an observation can probe a candidate's knowledge about the whys and wherefores and inquire about how they would act differently under different circumstances. The argument is cogently made by Jessup (1991):

Two points may be made: (1) knowledge is required, in the context of practising an occupation or profession, not as an end in itself, but to ensure competent performance; and (2) knowledge is required to facilitate transfer of skills . . . [For this latter purpose] the assessment of knowledge should concentrate on:

a) the knowledge of the variation in circumstances that might be expected and how practices and procedures should be modified to meet different circumstances, over the range which is expected;

b) an understanding of the principles or theory which explain the nature of the function or activity to be assessed.

How much evidence is sufficient reasonably to ensure that a candidate can perform competently in the required range of situations is an issue which can only be resolved through empirical research. In assessment for NVQs, it is suggested that the evidence should be gathered from:

– performance demonstrations in at least one context;

Table 9.3: Unit C5 of the National Occupational Standards for Working with Young Children and their Families

C.5.6	Help children develop a positive self image and identity

Performance Criteria

5.6.1	Praise and other forms of recognition for children's personal qualities, achievements and behaviour are offered in a manner and with a frequency likely to enhance each child's self-image.
5.6.2	Planned activities and experiences provide opportunities to explore issues of self-image and identity in ways that are appropriate to the children's level of development.
5.6.3	Learning materials and resources provide positive and non-stereotypical images of children and adults of both genders and various racial origins.
5.6.4	Effective use is made of resources and networks in the local community to introduce positive role models for all children, including those with disabilities.
5.6.5	Children are encouraged to explore a variety of roles and identities in their play, and discussion helps them identify with and take pride in their own racial and sexual identity.
5.6.6	Signs of extremely low self-image or disturbed identity development are accurately recognised and advice sought from an appropriate person as soon as possible consistent with the candidate's role and responsibilities.
RANGE	Age band: 1 to 4; 4 to 7 years. Characteristics of children: children of white European origin; other ethnic origins; children with special needs; abused children; children using one language; children using more than one language; children who have difficulty with self image and identity and children who do not.

Examples and definitions to clarify terms used in the range or performance criteria.

5.6.2	examples of opportunities to explore self-image and identity: games with mirrors, representing self in pictures, activities that require children to describe themselves, their likes and dislikes, life story books, etc.
5.6.3	examples of positive and non-stereotypical images: black inventors and their inventions, women as successful business people, disabled people in influential positions such as M.P. or achieving success in sports.
5.6.4	examples of use of resources and networks in the community: taking children to visit local workplaces and community groups, inviting local people to talk to children about their roles and lifestyles or to demonstrate 'signing', etc.
5.6.6	examples of signs of extremely low self-image or disturbed identity development: expressing consistent dislike of self, overcompliance or saying own wishes don't matter, not taking pride in personal appearance, appearing not to care what happens to his/herself, denying racial origins, trying to wash away evidence of skin colour, rejection of other disabled people, etc. examples of appropriate person: senior colleague, social worker, clinical psychologist, etc.

- additional performance demonstrations in varied contexts, if these occur naturally as part of the candidate's employment or are required in training. (Otherwise a range of professional performance demonstrations for the purpose of assessment could only be justified for elements where the cost of errors in assessment is very high);

- questioning to ensure understanding of the principles to explain the nature of the activity and performance required;

- questioning to ensure knowledge of variation in response required in relation to main variations in situations which might be presented.

The assessment decision is made on the accumulation of evidence from these different categories. If there is a considerable volume of performance evidence, the need for additional evidence from questioning would be correspondingly less. (Jessup, 1991, pp. 123–4)

Along with other authors, Jessup describes knowledge evidence as supplementary evidence but this, perhaps, is a misnomer. The total collection of evidence from all sources combined guides the judgment of competence; and there is no supplementary judgment. As suggested in Chapter 1 there are some problems with this particular use of the term 'knowledge', and this is further discussed in Chapter 10.

A good example of such a full specification is depicted in Table 9.3. It comes from the National Occupational Standards for Working with Young Children and their Families. The unit C5, 'Promote children's social and emotional development' is one of eleven core units required (with four additional units) for a Level 3 qualification. C5 comprises six elements:

- C.5.1 help children to relate to others;
- C.5.2 help children to develop self-reliance and self-esteem;
- C.5.3 help children to recognize and deal with their feelings;
- C.5.4 prepare children for moving on to new settings;
- C.5.5 help children to adjust to the care/education setting; and
- C.5.6 help children to develop a positive self-image and identity.

Table 9.4 gives the full specification of the last element, C.5.6. In addition to its title, there are six performance criteria, a range statement, an explanation of terms and a list of evidence requirements, subdivided into performance evidence and knowledge evidence.

Table 9.4:   Specification of Element C.5.6 (Evidence Requirements)

Performance Evidence

The preferred methods of assessment are:-

1. Direct observation of performance in the workplace especially with regard to C.5.6.1, C.5.6.5.
2. Oral questioning contingent on aspects of performance to cover performance criteria or parts of the range that are not readily observable.
3. Interrogation of candidate's rationale for activities/performance.
4. Reflective accounts of the candidate's own practice and evaluation of his/her personal effectiveness in planning activities, providing experiences and using resources in the community to help children develop a positive self image and identity.
5. Plans and other evidence of preparation for activities or routines.
6. Case studies and assignments.
7. Child observations and assessments of development.
8. Evidence of prior achievement.

Where performance is not directly observed, any evidence should be authenticated, preferably by colleagues, supervisors, parents or other appropriate person or by detailed questioning of the candidate by the assessor to establish authenticity.

Where appropriate, written and oral evidence may be supplemented by diagrams, photographs or other practical or audio visual materials.

Knowledge Evidence

Evidence of an appropriate level of knowledge and understanding in the following areas is required to be demonstrated from the above assessment process supplemented as necessary from oral or written questions or other knowledge tests or from evidence or prior learning.

C.5.6.a Knowledge of the development of self-image and identity in young children 6 weeks – 8 years.
C.5.6.b The special needs with regard to identity development of black and ethnic minority children in a predominantly white society.
C.5.6.c The difficulties which may be experienced by children with special needs, abused children and those who are HIV positive in developing a positive self-image and identity.
C.5.6.d The special needs that bilingual children may have with regard to identity.
C.5.6.e Methods of showing approval for children's efforts and why this is important for a child's self-image.
C.5.6.f The planning, provision and evaluation of activities and experiences which explore issues of self-image and identity in accordance with appropriate developmental levels.
C.5.6.g The importance of selecting and providing materials and resources which promote positive and non-stereotypical views of children and adults and provide positive role models.
C.5.6.h Strategies for the promotion among colleagues and other adults including parents of the realisation of the importance of a non-stereotypical view of children and adults.
C.5.6.i A variety of techniques and resources to encourage active exploration among children of different roles and identities in their play.
C.5.6.j The importance of discussion, planned and incidental, of gender, race, culture, religion and disability, in the promotion of positive identity.
C.5.6.k Patterns of behaviour in young children which may be symptomatic of poor self-image or disturbed identity and when and to whom appropriate referral should be made.
C.5.6.l The roles of professional workers to whom candidate can refer children for specialist advice and/or treatment e.g., senior colleague, social worker, educational psychologist, clinical psychologist.

Chapter 10

The Assessment of Competence in the Professions

This chapter discusses and expands upon the work of a research project directed by the author to study current British practice in the formal assessment of professional competence for the purposes of qualification, registration or membership of professional bodies.[1] It comprises both a description of current practice and a policy analysis in which current practice is compared with the recently developed system of National Vocational Qualifications, discussed in the previous chapter. The evidence cited is derived from case studies of eleven professional groups, chosen from four groupings:

- Engineering and construction
    Architecture
    Chartered surveying
    Civil engineering
    Electrical engineering
- Health and caring professions
    Nursing
    Optometry
    Social work
- Teaching
    Teaching in Scotland
- Business and management
    Management accountancy
    Management (industrial)
    Management (personnel)

The subsequent discussion of issues is based on consultation with a wider group of professions and interested parties. Its purpose is to consider both ways in which current practice might be achieved and ways in which the NVQ/SVQ system might be adjusted to better meet the needs identified by the professions. It should be noted however, that none of the issues raised are exclusive to occupations claiming professional status, that is the adjustments might benefit other occupations as well. The research did not cover academic qualifications giving exemption from professional examinations if they made no claim to assess professional performance or knowledge in use in professional contexts. This was a matter of imposing realistic constraints on the scope of the research, not a judgment that such qualifications were irrelevant. The relationship between academic qualifications based on propositional knowledge and practical professional performance was discussed in Part 1 and will be further discussed in Part 3.

The principal questions which shaped our collection of evidence were:

What are the principal routes to accreditation?
What precisely is being assessed?
How is evidence of individual performance/achievement collected?
By whom is the evidence collected?
How are the various pieces of evidence assessed?
What is the outcome of assessment?
What quality assurance procedures are in use?

Three patterns of assessment of competence were identified:

- Performance in the workplace is assessed during a period of practical experience subsequent to completion of an academic qualification in higher education;
- On-the-job assessment forms an integral part of the academic qualification, which then leads directly to professional recognition; and
- Assessment of practical performance is conducted both within the academic course and during a subsequent period of professional preparation.

We found it useful to discuss evidence of professional competence under two main headings: performance and capability. Performance evidence does, of course, provide evidence of capability; but the term 'capability evidence' is used to refer to evidence not directly derived from normal performance on-the-job. Sometimes the purpose of capability evidence was to supplement performance evidence, sometimes it was to ascertain the candidate's potential to perform in the future. Its scope encompassed the following categories of capability:

- underpinning knowledge and understanding of concepts, theories, facts and procedures;
- the personal skills and qualities required for a professional approach to the conduct of one's work; and
- the cognitive processes which constitute professional thinking

Many professions do not, as yet, have documents specifically designed to communicate their occupational standards. This makes it difficult to find out what qualified people are competent to do and to judge the validity of their assessment systems. In particular, it is difficult for those unfamiliar with the often unwritten traditions of a profession to distinguish those situations and circumstances in which newly qualified professionals are expected to be competent from those in which they still need guidance from senior colleagues. Nevertheless, candidates are assessed in most of the key areas of their professional work and across a wide range of relevant skills.

Our discussions revealed no dissent from the NCVQ/SCOTVEC principle that evidence based directly on performance in the workplace should be given a high priority; though many felt that the proportion of such evidence might be rather lower for higher-level occupations in order to accommodate demands for a much larger knowledge base, not all of which could be assessed through evidence based on performance. Table 10.1 summarizes the sources of evidence currently used in the eleven case-study professions, and gives some indication of the range and balance of evidence needed to assess professional competence.

Evidence Based on Performance

Comparison between the professions suggests that much of the variation in types of performance evidence is attributable to the different opportunities presented by different kinds of professional work. But, there is also a significant element of choice. The most convenient kinds of performance evidence are naturally occurring products, which can be collected for assessment without incurring significant extra cost; and can also be made available for verification of that assessment. Most products however, cannot be judged as self-sufficient pieces of evidence. A survey has to be checked for its accuracy and for possible omissions by an independent surveyor. A report, purporting to assess a client's needs, may need to be checked against the client's own views and/or independent professional assessment. A lesson plan has to be judged in terms of its appropriateness for the class concerned. Even an architect's or an engineer's design will have to be examined in relation to the context and the brief. Nevertheless, sampling across the expected range of performance is easier when these are naturally occurring products. Candidates can be questioned about their work in a very precise way; and decisions are easier to explain to fellow assessors or verifiers when there is a product available for examination which can serve as a concrete point of reference.

For many types of competence, however, direct observation is the most valid and sometimes the only acceptable method of collecting evidence. In most cases this is accompanied by some kind of informal questioning of the candidates to discover their analysis of the task or situation, their reasons for their actions and their evaluation of what occurred. Sometimes this is extended to questioning clients or other people present. Questioning of candidates may also be used to extend the range of the evidence collected by asking about what they would have done if certain things had happened or if certain features of the situation had been different. When an appropriate assessor is

Table 10.1: *Sources of Evidence Used in the Case-study Professions*

	Source of evidence	Profession										
		Arch	Svy	Civ	Elec	Nurs	Opto	SocW	Teach	Man Acc	Ind M	Pers M
P	Direct observation (Normal practise)	x	x	x	x	x	x	x	x		+	
P	Indirect observation (video-recording)						x	x	x		+	
P	Direct observation (Simplified practise)	x	x	x	x	x	x	x	x		+	
CP	Observation (role-playing or simulation exercise)	x	x	x			x	x	x		+	x
PC	Viva voce examination (or interview)	x		x		x	x	x			+	
P	Products of normal professional work	x	x	x	x	x	x	x	x	x	x	x
C	Reflective reports on work (or interview)	x	x	x	x			x		x	x	x
PC	Log-books/other portfolio evidence	x	x	x	x		x			x	x	
CP	Project Reports (work-related)	x	x	x	x	x		x			x	x
C	Assignments	x	x	x		x		x	x		x	x
C	Written Examinations	x	x	x	x	x	x	x	x	x		x

P= Performance evidence   C= Capability evidence

PC= Mainly Performance evidence, but also capability, depending on context

CP= Mainly Capability evidence, but also performance, depending on context

x Required   + Decision delegated to Assessment Centres

frequently present to observe performance and question the candidate, it is relatively easy for assessor training to ensure that a proper sample is used. But this becomes more difficult when special arrangements have to be made for an assessor to be present. In such circumstances, practicality and cost will restrict observation to a small sample of behaviour and the possibility of an observer effect will also have to be considered. When work has to be reorganized to ensure that particular things happen when an assessor is visiting, we are moving towards simplified practice rather than natural observation. Sometimes the directly observed sample can be expanded (or even replaced) by recordings of performance; though the intrusive effects of recording have to be carefully considered. One advantage of recordings is that they can be readily used for verification of the initial assessment, provided they are accompanied by appropriate contextual information.

Simulated exercises and observation of simplified practice are usually presented as 'second-best' solutions to the validity problem. The case for using them is strongest when the situations to which the candidate is expected to respond are very rare, dangerous or very expensive to set up. However, there can be other good reasons for using these methods. It may be possible to cover a wider range of situations more quickly; and assessment is easier to conduct in simple situations when attention can be more precisely focused on agreed criteria. However, simplification always raises the problem of transfer. When is it reasonable to infer that performing well in simplified situations, when there is less distraction and pressure, is sufficient evidence of competence in more complex and more crowded situations?

Further evidence provided by the candidate can serve a variety of purposes. Witness reports of corroboration or authenticity are simple to collect and verify. Logbooks provide a good basis for questioning, but cannot be treated as evidence unless there is some indication of the quality of work reported. If witnesses comment on quality, they become *de facto* assessors whose independence and reliability of judgment have to be verified. Reflective reports by candidates on their own professional work can be valuable for extending the range of what has been directly observed, especially if corroborated by other forms of evidence. Sometimes, however, they may be more appropriately considered as evidence of capability rather than performance. Like logbooks, they provide a useful basis for further oral questioning.

Evidence of Capability

The main purposes served by evidence of capability are as follows:

- To supplement performance evidence and extend the range of what may be inferred from it by demonstrating that the candidate has the necessary knowledge and skills to perform in a wider range of situations than those observed. (NB. This assumes that the ability to use

    such knowledge and to integrate skills into 'real' performance is suf-
    ficiently covered by the performance evidence).

- To assess the quality of a candidate's cognitive processes, which by
  definition cannot be directly observed. This includes the ability to
  understand clients, analyse problems and situations, discuss the relative merits of alternative approaches, and evaluate the professional
  practice they observe.
- To indicate that the candidate has a knowledge base that will serve as
  a foundation for future practice. This can range from knowledge about
  techniques, which are still at the pilot stage or about to be introduced,
  to a critical understanding of the concepts, theories and principles
  which underpin current practice; so that they can understand the significance of innovations and properly evaluate their work.
- To understand the role played by their profession in society, both
  through direct interaction with clients and through their contribution
  to employing organizations and government; together with the issues
  which arise as a result.

Other factors needing consideration include:

- The degree of responsibility given to professionals is usually high,
  because they frequently deal with unique cases about which nobody
  else is sufficiently informed to make a judgment. Predicting performance in such cases necessarily involves making inferences; and these
  will frequently need to draw on capability evidence as well as performance evidence.
- Learning from experience is extremely important in professional development, and requires an ability to conceptualize and an ability to
  evaluate (see Chapters 5 and 6).
- As a result, professionals are not only users of knowledge, they are
  also creators of knowledge. Several professions stressed the importance of creativity (see Chapter 3).
- It is important for professionals to sustain a critical and evaluative
  attitude towards practice, so that they seek to improve it and do not
  lapse into complacency (see Chapter 5).
- The opportunities for trainees to demonstrate some of these qualities
  at work may be limited, until two or three years after qualification;
  yet they are still very important.

In deciding what kinds of evidence to use in assessing capability the
following points need to be taken into account:

- Capability is essentially concerned with knowledge in use. Knowledge that does not get used does not get incorporated into a person's

action knowledge and does not contribute to their capability (see Chapter 4).

- The context of use is also extremely important. The greater the gap between the context of use for assessment purposes and the work-context, the greater the validity problem will be and the weaker the inference that the 'capability' will eventually contribute to performance (see Chapters 2 and 3).
- The level of integration involved in knowledge use is a particularly important aspect of this problem (see Chapters 7 and 8).
- The validity gap can be significantly narrowed by the appropriate design of assessment tasks.
- While integrative assignments such as projects linked to real work situations may be strong on validity, they necessarily reduce the range of knowledge which can be demonstrated.
- Combinations of types of evidence are needed, if both range of knowledge and use of knowledge are to be assessed.

There is a considerable scope for the more imaginative design of traditional kinds of assignment.

Handling Competence in Ethical Issues

Professional associations frequently expressed concern about how competence-based qualifications could handle ethical issues of the kind raised by codes of conduct or codes of professional practice. This problem is not peculiar to competence-based models but applies to qualifications in general. Qualifications are based on evidence of what candidates can do at the time and in the context of the relevant assessment activities; but they are commonly interpreted by employers as having a predictive dimension. Codes of conduct on the other hand are not primarily about what professionals *can* do but about what they *will* do. Assessment for a professional qualification can confirm, if properly designed, that a person is capable of following a code of conduct and that he or she has adhered to the code while a student or trainee. But it cannot guarantee that that person will continue to follow that code throughout their professional life. This is an area where the collection of evidence of current performance is not always easy; and predictive inferences about attitudes and dispositions are much less reliable than for other aspects of performance. Nevertheless, the manner in which professional education, training and assessment is conducted can help to develop a strong sense of commitment to the code at the time of qualification. Although the capability to follow a code of conduct can and should be incorporated into the assessment of competence for qualification purposes, there is still a need for a code of conduct that is separate from the qualification so that it can be properly monitored throughout a professional's career.

The problem of how best to incorporate ethics into occupational standards was addressed in a later project (Steadman *et al.*, 1994). This recognized four sets of values impinging on ethical conduct at work, all derived from the general domain of moral and social values espoused by individuals or groups in wider society: legal values, values of the profession, values of individual professionals and, except for those who are self-employed, values of employing organizations. Professionals have to be competent in recognizing and applying the values appropriate to the situations they encounter, and able to resolve any conflicts between them. Some values may be embedded in recognized procedures or practices which are normally followed without question, for example in accountancy. Others may impinge on areas where professionals have personal discretion and responsibility. In all cases professionals will need to be aware of, and understand, the relevant ethical issues and to recognize where decisions have an ethical dimension. They will need to understand and apply the relevant moral principles and codes of conduct, to reason in areas of ethical complexity, and to manage complex ethical responsibilities and value conflicts.

One general problem highlighted by the issue of ethical competence is the reluctance of some competence developers to give sufficient attention to the more integrating aspects of competence emphasized in the 'Job Competence Model'. Some groups have found it appropriate to have a special unit of competence devoted to ethical issues in addition to embedding ethical considerations in other standards. More recently the construction professions have extended this practice to include other generic aspects of professional competence such as giving advice and problem-solving. Their generic unit (depicted in Tables 7.2–7.4) provides an interesting example of the generic competence approach (see Chapter 8) being incorporated within the more specific competence oriented NVQ/SVQ system.

The Implementation of Assessment

Assessment and verification procedures are well established in the higher-education context but rather patchy for workplace assessment. Although most professions provide some training for assessors, several lack explicit criteria for assessment in the workplace. While it may seem reasonable to claim that assessments made by experienced practitioners have a degree of validity, the lack of explicit criteria and/or verification procedures weakens their public accountability.

The issue of assessment criteria is necessarily linked with that of standards. Ideally, the assessment process should begin with (1) a collection of evidence about performance and capability (2) an indication of the standards of competence about which judgments have to be made (3) cross-referencing to indicate which pieces of evidence should be used for each distinct judgment of competence. Whereas traditional assessment systems have made separate judgments about each piece of evidence; judgments of competence have to rest on separate decisions about each element of competence, taking into account all the relevant sources of evidence. Thus assessment criteria 'belong' to elements of competence not to pieces of evidence. This takes advantage of the well-established principle that combining different kinds of evidence significantly improves reliability. Moreover, it need not result in the atomization of the assessment process, because some pieces of evidence may be relevant to more than one element.

Standards designed to meet the requirements of NCVQ and SCOTVEC will include performance criteria, which may be sufficiently specific to function as assessment criteria with minimal supplementary guidance. Other standards may be less detailed, in which case additional assessment criteria will need to be developed to improve the reliability and validity of the assessment process. Where there are no standards, however, the validity problem is much greater; because the assessment specifications and criteria are the only available definition of competence. Thus they have an additional function as proxy-standards, and have to take full responsibility for indicating the nature of the competence which is being assessed.

We need to recognize, however, that even the most detailed criteria leave some scope for variation in their interpretation. The problem is to combine written guidance on assessment with the training of assessors to get the desired level of agreement and standardization. Evidence suggests that once established by training and regular communication, a community of assessors is able to ensure sufficiently standard use of criteria; but that it is easy for standardization to slip if training and communication are not regularly maintained.[2] Such a community, however, must have assessment criteria that are limited in number and easy to use. Hence the function of assessment criteria should be to focus on areas where differences of interpretation are most likely to arise; they simply get in the way when they state the obvious. Overemphasis on lengthy and highly specific lists of criteria at the expense of developing and maintaining the quality of individual assessors is counterproductive. But lack of appropriate assessment criteria will tend to make inter-assessor consensus a social achievement rather than a valid judgment of a particular competence.

The training of assessors and verifiers is another essential component of quality assurance; because assessment and verification are themselves professional processes requiring special expertise. In particular, assessors are required:

- to know and to understand the profession's system of assessment;
- to interpret its occupational standards in the agreed manner;
- to collect valid and reliable evidence by techniques such as observation, oral questioning and setting examinations; and
- to apply agreed procedures and criteria in making professional judgments of competence.

All these types of expertise are unlikely to be acquired without both training and active membership of a community of assessors. Verifiers should then receive additional training for observing assessors at work, playing a leadership role in the community of assessors and using independent assessment of a sample of evidence for appropriate verification purposes.

The Concept of Capability Revisited

The word 'capability' carries two meanings (SOED). First, it is described as 'the quality of being capable', that is of being able to do things; and in this sense it is almost synonymous with competence but with less of a normative connotation (see Chapter 8). The second meaning of capability is that of 'an undeveloped faculty or property, a condition capable of being turned to use'. The famous landscape architect Capability Brown got his nickname from his habit of saying that the grounds that he was about to convert into beautiful, yet seemingly natural, landscape had capabilities. Thus the second meaning refers not to the state of already being competent but to the capacity to become competent. The usefulness of the capability construct for professional education lies in holding these two meanings together in some kind of balance. In its first sense capability has a present orientation and refers to the capacity to perform the work of the profession: capability is both necessary for current performance and enables that performance. In its second sense, capability can be said to provide a basis for developing future competence, including the possession of the knowledge and skills deemed necessary for future professional work.

The word 'foundation' is frequently used when justifying the teaching of theoretical knowledge to aspiring professionals, with the implication that a critical understanding of concepts, theories and principles is needed for professionals to 'go beyond the information given' and reason what to do when confronted with new situations: this applies both to extending the range of personal competence and to being able to handle future, unanticipated problems. However, this argument also applies to capabilities other than theoretical knowledge. Many professions emphasize the need for interpersonal skills, the ability to work in teams and cognitive skills such as problem-solving, all of which can be developed and demonstrated in practice-relevant ways outside the normal professional work-context. Sometimes developing capabilities of this kind is better pursued outside the work-context, at least in the initial stages. Sometimes there is little opportunity to use such capabilities in the work-context: for example, although it is important for professionals to be able to evaluate current practice in organizations, such behaviour is rarely welcomed from students or even from newly qualified professionals. Opportunities to consider ethical issues pertinent to professional codes of conduct may also be limited. So capability evidence beyond, but also including, theoretical knowledge has an important part to play in the assessment of professional competence.

Greater use of the capability construct would help to redress two significant weaknesses in the way the NVQ/SVQ system is currently developing: the ambiguous treatment of 'knowledge' arising from its late introduction into the system; and the rather dubious stretching of the term 'performance' to satisfy the assessment criteria. Whereas our study of the assessment of competence in the professions led us to develop the construct of capability evidence to describe aspects of evidence other than performance evidence which made an important contribution to judgments of professional competence, the NVQ/SVQ model seems to be stuck with the term 'knowledge and understanding'. If this term was understood in the very broad sense defined in Chapter 1 and elucidated in Chapters 2–7, there might be no problem. But clearly it is not understood in this way, and a very recent Employment Department briefing note on the topic (ED, December 1993) makes no attempt to establish such a definition. The closest it gets to including non-propositional knowledge is when it states that:

> Knowledge and understanding is about knowing what should be done, how (and perhaps where and when) it should be done, why it should be done and what should be done if circumstances change. (ED, 1993, p. 5)

This largely falls within the category 'knowledge of practice' but does not allude to other relevant categories discussed in Chapter 5 such as knowledge of people and knowledge of situations. There is little hint of the rich range of capabilities covered by the capability evidence described at the beginning of this chapter. Worse still, many published sets of occupational standards have interpreted knowledge and understanding as referring only to propositional knowledge.

Apart from the late arrival of knowledge and understanding on the NCVQ scene, the problem has been exacerbated by the assumption that because knowledge and understanding is embedded in competent performance, its presence in candidates can be inferred from their performance. The alternative, and much neglected, explanation is that it is somebody else's knowledge and understanding that is embedded in that performance. Apprenticeship learning, in particular, is liable to result in competent performance which is not based on knowledge and understanding. Untrained mentors are likely to show rather than explain, and may even have difficulty in providing an appropriate explanation because they have become so immersed in the taken-for-granted world of that particular work-context. The argument for getting a balance of performance evidence and capability evidence depends not only on efficiency and the possible lack of sufficient opportunities to collect a wide range of performance evidence, but also on validity. Appropriate capability evidence can often provide more valid evidence of underpinning knowledge and understanding than performance evidence, and that too has to be taken into account when designing an assessment system.

Another consequence of adopting the term 'knowledge and understanding' without insisting on a broader definition than commonly assumed has been to create a gap between what are coming to be described as knowledge evidence and performance evidence. The gap excludes many useful assessment methods; and is causing people to try and incorporate them by extending the definition of performance beyond all credibility. I prefer to endorse the principle of NCVQ assessment criterion 4 that performance should refer to performance in the workplace under normal or near-normal conditions; because the notion of a performance-based qualification becomes meaningless if the meaning of the word 'performance' is stretched too far, perhaps even to include performance on a written examination. This can be further clarified by adding a second, very similar, principle that performance evidence should be confined to tasks which form a normal part of the job and are not specially introduced for assessment purposes alone. Thus many projects and assignments which are used to demonstrate professional knowledge and thinking cannot be classified as performance evidence.[3] Neither do they sit easily under the heading 'knowledge and understanding'. They are most naturally classified as capability evidence. This does not diminish their importance for the assessment of competence, but properly reminds us that their incorporation into normal professional work is being inferred rather than directly demonstrated. Another consequence should be to regard portfolio evidence as a subset of the total evidence collected and not as a single method of collection, because portfolios often comprise a mixture of performance and capability evidence. In some cases the distinction between capability evidence and performance evidence is not clearcut. When definitions refer to normal working conditions or normal professional work the boundary is fuzzy, but such situations are easily noted and present no practical difficulties in the design of assessment systems.

To conclude, therefore, we may note that without sufficient performance evidence, judgments of competence will be unreliable, invalid and lack credibility. But experience also suggests three reasons why capability evidence is likely to be needed:

- It may complement and strengthen performance evidence, either by improving the confidence of the assessor or by extending the range over which competence may be reliably inferred.
- It may be the most practicable alternative when there is little opportunity for candidates to provide performance evidence. For example, in some professions those not yet or recently qualified may have little real contact with some kinds of client, are not expected to play a prominent role in team discussions and are discouraged from evaluating common practice.
- It may provide some assurance that candidates have sufficient

conceptual, perceptual and ethical knowledge to continue to learn, to grow professionally and to respond flexibly to future, yet unforeseen, challenges and circumstances.

The Role of Occupational Standards

All professions should have public statements about what their qualified members are competent to do and what people can reasonably expect from them. These should comprise both minimum occupational standards and codes of professional conduct. They could also include information about more specialist services provided by members with additional expertise and/or further qualifications. While most of the requirements of a code of conduct can and should be embedded in occupational standards, in my view it is nevertheless important to have a separate statement of the ethical foundations of the work of a profession and the commitments made by its members. These ethical issues are more fully discussed in Chapter 11.

Other purposes for which occupational standards are needed include:

- To inform the public and employers about the claims to competence of the profession, an essential starting point for any public discussions about the role of the profession and the strength of its quality assurance, as well as shaping the expectations of individual clients.
- To inform providers of professional education and training, both in higher education and in public or commercial practice, about the goals to be achieved by candidates for entry to the profession.
- Where appropriate, to be incorporated into regulations or criteria for the approval of courses and/or practice settings.
- To provide guidance for learners (and those who help them to learn through teaching, mentoring or supervision) about what they have to achieve.
- To provide a foundation for the design of valid assessment systems for professional qualifications.
- To establish European equivalences and/or criteria for granting professional status in the UK to those who have trained and practised abroad.

The same statements of standards are unlikely to be equally suitable for all these roles. In particular, the assessment role is likely to be the most demanding and to require the greatest attention to detail; because it has to produce decisions which are just, reliable and valid. It is worth considering whether some of its more detailed requirements might not be better satisfied through guidance notes on assessment, so as to make the standards themselves less lengthy and possibly more useful for other purposes.

The most contentious issue raised in our discussions about standards concerned the optimum level of specificity. Too little specificity can lead to lack of clarity, poor communication and diminished credibility. Too much specificity leads to cumbersome standards, which take too long to read, and to possible abuse of the system by people taking shortcuts. Sometimes the problem can be resolved by improved presentation; but often the natural tendency towards a uniform style of presentation can exacerbate the problem. Our consultations suggest that different parts of the same set of occupational standards may require different levels of specificity. Some aspects of professional work are learned, performed, perceived and judged holistically, i.e., the capacity of a teacher to control a class: these can be adequately described in fairly general terms. Others involve more discrete areas of competence which are separately acquired and demonstrated: these need to be described with greater specificity than some generic label which conveniently groups them. Some processes are regarded as having general applicability, e.g., active listening to clients, and do not therefore require separate specification for every kind of situation: others may entail situation-specific or task-specific variations which need spelling out. Trying to impose a uniform level of specificity which ignores these differences will often be counter-productive.

Another problem is needlessly created when over-enthusiastic proponents of standards try to invest them in an aura of perfectionism. Whichever purpose is being considered, one role of standards is to establish a reasonable level of agreement and common understanding about the definition of competence. Well-defined standards will do this more effectively than poorly-defined standards; but there are still limits to what written statements can achieve on their own. The area of common understanding could be expanded by additional conferences and workshops, and will improve still further when people continue to work together for a period of time, i.e., during the establishment of a verification process. But total uniformity of interpretation is an unattainable goal. Trying too hard to produce a fool-proof system will only make intelligent people feel that they are being treated like fools.

At a more practical level, the formulation of standards necessarily involves a great deal of professional judgment. While it is vital that standards are based on thorough analysis of the nature of professional work and the knowledge base that informs it, there is no standard version of what professional works entails which can serve as a single point of reference. The variations in work and in working practice between one job context and another can be quite important. Hence compromises and judgments have to be made about precisely what will be taken as the standard; and issues of the range of expected competence will be particularly difficult to resolve. In addition, a balance has to be struck between current practice and anticipated future practice, or allowance for change built into the standards themselves: otherwise new entrants to the profession may be judged by criteria which are already out-of-date. Both the methodology used to derive the standards and the professional judgments made in deciding their final form and content could be made explicit in a document explaining the rationale for the standards.

Otherwise people may believe that decisions have been arbitrary or ill-informed; and the standards will fail to gain the full confidence of the various stakeholders. It can also be useful to put out markers for special attention when the standards are next reviewed.

Hitherto, there has been little public discussion about the presentation of standards, in spite of its undoubted significance. For example the adoption of a uniform list structure of units and elements of competence gives the impression that they are all of equivalent importance and difficulty, even though this is rarely true in practice. This could be remedied by sequencing (starting with units perceived as most central to a profession's identity) and by accompanying comments on the importance and/or difficulty of particular sections: some units might even be called double units. While this has no logical justification in a system where all units have to be passed, the psychological significance is still very great. The ability to identify with a set of standards enhances its credibility. Other presentational devices such as overviews, and diagrams could also be used rather more, especially to convey a feeling of coherence rather than segmentation. We believe that this presentational problem has been partly created by people treating the results of a functional analysis as the only official mode of representing standards, instead of addressing the problem of finding the most appropriate mode of representation for each particular purpose.

Professional educators, for example, should treat the compendia of standards resulting from functional analysis as foundations for course design rather than substitutes for it. Like the outcomes of a training needs analysis standards do not in themselves constitute a design. To convert them into a course design is not a simple logical task but a creative problem-solving process requiring the synthesis of many dimensions and perspectives. Thus models of professional action are needed which integrate the various functions and elements and minimize duplication of effort. Such integration is needed both for teaching and for assessment purposes, not only to improve efficiency and effectiveness but also to improve the validity of the fragmented representation of competence which inevitably results from functional analysis. Hitherto, the assumption made by the NVQ system has been that standards can be converted into qualifications without any intervening design stage. Until that assumption is challenged, many of the perceived weaknesses of the NVQ system will persist.

The Design of Assessment Systems

The prime reason for having a professional qualification can be seen as quality assurance. The public want to be assured that people designated as qualified are competent to perform the roles and tasks normally undertaken by members of their profession. Where the consequences of incompetence are likely to be serious, the legal right to practise may depend on having the appropriate qualification. Where there is no specific legislation, the public still want the certainty of being able to rely on the competence of those with professional qualifications. Without this assurance of competence the qualification is devalued and the purpose of having a profession is defeated.

Employers also want to be certain that all qualified persons can take on the responsibilities normally accorded to employees of professional status without jeopardizing their own quality-assurance systems. In many cases the qualified status of professional staff is the central feature of an organization's quality-assurance system. The assessment system linked to the qualification must not only be capable of providing this assurance of competence but must be *seen* to provide it by both the public and employers of professional people. Thus an assessment system must be sufficiently robust to assure both the general public and employers of professionals that qualified persons are competent in certain designated areas of work.

Even with good implementation, there are many problems in making valid and reliable judgments in professional occupations due to the range and complexity of the work. Assessment systems need to be carefully designed to use appropriate mixes of different kinds of evidence; and evaluated for their cost and effectiveness. In practice, assessment systems in the professions have gradually evolved from a combination of qualifying examinations (see Chapter 8) and employers' reports to the more sophisticated systems reported above. But research into even the latest systems has been very limited. In these circumstances the more radical alternative offered by the NVQ system can be attractive.

Unlike most of the current assessment systems surveyed, the radical alternative devolves decision-making about assessment methods to individual assessors. Assessors are advised to collect any mix of evidence which enables them to make a valid judgment of competence, with due attention to local circumstances, cost and convenience. However, they are still expected to be extremely comprehensive, so that candidates are advised to provide sufficient evidence for their competence to be judged in each separate element. This contrasts favourably with the more traditional approach which prescribes what evidence will be collected and then expects the assessor to make judgments of competence without necessarily having sufficient evidence to do so. But this apparent advantage depends on assessors being able to properly implement the system. So far there is little evidence that they can be relied upon to do so, partly for conceptual reasons and partly because of their heavy workload. There is less chance of individual assessors being able to design an assessment system that takes advantage of evidence covering several elements while still ensuring sufficient evidence for each element: an atomistic approach is more likely to result that is more time-consuming for all concerned and likely to lead to ill-considered shortcuts. Even trained assessors may lack knowledge about the technical aspects of assessment, such as sources of bias and inaccuracy, sampling and the reliability of judgments based on different combinations of evidence.

The existence of these difficulties is denied by some of the more naïve claims made on behalf of this devolved approach, namely the assertion that:

> It is not so important that their assessments are in line with other assessors but that all assessors interpret the criteria correctly. (Mitchell and Cuthbert, 1989, p. 36)

or the circular argument that validity is achieved by ensuring the evidence is sufficient. A sensible compromise might be to offer a choice of approved assessment patterns which have been carefully designed and tested and for which appropriate training using exemplars is available. More research is needed into the reliability and validity of devolved systems, before they become accepted as normal practice.

Progression and Continuity of Learning

One meaning of 'competence', we noted in Chapter 8, regards competence as a stage on the way to proficiency and expertise. A competent professional is no longer a novice or a beginner and can be trusted with a degree of responsibility in those areas within the range of his or her competence, but has not yet become proficient or expert. This contrasts with those definitions of competence adopted by most competency-based systems of training and education, which assume a binary scale by confining assessment decisions to judging whether a candidate is competent or not yet competent. In Chapter 6 we suggested that binary scales were inappropriate for assessing most areas of professional knowledge and argued that they were incompatible with the notion of lifelong learning. It was still necessary to make judgments of competence, but these did not need to be situated within a conception of competence that was tied to a binary scale. In this context we should note that the concept of a binary scale did not originate with the introduction of competency-based approaches to training. It is inherent in the concept of a qualification: either somebody *is* qualified or *is not* qualified.

The current binary concept of a professional qualification developed in England during the nineteenth century and is rarely challenged. Indeed it is noticeable that where the dual-qualification system has been adopted, academic awards have been classified while the assessment of professional competence has remained as a binary pass–fail judgment. The arguments involved are best illustrated in those situations where assessment of professional competence has been embedded within an academic degree. Normally the degree itself is classified, as are its component academic courses. The debate is about whether or not the practical professional components of the degree should also be classified; and there is considerable variation in practice. The arguments in favour of classification are mainly based on status, to assess practical professional work on a pass–fail basis is to devalue its importance. The arguments against classification are based on fairness and predictive inference. The fairness argument is based on considerable variations in the levels of challenge and support provided by different placements. While it is reasonable to expect all successful candidates to cope in difficult circumstances, such as teaching in an inner-city school or nursing on an understaffed ward, the probability of earning a high grade will be lower. Hence any grading system is inherently unfair. The inference argument is that awarding grades for professional performance on training placements would mislead future employers because they have little predictive validity. Although classified academic awards provide a reasonable, though frequently overestimated, prediction of future performance in quasi-academic forms of work, grades for professional performance come so early in a person's professional career that they give little indication of a person's future capability. The relative merits of these arguments will vary from one profession to another, but they raise some important questions. The fairness argument suggests that in some professions, judgments of competent performance in favourable, supportive contexts provide insufficient evidence for assuming that competence can be transferred to more challenging contexts. The predictive argument suggests that judgments of the comparative capabilities of two professionals at the point of qualification will no longer apply when those same two people have become more proficient after a further period of professional experience. We shall return to these issues later when we discuss different forms of progression.

Historical tradition has shaped much more than the pattern of professional qualifications; it has also shaped the standard of performance associated with the possession of those qualifications. This can manifest itself in a number of different ways. Chapter 8 described the variation in expectations of newly qualified professionals, both between professions and across different areas of work within the same profession. These expectations probably owe more to historical traditions than to current paper specifications of the qualification concerned. Often they are embedded in the way in which work is organized and allocated, which makes it difficult to change the learning opportunities provided.

Upgrading qualifications also threatens those who qualified under previous systems with being overtaken in their careers by a more highly esteemed new generation. Their response may well be to reassert the historical expectations. Such expectations, however, should not be seen only as constraints. They can add reliability and security to a qualification system. The majority of professionals who start their careers in organizations encounter both quality assurance and a context for continuing professional learning. Although both may be in need of improvement, they nevertheless guarantee that eventually that professional becomes proficient in the areas of work to which they are allocated. This additional quality assurance can and, indeed, is often expected to remediate any weaknesses in the qualification system itself. The greatest risk is when newly qualified professionals become either self-employed or get barely competent or non-professional supervisors, i.e., where there is no tradition of developing the proficiency and/or broadening the range of competence of newly qualified professionals.

The length of training also affects the extent to which a qualification is narrow or broad in scope, or encourages learners to progress beyond competence in some areas of professional work. This, in turn, has been influenced by the aspirations of professions or would-be professions seeking the status accorded to longer training periods and higher-level qualifications, and by financial factors. So it is pertinent to ask whether the length of training has determined expectations of competence rather than being determined by the perceived requirements of the profession. Perhaps both interactions are significant. Now that most professional education includes a substantial period of higher education, much of its cost falls on government. Hence recent government pressure to reduce the length of training for architects, and its refusal to lengthen the postgraduate training period for primary teachers beyond thirty-six weeks in spite of the increased expectations created by its own policies for the primary-school curriculum and its assessment. With internships, however, the cost of providing training falls on employers who may compensate by getting trainees to do work that might otherwise be done at greater cost. Perhaps the best known example is that of junior hospital doctors, who are required to work for excessively long hours on tasks which have little educational value, especially during their pre-registration year (Lowry, 1993). Ameliorating this problem, which has evolved since medical education became hospital-based in the middle of the nineteenth century, can only be achieved by reallocating some of their current work at greater cost to the hospitals concerned. In many occupations the dividing line between practice-based learning and the exploitation of cheap labour is difficult to discern.

A new but very significant factor affecting length of training is the transferability of qualifications across national boundaries. The European Union is committed to interchangeable qualifications and gradually trying to establish equivalencies. Many would argue that these ought to be competency-based, and much of the Australian work on professional competencies has been sponsored by the National Office of Overseas Skills Recognition. But the prospect of negotiating international agreement on competencies conjures up images of a twenty-year cycle of GATT talks. Not only is the level of detail very considerable, but the nature of professional work often differs significantly from one country to another. We can safely assume that the length of the training period and the coverage given to key areas of professional knowledge will continue to be the main basis for negotiating such equivalencies.

Given the range of factors to be taken into consideration when fixing the length of initial qualifications, it seems more constructive both to make the most of the time on offer and to ensure that the necessary post-qualification training is firmly in place. Qualification may signify a critical change in the status of a professional and mark a decline in the amount of time formally allocated to professional learning; but should not be regarded as a break in the learning process itself. Arguments about the length of initial training and the point of qualification should not be allowed to divert us from following through the implications of the models of professional learning discussed in the earlier chapters. These clearly indicate the need to regard professional learning as a lifelong process and to establish a framework for it which is coherent and continuous, quite independently of any qualifications which might be acquired *en route*. This framework will need to recognize both the public need for quality assurance and the well-established finding that in all learning contexts people learn different things and learn them at different rates. However, developing such a framework will also involve challenging several commonly held assumptions.

First the qualification system itself needs to become more flexible. Basic qualifications can indicate competence only in designated areas of professional work under a given range of circumstances; but they can be designed to allow later additions after qualification, and some of these could be a requirement for remaining on the register. Later specialist qualifications could be designed in a similar way, with scope for later enhancements. Then finally, in order to maintain the claim that all qualified persons are competent, serious consideration might need to be given to date-stamping qualifications linked to a system of five or ten yearly updates.

The second assumption to be challenged is that time spent on further learning after being assessed as competent is wasted, a frequent claim by advocates of competency-based training. A more constructive perspective is to regard formal training periods as learning contracts with the following aims:

- to ensure the necessary minimum competencies;
- to take advantage beyond this of learning opportunities available in educational and workplace settings; and
- to be responsive to the qualities and preferences of individual learners.

This proposal should not be interpreted as eschewing the special advantages of groupwork for many educational purposes nor as neglecting resource constraints. Rather it offers the opportunity to work with an agreed model of progression which begins before qualification and continues after qualification; and to develop habits of self-assessment, target setting and planned learning which are important for continuing professional development.

In most professions this model of progression should take into account during the period before and soon after qualification the following kinds of progress:

- extending competence over a wider range of situations and contexts;
- becoming more independent of support and advice;
- routinization of certain tasks;
- coping with a heavier workload and getting more done;
- becoming competent in further roles and activities;

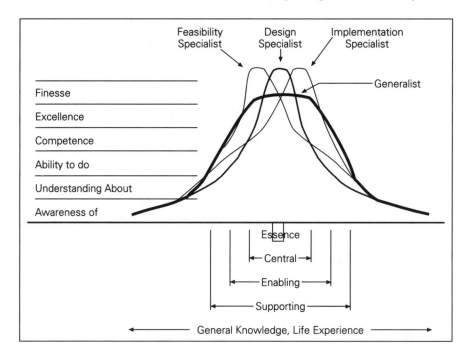

Figure 10.1: Professional Architects' Expected Pattern of Competencies

- extending professional capability; and
- improving the quality of some aspects of one's work.

Examples with which I am familiar do not attempt to formalize all these aspects of progression, but do at least aim to provide continuity of learning before and after qualification. One example from my own university is a profile intended to depict achievement in various aspects of teaching performance during training, which is identical with that used for the formative evaluation of newly qualified teachers in neighbouring school districts. Like many such documents it has to be extremely simple or mentors will not use it.

A more sophisticated model has been developed for architects by Cowdroy (1992), which takes into account both levels of achievement and breadth of achievement. Figure 10.1 indicates the different pattern of competencies expected of mature professional architects who are either specialists or generalists.

While Figure 10.2 suggests the level likely to be reached at the time of graduation by passable and top graduates.

More detailed breakdown of areas of competence according to either the 'project cycle' or the 'office cycle' leads to profiles for use in planning continuing professional development. Although these frameworks can be used to support course design, they will not be competency-linked in any real sense

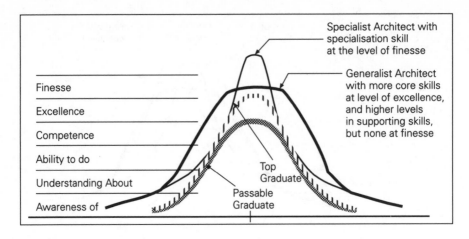

Specialist Architect with
specialisation skill
at the level of finesse

Generalist Architect
with more core skills
at level of excellence,
and higher levels
in supporting skills,
but none at finesse

Finesse

Excellence

Competence

Ability to do

Understanding About

Awareness of

Top
Graduate

Passable
Graduate

Figure 10.2: Competency Distribution of Professional and Graduating Architects

unless they are also reflected in the scheme of assessment. Currently assessment schemes which support the principle of lifelong professional learning are almost non-existent; and we are concerned that the adoption of competency-based systems will exacerbate this problem. At the very least, therefore, we recommend that assessment systems should be capable of recording achievement beyond competence in a manner which takes into account the types of progression listed above. Such systems should also be coherent, though not necessarily identical, with those being developed for recording continuing professional development or accrediting post-qualification learning.

Notes

1. The author wishes to acknowledge the contribution of Gerald Cole to this chapter, which is largely based on two articles from Issue 21 of *Competence and Assessment*. The research described was funded by the Employment Department from whom a full report is available in two volumes, *Policy Analysis* and *Case Studies*. However, the opinions expressed in that report, *Assessing Competence in the Professions* (Eraut and Cole, 1993), and in this chapter are those of its authors, not those of the Employment Department.
2. These issues are discussed with considerable cogency by Wolf (1993).
3. This issue is more fully discussed in Gealey (1993).

Part 3

Professional Accountability

The concluding chapter returns once more to some of the issues raised in the opening chapter. What is the role of the professions in society, and which of the claims associated with the ideology of professionalism are necessary for the proper discharge of that role.

The central argument of the chapter is that it is the duty of professionals to pursue the interests of their clients and other stakeholders. This moral accountability is not confined to direct contact between professionals and clients, because most professionals work in organizations. These organizations are themselves accountable for their actions to clients and stakeholders, and professionals for their contribution to such organizational behaviour.

This raises the question of the outcomes of professional or organizational action; and the principle of giving primary consideration to outcomes for clients is explored through a series of examples, many of which are characterized by complexity and uncertainty. Nevertheless careful examination of professional accountabilities and thinking focused on outcomes for clients discloses aspects of professional expertise which are often neglected. They need to be given greater priority in professional preparation and continuing education.

Finally the constraints on quality of service and hence on professional accountability are noted. Some come from organizational policies and culture, some from external pressure. The growing involvement of government in mandating accountability procedures is discussed, together with concern about its distorting effects on the character of professional work. Will too much externally imposed accountability irretrievably weaken the moral accountabilities expected of all professionals?

Chapter 11

Professional Accountability and Outcomes for Clients

The Changing Pattern of Professional Accountability

Three central features of the ideology of professionalism are a specialist knowledge-base, autonomy and service. Each has been significantly affected by social and cultural changes over the last two decades. Expansion of the knowledge base has led to increasing specialism within many professions and to increasing numbers of professions, so that a single client needing a service, for example, in health care or construction, may encounter both several specialisms within the same profession e.g., medicine or engineering, and members of several different professions. The result is not only increased complexity for the client but a web of intraprofessional and interprofessional relationships in which mutual accountabilities are easily obscured.

Simultaneously with this expansion, specialist knowledge has begun to be challenged and criticized in a number of ways. Where knowledge creation is based on research, questions are raised about the priority given to different areas of research and the lines along which inquiries subsequently develop. There is suspicion that the strength of evidence underpinning important findings or conclusion is exaggerated and the risks of error underemphasized. There is recognition that professionals tend to frame problems and issues in particular ways and that this affects how their specialist knowledge gets used. Above all, people are asking whose interests are served by the way in which specialist knowledge is created, selected, represented and used. This is an area where accountability lies not so much with individual professionals as with the collective membership or leadership of a profession; and to some extent with government which is exerting increasing influence on the direction of research and on issues of professional development.

The specialist knowledge base of a profession also confers status upon it and provides the centerpiece of its claim to autonomy, the argument being that only fellow members of the profession are sufficiently knowledgeable to judge the work of their colleagues. The need to legitimate their knowledge base has been an important factor, together with quality of intake and access to government funding, in causing the newer professions to move their training into the higher-education sector. A further consequence has been the drive towards framing the knowledge base mainly in scientific and technical terms, with concomitant marginalization of interpersonal skills, moral thinking and other forms of professional expertise. Part 1 was largely concerned with the epistemological and empirical arguments in favour of a more balanced perspective. This chapter takes up some of the moral arguments.

The ideal of autonomy applies at two levels. At the level of the whole profession, the argument is that only the profession itself can define and judge the competence and good conduct of its members, because only they have the requisite knowledge. At the level of the individual, the argument is about control of one's own work; and this may even be extended to some individual practitioners rejecting the recommendations of their own professional body, though not transgressing its regulations. In practice, there is a continuum of power accorded to different professions at both these levels; and growing criticism of the way in which that power is used. We should note however, that this criticism is no less when some of these powers are exerted by higher education or by government. First, there is scepticism about peer disciplinary committees as a device for ensuring good conduct, and about the low chances of complaints even entering the formal system. Second, there are doubts about the effectiveness of professional guarantees of the competence of all their members.

While there are good arguments for wider public participation in the setting of standards of probity and competence, especially when technical perspectives have overshadowed responsiveness towards clients, the main focus of criticism has been ineffective implementation of standards. This focus on occasional incompetence rather than debatable policies is probably a natural consequence of the important role played by media which prefer stories to issues. Ironically, assurance of competence probably owes more to the employers of professionals than to the professional bodies themselves.

Both the autonomy and the service aspects of the ideology of professionalism assume that professionals are self-employed or partners in small practices. However, the proportion of professionals employed in this way is quite small. Much larger numbers are employed in the public sector, industry and commerce, where concepts of professional service and autonomy differ from those promoted by the professional bodies. Individual professionals in these situations may not be greatly helped by traditional formulations of the ideology of professionalism, nor by the dominant focus of public and academic discussion on the élite professions of law and medicine. That level of power and status is but a dream for most professional workers, for whom the pursuit of 'autonomy' is primarily a strategy to secure the maximum degree of freedom in their daily practice and a significant role in determining those organizational policies which most affect them. Research comparing the relative autonomy of people from strong professions, weak professions and occupations not claiming professional status would be of considerable interest, especially when comparisons can be made within the same organization or across public and private sectors.

Logically, the greater one's autonomy, the greater one's responsibility;

and therefore the greater one's accountability. But for social and historical reasons that is not how it is perceived. Accountability has been presented to professional workers more as an external control mechanism than as a strengthening of their moral and professional obligations: and hence as a threat to autonomy rather than a consequence of it.

The service ideal is based on the belief that professional action should be based on the needs of the client alone, and not on the needs of the professional nor even those of society. But historically, the assumption has been that because of their specialist knowledge it is only the professionals who can determine what their clients needs are. This assumption has been increasingly challenged and concepts such as client *rights* and client *choice* are widely accepted in many countries, though not fully implemented. More problematic still is the issue of children's rights, which have become increasingly protected by a legal framework but still pose many difficult dilemmas for professionals who work with children (Barnett, 1987). Adjusting the power relationship, however, does not resolve difficult questions about who *are* the clients and whose clients they are. Are teachers, for example, meant to be serving pupils, their parents, their school, their local community, employers or the nation? Other public-sector professionals, such as social workers or librarians may even be concerned about their lack of service to potential clients. It should also be noted that for these and many other professions, these clients are not clients of the individual professional but of the organization which employs them. It is the school rather than individual teachers that enrols pupils as clients, and usually the school district which carries the legal responsibility. Those seeking legal advice become clients of the practice/partnership not clients of individual lawyers.

Once we recognize that it is employing organizations which usually provide the service, other accountability relationships can be taken into consideration. The basic principle of 'moral accountability' is that people are accountable for the effects of their actions insofar as those effects are reasonably foreseeable. The same principle can be applied to the moral accountability of organizations, so that all those people likely to be affected by the actions of an organization can be properly described as its stakeholders. The term 'stakeholder' is broader than that of client or service user and enables a wider set of accountability relationships to be considered, including special-interest groups, the local community and the environment. It should also be noted that many stakeholders have multiple roles, e.g., they may be both clients and taxpayers.

These accountability relationships are depicted in Table 11.1, which also indicates moral accountability relationships between employers, individual workers and work teams.

Many of the relationships depicted above will also include a contractual or legal dimension governed by commercial law, employment law, planning law, etc.; and will be subject to laws relating to negligence or tort. Moral accountabilities usually extend beyond this minimal legal framework; though

Table 11.1:   Moral Accountabilities at Work

Agents and organizations	External stakeholders
Individual workers Team/Department Employing organization 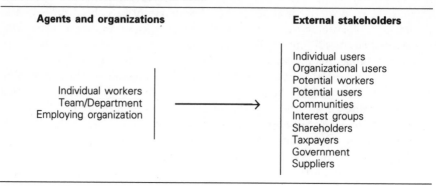	Individual users Organizational users Potential workers Potential users Communities Interest groups Shareholders Taxpayers Government Suppliers

it is reasonable to predict that when legal considerations are prominent, moral considerations are liable to get displaced. Indeed, Svensson (1990) has noted that architects whose work is strongly framed by rules, norms and ordinances seldom refer to ethical issues; whereas psychologists whose work is comparatively unregulated often refer to ethical issues and ethical rules.

The huge difference between Britain and North America in the extent of litigation over professional work probably derives from the general acceptance by British law of the validity of the ideology of professionalism for the élite professions such as doctors, academics and the lawyers themselves. This is clearly expounded by Montgomery (1989) who also comments on the law's failure to adapt to the delivery of cooperative care by multiprofessional teams. Copp (1988) reports cases where nurses were dismissed for refusing to administer treatments which they deemed harmful to a patient. Though it was management who dismissed them, it was medical orders which were challenged and the dismissals were upheld by the courts without recourse to any independent review of the merits of the clinical decisions.

Another form of contractual accountability is that between employing organizations and their professional employees. In this context one finds both vigorous assertions of autonomy by some professionals and a widespread belief among managers that the management of professionals is a major problem (Raelin, 1986). The power conflict is most marked with the most prestigious groups of professionals, especially doctors and academics. There are also significant differences between situations where the managers are promoted members of the same profession and those where they have had quite separate career paths. Beneath the rhetoric, however, one has to look very carefully to decide when the conflict concerns personal power and when it derives from different views about the interests of the client. For example, it is quite common for managers and professionals to give different priorities to different stakeholders. Professionals tend to focus almost entirely on the interests of individual clients, while managers have to consider the total population of current and potential clients and other stakeholders such as politicians and taxpayers or shareholders. A further complication arises when third parties are affected by advice given by a professional to a client, an issue discussed in considerable depth by Schwartz (1978) with reference to the accountability of American lawyers.

A different kind of relationship from those depicted in the left-hand column of Table 11.1 is best described as 'professional accountability'. This encompasses both the relationship between individual professionals and their colleagues in their workplace, and the relationship with their professional organization. The more positive aspects of professional accountability concern upholding professional standards of competence and behaviour. More questionable is the demand of loyalty to fellow-professionals which forbids any public criticism. Its primary purpose is to avoid bringing the profession into disrepute, but it also serves to sustain a false public view of the certainty of professional knowledge and to avoid disclosing that any member of a profession might be less than totally competent. A recent article in the *New Scientist* (Beder, 1993) described two separate cases in which Australian engineers, who publicly complained about unprofessional behaviour by colleagues which threatened the local environment, were subsequently arraigned by their professional body for bringing their profession into disrepute. This problem derives from the professional organizations themselves rather more than their individual members. They must surely be accountable, at least in the moral sense, for the way in which they present themselves to the public, for failures to sustain their claims about the competence and altruistic behaviour of their members, and for the ways in which they seek to develop the role of their profession in society as a whole.

Of equal importance, though perhaps less explicit, is the subtle manner in which the internalized norms of the profession create a form of self-accountability or professional conscience. One common problem is that many such norms are based on the professions' preferred views of themselves rather than working realities. Theories are promulgated which accord with the traditional ideology of professionalism but assume a mythical age, past or future, in which professionals have infinite time and resources to meet their clients' needs. Although such theories are ill-matched to the busy, crowded, resource-starved realities of current professional life, they still frame the 'ideal-type professional' against whom conscientious service-providers evaluate their work. The resultant guilt is accentuated when formal accountability mechanisms take the professions' claims for granted and treat their espoused capabilities as reality. This phenomenon helps to explain the increasing burn-out of professional workers. However, there are also some contrasting examples of norms developed to enable professionals to cope with external demands. Many soon learn that to 'cover your back' against possible liability or criticism overrides concern for the client; and Stelling and Bucher (1973) describe how medical students acquire a 'vocabulary of realism' which virtually annihilates the concept of 'making a mistake'. Can professionals, their employers and the public find a proper balance between the guilt-ridden and the callous?

We are now ready to consider how an appropriately modified ideology of professionalism might inform the complex interplay between professional, moral and contractual accountability within relationships between agents/agencies and their clients or stakeholders. Since most professionals are employed by organizations which carry overall responsibility for the services they provide, we need to examine both what it means for an organization to be morally accountable for its actions and what this implies for its professional workers. Let us begin with accountability to clients or service users. Treating clients in a manner congruent with the ideal of professionalism entails the following kinds of obligation:

- Access   : equity among clients, convenience for clients.
- Cost   : in time as well as money.
- Relationships : good communication, friendly and respectful manner, responsive, relieving rather than causing distress.
- Quality   : of process, of judgment, of service, of outcome.

From this it follows that individual professionals within organizations are morally obliged to develop and sustain such organizational practices; provided that in so doing they will be properly serving their clients. It must be recognized, however, that there are many occasions when professional values may conflict with organizational policy. An educational counsellor, for example, is expected to reduce drop-out rates even though withdrawal from a course might be the most beneficial outcome for some student clients (Bond, 1992). None of these obligations are confined to professional workers; and the close similarity to principles of quality management is worth noting. Professionals do not have any exclusive claim on the concept of client-centredness nor that of moral accountability. If distinctive, the professional element must reside in the need for quality judgments in complex cases (see Chapter 7).

In public-sector organizations, there are also important moral accountabilities to stakeholders who are not necessarily clients, i.e., to the community and to taxpayers, as well as contractual accountability to government. Thus principles such as responsiveness to stakeholders and changing needs, stewardship of the resources received from the community in order to achieve maximum benefit for the community, and internal accountability to employees, lead to additional obligations of the following kind:

- communication with stakeholders;
- selection and prioritization of services;
- policy development and review;
- overall efficiency, economy and effectiveness;
- continuing development of the organizational knowledge base; and
- continuing development of employees.

Once more, there is a strong argument that professional workers should be obligated to develop, sustain and support these organizational activities, thus extending the concept of professional service to stakeholders as well as to clients.

This extended definition of professional duties to the development and support of client and stakeholder-orientated activities of the kind listed above, needs to be reflected in initial and continuing professional education. Not only do they demand attitudes which conflict with those engendered during socialization into some professions, but they require competences which may not be significantly developed under present systems of professional preparation. While the client-centred obligations in the first list above clearly belong in initial training, the stakeholder-centred obligations in the second list might be better handled in a mandatory system of post-qualification education.

Another logical consequence of these accountability relationships is that competence itself has to be defined according to criteria linked to outcomes for clients and stakeholders. This will not automatically lead to the same definition as that put forward by the profession as its preferred view nor will it coincide with current normative practice within the profession. It is possible, therefore, that those who focus the spotlight of public accountability on the issue of professional incompetence have not selected the most important target.

Because, for every incompetent professional, there are probably several who are competently doing the wrong thing. The apparent contradiction stems from the application of two different sets of criteria: one relatively narrow set of criteria judges competence according to the task rather than the occupational role, the broader set judges right and wrong according to the most beneficial outcomes for the client. The traditional concern of professional education with the outcomes of training is insufficient. We now have to take equal cognizance of the outcomes which result from the actions of those who have been trained, i.e., the outcomes *beyond* the outcomes of training.

The Outcomes of Professional Action

The principal purpose of this section is to highlight the problems of outcomes-based evaluations of professional work; and in so doing to draw attention to the wide range of professional knowledge that might be necessary for a professional to be truly accountable to his or her clients. Four types of problem are readily identified:

- the relative significance of short-term and long-term outcomes;
- considering indirect (or secondary) outcomes as well as direct outcomes;
- ambiguities in the causal connection between professional action and subsequent outcomes; and

- whether professional actions are the prime responsibility of an individual, a team or a whole organization.

The extent of these problems will become clearer if we discuss some examples; and I have selected these to cover several different types of professional action: designs, reports, consultations, decisions and ongoing processes.

The Design of a Building

When an architect designs a building there are several types of outcome. First the design itself emerges, and is clearly considered sufficient evidence for the *cognoscenti* to judge, as for example in architectural competitions. Less sophisticated people will want to withhold even their aesthetic judgment until the building has been constructed, finding it difficult to judge the scale, texture, and relationship to the environment from drawings or even from models. At this stage, however, issues such as quality of construction, choice of materials and interior decoration will affect perception of the original design. Unless the building is small, it will have been designed by a whole team of architects, and other professional groups will also have contributed — quantity surveyors, building service engineers, building technologists, etc. Their necessary mutual adjustment will render problematic the attribution of responsibility for a significant number of decisions. Another surprising aspect is likely to be the level of uncertainty about the life expectancy of the building, especially if new materials or construction methods have been used.

It is possible, even common, to consider the building as a product without paying attention to its function, thus ignoring the third type of outcome which concerns useability. Who will live and/or work in the building, and how will they find the experience? Will there be any systematic assessment of user experience and will it be relayed back to the architect? There is probably some relevant research on user responses to buildings, but how far has it been disseminated or given widespread attention? Again, there will be problems of attributing responsibility for any dissatisfaction with the final outcomes. Was it the architect's original brief that was wrong, the prototype design to which the clients agreed, the plans drawn up for furnishing and using the space, or the traditional work habits of the unprepared occupants? People often complain of insufficient or ineffective consultation; but does this result from the architects' neglect or lack of consultation skills, from the hierarchical nature of the client organization or from collusion between them to do a rush job and keep the price down?

Reports

Reports will usually involve some form of investigation or collection of evidence, possibly followed by an analysis of the implications or the respective merits of different interpretations or courses of action: they may conclude with recommendations or points for discussion. But to what level of thoroughness is the investigation pursued? How are decisions made about what tests or techniques to use, when cost is a major consideration? Are there clues which affect the probability of further inquiry being worthwhile? Some assessment of risk or pay-off is likely to be involved, but this may be highly intuitive. Will there be outcomes data to confirm or disconfirm that decision? Probably not, if the professional ethos is one of concealing one's doubts from one's clients and communicating an air of certainty.

Both the analysis and the presentation of a report may be judged either for their intrinsic content (presumably by fellow-professionals using criteria of accuracy and inclusion of vital information) or for their impact on various audiences. Have readers understood and noted the issues and the information which needed to be drawn to their attention? If they have not, can the report be said to have been adequately prepared? Or, to ask an even more difficult question, have the intended recipients taken appropriate subsequent action? One could argue that this last type of outcome is beyond the responsibility of the report writer. But evidence from the evaluation literature suggests that reporting needs to be viewed as a process rather than a product in situations where cognitive or attitudinal change is envisaged: it takes time for people to digest and accommodate to new ideas or new information. Presumably an outcomes-focused evaluation of professional work would be concerned about whether professionals knew how to influence their audiences.

This process aspect of report-writing is well recognized by town planners and social workers, for whom the process of consulting a range of interested parties is crucial for credibility and will usually have a major effort on the acceptability of their recommendations. Some would argue that it is the responses to a report which are the real outcomes, even when they depend on many factors beyond the reporter's control.

Consultations

In some aspects, consultations resemble the reporting process without the report. Although they ensure a period of direct interaction between a professional and a client, the circumstances may not always be propitious for achieving the most beneficial outcome. Typical handicaps include:

- time pressures which curtail conversation;
- limited opportunities for either party to reflect, think or consult;
- little, if any, prior acquaintance between the people involved; and
- tensions which impede both communication and the client's ability to remember what advice was given.

Elsewhere I have analysed in some detail how these and other factors, such as hidden agendas, impinge on teacher–parent consultations about children's progress at school; and suggested that the way consultations are organized can be as important as how they are conducted when they eventually occur (Eraut, 1988). Thus the quality of consultation depends on management as well as the skills of individual professionals.

Ideally, the sequence of outcomes will be as follows:

1. The professional makes an accurate assessment of the client's needs and preferences.
2. Good advice is given, because the professional is aware of all the relevant options and can assess their relative benefits for the client.
3. The client understands and remembers the advice.
4. The client acts on the advice.
5. The final outcomes are as predicted.

Again, it could be argued that the fourth outcome is the sole responsibility of the client; but there could also be circumstances in which the failure to anticipate and discuss barriers to a client following good advice could be partly the responsibility of the professional. The need for skill and metacognitive control when giving and receiving information was discussed in Chapter 6.

Decisions

Decision-making was discussed at some length in Chapter 7, where we noted the tension between rapid, intuitive, decision-making based on experience and deliberative decision-making which incorporates an element of analysis. Making a good decision in the deliberative mode will depend on:

- the right analysis of the problem or situation;
- considering the full range of options for action and assessing their risks and benefits; and
- finding the best fit between the situations and one of the decision options (which could of course include a decision to wait until further information became available).

A profession-centred approach would argue that in order to make good decisions, a professional needs to be a good investigator, knowledgeable about options, able to reason critically and able to learn from experience. Learning from experience involves reflecting on particular issues in the light of their eventual outcomes; and knowledge about options should incorporate evidence from outcomes, reported in the literature or by colleagues. Such evidence does not on its own guarantee the right conclusion, because many factors affect outcomes; but critical thinking which compares and contrasts evidence from several cases is likely to improve the quality of decision-making. However, even this may depend on whether the original analysis of the problem was appropriate. Nevertheless, some decisions will be capable of being routinized and executed in an intuitive mode.

In contrast, a client-centred approach will argue that the problems and perspectives of individual clients cannot be routinized. Not only will there be a unique client 'definition of the problem or situation', but the proper evaluation of options will depend on the client's preferences and circumstances. Neither can be assumed or taken for granted. Hence decision-making has to incorporate an element of consultation. The skill requirements and time requirements for good consultation have to be added to those listed above for profession-centred decision-making.

Ongoing Processes

Prolonged periods of contact characterize work in some helping professions, for example teaching and psychiatric nursing. Professional intervention is then seen more as an ongoing process than a small number of distinct decisions. This can be a disadvantage, when tradition and custom prevail, and there is little deliberative decision-making involving the genuine exploration of alternative policies and practices. Moreover, evaluation tends to be in terms of instant client response rather than medium or long-term outcomes. Outcome priorities which tend to go against the grain include developing client independence of professional support and changing client attitudes in order to affect long-term behaviour.

Another feature of prolonged periods of contact is that they often take place in organizational settings, where the influences of management style, policy and climate transcend those of individual professionals. It is surely no accident that research on school effectiveness appears to be more conclusive than that on teacher effectiveness. We shall return to this issue when we discuss the role of organizations in professional accountability.

The Implications of a Focus on Outcomes

One conclusion to be drawn from the foregoing analysis is that the evaluation of professional work needs to take into account longer-term outcomes and a wider range of outcomes than is normal in most professions. This problem has arisen for a number of reasons. Where the professional is paid for a specific service, his or her interest ceases (at least in the pecuniary sense) as soon as that service has been completed. Further pursuit of outcomes evidence may be regarded as too intrusive, too expensive or something to be left to researchers. It is likely to take time and effort which might otherwise be devoted to other clients. A more cynical explanation might be that a professional's interest in self-evaluation is limited to the outcomes *for the professional* — the construction of a building, the production of a report, the completion of treatment, the end of a consultation, the conclusion of a process, etc. — and takes little notice, beyond polite expressions of concern, of the outcomes *for the client*.

This brings us back to the ideology of professionalism, and the informal concordat by which it was believed that expert knowledge was protected from abuse by being entrusted to self-governing professions dedicated to the service of their clients. However, the Victorian concept of service preceded universal suffrage and was essentially profession-centred. Except when clients were exceptionally powerful it was the professional alone who decided what their needs were: the client's contribution was relatively small. Restoring the client's role from that of object to that of subject in accord with the expectations of the twenty-first century entails giving primacy of attention to the outcomes for the client.

This concern for outcomes may affect not only the evaluation of professional work, but also its very nature. Outcomes become part of the content of professional discourse: the professional seeks to ascertain client preferences and priorities with respect to outcomes, the client seeks advice on the probable outcomes of the range of alternative courses of action about which the professional is able to provide information. Clarity of communication is vital for the success of these kinds of consultations, but is inhibited by understandable differences of perspective. The professional has to estimate probabilities and may not be too confident about the figures: the client is looking for certainties.

Introducing a focus on outcomes broadens the range of relevant professional knowledge with considerable implications for training programmes and even for research. Where possible a professional needs to have access to data on possible types of outcomes and their relative frequency of occurrence, to know how the likelihood of each outcome is affected by situational factors and to be able to ascertain the significant factors in the case or situation being considered. Even when accurate information is unavailable, and estimates become very subjective, this line of reasoning may need to be followed and the client informed about the level of uncertainty; for to hide such uncertainties from clients would only be morally defensible under very special circumstances. Technical information about outcome probabilities at a local level may be collected systematically by monitoring or audit procedures or by regular outcome reviews; but this will often need backing by funded research with larger samples which can collect more reliable evidence on factors covering the observed variations in outcomes. General information about the relative values placed on various outcomes requires survey data, though one should never assume that any particular client will agree with the views of the average person. Keeping up-to-date with such information, and often at a local level trying to collect it as well, can be a very demanding activity but it lies at the heart of client-centred reasoning and decision-making.

We should not assume, however, that all professional situations lend themselves to this kind of analysis; nor that outcomes-focused thinking is a purely technical process. There are also moral and affective dimensions to be taken into account. As suggested in Chapter 10, many kinds of ethical issues can arise during professional work which need to be recognized, thought through, discussed if necessary and acted upon. Important values may come into conflict or be difficult to interpret; and the interests of various stakeholders will frequently fail to coincide. Ethical problems can also be emotionally very demanding, as can a significant number of client encounters; thus placing yet another significant demand on training and on organizations employing professional workers who have to cope with continuing emotional pressures. Currently few professionals get sufficient training or managerial support for handling ethical issues and emotional stress; yet if these aspects of their work are not well handled, or even subject to avoidance strategies, the consequences for clients can be serious.

At this point it is important to emphasize the close link between being client-centred and continuing to develop one's professional knowledge. Chapters 5 and 6 in particular stressed the complex ways in which professionals acquire information about people and situations. In most professions there is not only that stock of generalizable knowledge which I have called the knowledge base, there is also specific knowledge to be freshly acquired about individual clients, situations, problems, cases, etc. Getting this specific knowledge will usually be the responsibility of the person or team 'on the spot', at least in the first instance; and they will also be the main users of that knowledge. Nobody else knows enough about that particular case to be able to jump in and immediately tell the local team what to do. There is a convincing argument that whenever decisions are so distinctive that each case requires a separate process of inquiry and judgment (and the principle of client-centredness implies that this should be the normal assumption), responsibility has to be devolved to the individual professional or team.

We should note, however, that such professional judgment requires each individual professional to have the knowledge and skills to acquire and interpret the most relevant information, a sufficient repertoire of possible courses of action and ways of adapting them to individual circumstances, and the experience and wisdom to make an optimal set of decisions, adjusting to new information as it becomes available. He or she will usually also need to be capable of, and disposed towards, working with their colleagues for the benefit of current clients; and to continue to develop their expertise for the benefit of future clients.

Such devolution is good management, provided there has been good training. To fail to delegate can be inefficient and wasteful, and to interfere without sufficient knowledge is to jeopardize the quality of service. But I do not regard professional autonomy as a birthright; or perhaps I should call it a 'qualification right'. It does not justify opposition to monitoring or appraisal that is genuinely based on client-centred principles; nor does it justify isolation from collegial or organizational discussion of practice. Quite the opposite. Self-monitoring with periodic external auditing and consultation is an important part of continuing professional development. Not only must the individual professional learn from his or her own experience and that of colleagues, but so also must the organization learn if it is to provide a quality service to clients. Indeed, it is as important for an organization to foster and use the experiential and collegial learning of its members as it is to have a monitoring system.

Thus the accountability of individual professionals includes:

- a moral commitment to serve the interests of clients;
- a professional obligation to self-monitor and to periodically review the effectiveness of one's practice;
- a professional obligation to expand one's repertoire, to reflect on one's experience and to develop one's expertise;
- an obligation that is professional as well as contractual to contribute to the quality of one's organization; and
- an obligation to reflect upon and contribute to discussions about the changing role of one's profession in wider society.

At first sight, these views of accountability may seem a little idealized; but I believe they provide a framework which enables us to be more realistic about what professionals can and do achieve. A great deal of the theory of professional practice is predicated upon the assumption of almost limitless time with a single client. This causes a gap between professionals' aspirations and their practice which becomes an endless source of stress and frustration, and often causes burn-out. It also causes a defensiveness, and insecurity which impedes communication with the public. Who wants to talk about their practice if they know they are bound to be found wanting? Yet a community needs to nourish its professionals; and it is only with its support that some of these tensions will be resolved.

The most difficult problem for some professions is that their service is rationed. The nurse or the teacher has to distribute their attention among a crowd of clients; the doctor's waiting room fills up if he or she spends a long time with a patient; the social worker has to limit the number of visits. All public-sector professionals wonder whether the people they see are those who are most in need of their services. Again, current professional preparation can be exceedingly unhelpful; because it tends to inculcate an idealized form of service which cannot possibly be delivered with the resources society is prepared to provide. Hence professionals are often ill-prepared to cope with the rationing of their services; and given little support by a society which either ignores their pleas on behalf of the needy or expects them to cope with rationing by overworking and pretending that rationing doesn't exist.

This is one reason why I believe there should be external participation in reviews of policy and practice in public-sector organizations. There are not only the clients to be considered, but those who pay for public services. If the taxpayers or their representatives are not aware of the effects on an organization of increasing or decreasing the level of resourcing, they will forever assume that efficiency gains are still possible. Wider participation is not just

a democratic principle. Organizations need the greater involvement and support of their clients and their community so that decisions can be shared about
what can be reasonably achieved and what should be prioritized. In the long-
term I believe this is essential for sustaining morale. The price of autonomy
is dissatisfaction and stress. Thus the essence of my argument is that, unless
the professions renegotiate their role in society with the laity, they will be
destroyed by the current growth of pressures upon them.

Accountability in Organizations

Hitherto the emphasis of our discussion about organizations has been on the
accountability of professionals to their organizations being part of their moral
and professional accountability to clients: because services to clients are significantly influenced if not wholly determined by organization policies and
practices. We have given less attention to the constraints which organizations
sometimes place on the exercise of professional accountability to clients and
consequent ethical issues; and the accountability of organizations to their internal stakeholders, including the professionals in their employment, has been
mentioned only briefly. It is difficult for professionals to sustain their accountability to clients or to the continuing development of their knowledge base
unless their employing organization has some genuine commitment to quality.

The nature of an organization's commitment to quality was briefly outlined in the opening part of this chapter; and elsewhere I have suggested that
some of the distinguishing features of a quality organization are that it:

- sustains an appropriate climate;
- serves the interests of its clients;
- supports and develops its staff;
- continually seeks to improve its policy and practice; and
- reviews, evaluates and controls its affairs on the basis of valid information about its quality, impact, and effect (Eraut, 1994).

Such advice, however, is more easily offered than implemented.

Two major problems in seeking to move organizations towards this quality
scenario are their internal culture and external expectations and influences.
Both have significant implications for professional accountability. While the
term 'organizational culture' is increasingly used in professional discussion, its
meaning is not necessarily very deep. In particular there is a tendency to
equate culture with people's attitudes and shared meanings and to neglect its
roots in daily activities and the way things get done (Schein, 1992). As a
result, people fail to recognize the extent to which the activities which constitute the daily life of an organization are not the creation of a single person
or group. They evolve without being planned, they carry organizational
knowledge which is different from the knowledge of individual members,

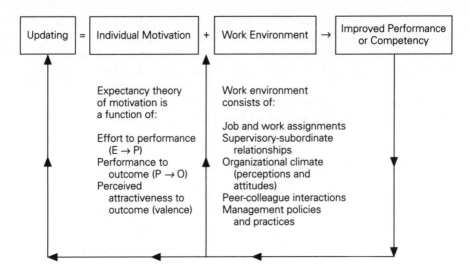

Figure 11.1:   The Dubin Model of Technical Updating

and they consume time and resources in ways that are difficult to analyse and retrieve (Blackler, 1993). Thus organizations as well as individuals have espoused theories which differ from the theories in use which underpin their activities; and find it difficult to allocate time to deliberation that is free from immediate demands and routines, for what Argyris and Schön (1978) would call double-loop learning. The worst case scenario is when prevailing activity systems continue to operate regardless of their impact on the quality of service or the quality of work. Learning comes to be regarded as a subversive activity, and all change is perceived as a threat to be defended against.

In contrast, research into maintaining professional competence (Willis and Dubin, 1990) has shown how a positive work environment can facilitate the maintenance of competence. Dubin's 'Model of Technical Updating' based on research with engineers provides a useful analysis of the principal factors affecting motivation to keep up-to-date (see Figure 11.1). Individual motivation is treated in terms of expectancy theory (Vroom, 1964), which predicts that people make rational choices based on expected pay-off. ($E \rightarrow P$) represents an individual's belief that effort E will be needed to produce performance P; and ($P \rightarrow O$) the belief that performance P will result in outcome O. Attaching value to visible outcomes (valences) then enables calculations to be made. Though presented as an individual factor, these relationships are not independent of the work context. Dubin (1990) lists the criteria most likely to lead to the five work-environment factors having a positive effect on motivation to keep up-to-date.

These are further developed by Farr and Middlebrooks (1990) who conclude:

Traditional approaches to the problem (of maintaining professional competence) seem to have primarily reduced the negative outcomes of professional development activities without increasing the positive outcomes. Challenging task assignments, an effective reward structure, and adequate feedback are ways that the organisation can strive to correct this imbalance. By rewarding and enhancing individual efforts and beliefs regarding professional development activities, the organisation can increase professionals' intrinsic motivation to enhance professional competence. Most important, organisations must first recognise those work environment factors that influence professionals' beliefs about the utility of professional development activities for obtaining valued outcomes, and then restructure the professionals' work environment appropriately. (Farr and Middlebrooks, 1990, p. 211)

The other factor affecting an organization's commitment to quality is the role of external demands and expectations. In the private sector the main influences are the market and principal stakeholders, though an increasing number of companies also have ethical codes of practice. The main concerns of government have been ensuring professional competency and moral behaviour, by influencing if not controlling professional education; and trying to ensure that its citizens get value for money in quasi-monopolistic situations, by fixing fees (as in dentistry) or increasing competition (as in conveyancing). Nevertheless, while tending to restrict rather than strengthen the power of individual professions, they have not tried to reverse the tide of professionalization. Indeed the government appears relatively unconcerned about the possible abuse of professional power in the private sector, as evidenced by the marked contrast between its determination to control the activities of schoolteachers with its *laissez-faire* attitude towards pensions advisers who harm their clients.

In the public sector, however, government control of the purse strings has always been the decisive factor. Moreover government is concerned not only with policy but also with efficiency and with quality. Financial constraints have been accompanied by a deluge of accountability measures which are transforming the nature of public-sector organizations. Table 11.2 indicates the range of accountability mechanisms now in use, and is almost certainly incomplete. It comprises both internal procedures, which are mandated or expected by the government and checked by external inspection or audit, and external procedures directly applied by the government.

These approaches cover a range of purposes, some of which can be conflicting. Charters, for example, are designed to identify and promote the rights of users, monitoring and accreditation to ensure quality, financial controls to reduce unit costs, and inspections to ensure conformity to particular principles or policies. However, the effects of these accountability measures have rarely

Table 11.2: *Approaches to Accountability and Quality Assurance*

Internal mechanisms	External mechanisms
Monitoring systems	Appointments to boards
Case review	Case inquiries
Internal audit	External audit
Internal review	External review
Public reporting	Financial control
Customer survey	Accreditation
Employee survey	Contracting
Market research	Inspection
Inspection	Standard setting
Standard setting	Public-performance indicators
Complaints procedures	Charters
	Regulations

been evaluated with any rigour, in spite of considerable debate and the exchange of anecdotal evidence.

What is undeniable is that, for good or ill, government accountability policies are changing the nature of professional work in the public sector and creating a volume of documentation, only previously associated with the European Community. Hence it is becoming increasingly urgent to ask which of these policies are strengthening the accountability links depicted in Table 11.1, which are providing value for money, and which are fit for their purpose? Agreeing with the declared aims of a policy should not be confused with accepting that the policy achieves those aims or that it is free from unanticipated or unpublicized side-effects.

Conrad (1985), for example, describes how regulation and indicators affect the behaviour of fostering agencies, often against their clients' interests. Performance indicators are particularly liable to produce unforeseen, though many would argue eminently foreseeable, side-effects. For example, outcome-based indicators designed to improve the quality of a service are likely to have the additional effect of reducing access to that service by potential clients who might be perceived as likely to depress the average score.

Another problem arises when a policy forces people and organizations into such a defensive posture that they lose sight of the consequences of their actions for clients and stakeholders. An interesting American example is Wiener and Kayser-Jones' (1989) report of professional defensiveness acting against the clients' interest in nursing homes for the elderly.

There is always some competition for the use of resources, particularly for professionals' time; and there will usually be some conflict between accountability measures which reflect the interests of different stakeholders. Hence the effect of any set of accountability measures on the balance of priorities has to be carefully studied. It rarely reflects the original intentions.

In the meantime, organizations in the public sector are finding it increasingly difficult to attend to their own definitions of quality or even those of their immediate clients. Practices are increasingly changed to maximize performance on external inspections and performance indicators, causing increasing alienation of professional workers and weakening commitment to moral accountabilities.

Appendix

Appendix 1: A Map of Headteacher Knowledge and Know-How

(adapted from a discussion paper for a University of Sussex research project and further developed in Chapter 5.)

This can be mapped into three dimensions.

1. Areas of responsibility — these provide the contexts for knowledge use.
2. Skills and processes.
3. Knowledge about people, practice, regulations, etc.

The following further categorization is highly provisional, but should serve as a useful base for further enquiry.

1. *Areas of responsibility*

Curriculum and training	School organization
Staff	Relations with local environment
Pupils	Relations with governmental system
Finance and resources	Self-management

2. *Skills and processes*

Collecting information and advice	Planning
Giving information and advice	Organizing/administering
Personal Relations	Coordinating and controlling
Handling groups	Political skills
Written Communication	Team building
External relations	Budgeting

3. *Knowledge about People*

External contacts and networks	*Practice*
Sources of advice	Practice in other schools
Friends in high places/low places	Decision options
Personal styles/characteristics	Latest reports
Local community	Issues under discussion

Regulations and Procedures	*Conceptual Frameworks*
Government systems	Theories of education
Law	Social science concepts
Local services	Educational research
National Curriculum	Socioeconomic trends

Appendix 2: A Map of Social Workers' Knowledge and Know-How

(adapted from Baskett, 1983)

1. Knowledge about resources and how to get them: the existence and worth of resources, what they can do and how they relate to needs, procedures for getting them and how to 'bend' them without 'breaking'.
2. Knowledge about organizations and subcultures, their norms and values and how to deal with them: especially the peer-group subculture, community-resource systems such as schools and courts, client subcultures and their own administration,
3. Knowledge of how to get knowledge: personal storage and retrieval systems, using several sources to establish veracity, using personal networks, skills in taking short cuts.
4. Knowledge of self and how one learns.
5. Formal knowledge, as found in books articles and higher-education courses.
6. Coping knowledge: practical precepts for coping with the pressures and contradictory demands of the work setting, e.g., 'Wait, it will work', 'Don't get sucked in', 'Tell 'em what they want to hear' and CYA 'Cover your ass'.

References

ALEXANDER, R. (1984) *Primary teaching*, Eastbourne, Holt, Rinehart and Winston.

ANDERSON, D.C. (1981) *Evaluating Curriculum Proposals*, London, Croom Helm.

ARGYRIS, C. and SCHÖN, D.A. (1974) *Theory in Practice: Increasing Professional Effectiveness*, San Francisco, Jossey-Bass.

ARGYRIS, C. and SCHÖN, D.A. (1978) *Organizational Learning: A Theory in Action Perspective*, Reading, Mass., Addison-Wesley.

ARMSTRONG, P. (1993) 'Professional knowledge and social mobility: Postwar changes in the knowledge-base of management accounting, *Work, Employment and Society*, 7, 1, pp. 1–21.

BARNETT, B. (1987) 'School psychology and children's rights', *School Psychology International*, 8, pp. 1–10.

BASKETT, H.K. (1983) *Continuing Professional Education in Social Work: An Examination of Knowledge Utilisation from a Field Perspective*, D.Phil. Thesis, Brighton, University of Sussex.

BECHER, A., ERAUT, M. and KNIGHT, J. (1981) *Policies for Educational Accountability*, London, Heinemann.

BEDER, S. (1993) 'Engineers, ethics and etiquette', *New Scientist*, 25 September, pp. 36–41.

BENNER, P. (1984) *From Novice to Expert: Excellence and Power in Clinical Nursing Practice*, Menlo Park, Calif., Addison-Wesley.

BENNETT, N. *et al.* (1984) *The Quality of Pupil Learning Experiences*, London, Lawrence Erlbaum Associates.

BERGENDAHL, G. (Ed) (1984) *Knowledge Policy and Knowledge Traditions in Higher Education*, Stockholm, Almquist and Wiksett International.

BERNSTEIN, B. (1971) 'On the classification and framing of educational knowledge', in YOUNG, M.F.D. (Ed) *Knowledge and Control*, London, Collier-Macmillan, pp. 47–69.

BETZ, B. and O'CONNELL, L. (1983) 'Changing doctor-patient relationships and the rise in concern for accountability', *Social Problems*, 31, 1, pp. 84–95.

BLACKLER, F. (1993) 'Knowledge and the theory of organizations: Organizations as activity systems and the reframing of management', *Journal of Management Studies*, 30, 6, pp. 863–84.

BLOOM, B.S. *et al.* (1956) *Taxonomy of Educational Objectives, Handbook, 1; Cognitive Domain*, New York, McKay.

BOND, T. (1992) 'Ethical issues in counselling in education', *British Journal of Guidance and Counselling*, 20, 1, pp. 51–63.

BORDAGE, G. and ZACKS, R. (1984) 'The structure of medical knowledge in the memories of medical students and general practitioners: Categories and prototypes', *Medical Education*, 18, pp. 406–16.

BOREHAM, N.C. (1987) 'Learning from experience in diagnostic problem solving', in RICHARDSON, J. *et al.* (Eds) *Student Learning: Research in Education and Cognitive Psychology*, Guildford, SRHE, pp. 89–97.

BOREHAM, N.C. (1988) 'Models of diagnosis and their implications for adult professional education', *Studies in the Education of Adults*, 20, pp. 95–108.

BOREHAM, N.C. (1989) 'Modelling medical decision-making under uncertainty', *British Journal of Educational Psychology*, 59, pp. 187–99.

BOYATZIS, R.E. (1982) *The Competent Manager: A Model for Effective Performance*, New York, Wiley.

BOYLAN, A. (1974) 'Clinical communication', *Nursing Times*, 28 November, pp. 185–89.

BROUDY, H.S. (1980) *Personal Communication.*

BROUDY, H.S., SMITH, B.O. and BURNETT, J. (1964) *Democracy and Excellence in American Secondary Education*, Chicago, Rand McNally.

BUCHLER, J. (1961) *The Concept of Method*, New York, Columbia University Press.

BUCHMANN, M. (1980) *Practitioners' Concepts: An Inquiry into the Wisdom of Practice*, Occasional Paper 29, Michigan State University, Institute for Research on Teaching.

BURGOYNE, J. and STUART, R. (1978) 'Managerial skills', in BURGOYNE, J. and STUART, R. (Eds) *Management Development: Context and Strategies*, Aldershot, Gower Press, pp. 51–73.

BURKE, J. (1991) 'Competence and higher education: Implications for institutions and professional bodies', in RAGGATT, P. and UNWIN, L. (Eds) *Change and Intervention: Vocational Education and Training*, London, The Falmer Press, pp. 22–46.

BURRAGE (1994) 'Routine and discreet relationships: Professional accreditation and the state in Britain', in BECHER, T. (Ed) *Governments and Professional Education*, Open University Press/SRHE, pp. 140–58.

CAIN, M. (1983) 'The general practice lawyer and the client: Towards a radical conception', in DINGWALL, R. and LEWIS, P. (Eds) *The Sociology of the Professions*, London, Macmillan, pp. 106–30.

CALDERHEAD, J. (Ed) (1988) *Teachers' Professional Learning*, London, The Falmer Press.

CANTOR, N. *et al.* (1980) 'Psychiatric diagnosis as prototype categorisation', *Journal of Abnormal Psychology*, 89, p. 181.

CARE SECTOR CONSORTIUM (1991) *National Occupational Standards for Staff Working with Young Children and their Families.*

CARR-SAUNDERS, A.M. and WILSON, P. (1933) *The Professions*, London, Frank Cass.

CHARTERED INSTITUTE OF MANAGEMENT ACCOUNTANTS (1992) *Draft Standards of Competence in Management Accountancy.*

CHOMSKY, N. (1968) *Language and Mind*, Harcourt, Brace and World.

CLARK, C. M. (1986) *Asking the Right Questions about Teacher Preparation: Contributions of Research on Teacher Thinking*, October, ISATT Conference Paper.

CONRAD, K. (1985) 'Promoting quality of care: The role of the Compliance Director', *Child Welfare*, LXIV, 6, pp. 639–49.

CONSTRUCTION INDUSTRY STANDING CONFERENCE (1993) *Draft Unit on Professional Competence*, London, CISC.

COPP, G. (1988) 'Professional accountability: The conflict', *Nursing Times*, 84, 43, pp. 42–4.

COWDROY, R. (1992) *Architects' Continuing Professional Development: A Strategic Framework*, University of Newcastle, NSW, Faculty of Architecture.

CRONBACH, L.J. *et al.* (1980) *Toward Reform of Program Evaluation*, San Francisco, Jossey-Bass.

DACUM, (1983) DACUM Booklets, British Columbia, Can., Ministry of Education.

DAY, C. (1981) *Classroom Based In-service Teacher Education: The Development and Evaluation of a Client-centred Model,* Occasional Paper 9, Brighton, University of Sussex Education Area.

DEBLING, G. (1989) 'The Employment Department/Training Agency Standards Programme and NVQs: Implications for education, in BURKE, J.W. (Ed) *Competency Based Education and Training*, London, The Falmer Press, pp. 77–94.

DEWEY, J. (1933) *How We Think — A Restatement of the Relation of Reflective Thinking to the Educative Process*, Boston, Heath.

DOWIE, J. and ELSTEIN, A. (Eds) (1988) *Professional Judgement: A Reader in Clinical Decision Making*, Cambridge, Cambridge University Press.

DREYFUS, H.L. and DREYFUS, S.E. (1986) *Mind over Machine: The Power of Human Intuition and Expertise in the Era of the Computer*, Oxford, Basil Blackwell.

DUBIN, S.S. (1990) 'Maintaining competence through updating', in WILLIS, S.L. and DUBIN, S.S. (Eds) *Maintaining Professional Competence*, San Francisco, Jossey-Bass, pp. 9–43.

DULEWICZ, V. (1989) 'Assessment centres as the route to competence', *Personnel Management*, November, pp. 56–9.

ELAM, S. (1972) *Performance-based Teacher Education: What is the State of the Art?* Washington, DC, AACTE.

ELKIN, G. (1990) 'Competency-based human resource development', *Industrial and Commercial Training*, 22, 4, pp. 20–25.

ELLIOTT, J. (1991) *Action Research for Educational Change*, Milton Keynes, Open University Press.

ELSTEIN, A.S. and BORDAGE, G. (1979) 'Psychology of clinical reasoning', in

STONE, G. *et al.* *Health Psychology — A Handbook*, San Francisco, Jossey-Bass.

ELSTEIN, A.S., SHULMAN, L.S. and SPRAFKA, S.A. (1978) *Medical Problem Solving: An Analysis of Clinical Reasoning*, Harvard, Mass., Harvard University Press.

EMPLOYMENT DEPARTMENT (1991) *Development of Assessable Standards for National Certification*, Guidance Note 8, Sheffield, Employment Department.

EMPLOYMENT DEPARTMENT (Ed) (1993) *Knowledge and Understanding: Its Place in Relation to NVQs and SVQs*, Briefing Paper No. 9, Sheffield, Employment Department.

ENTWISTLE, N.J. and ENTWISTLE, A. (1991) 'Contrasting forms of understanding for degree examinations: The student experience and its implications', *Higher Education*, 22, pp. 202–27.

ERAUT, M. (1978) 'Accountability at school level — some options and their implications', in BECHER, A. and MACLURE, S. (Eds) *Accountability in Education*, Windsor, NFER Publishing, pp. 152–99.

ERAUT, M. (1982) 'What is learned in in-service education and how? A knowledge use perspective', *British Journal of In-Service Education*, 9, 1, pp. 6–14.

ERAUT, M. (1988) 'Teacher Thought and Action Outside the Classroom', Invited Paper for ISATT Conference, Nottingham, September.

ERAUT, M. (1989) 'Initial teacher training and the NVQ model', in BURKE, J. (Ed) *Competency Based Education and Training*, London, The Falmer Press, pp. 171–85.

ERAUT, M. (1990) 'Identifying knowledge which underpins performance', in BLACK, H. and WOLF, A. (Eds) *Knowledge and Competence: Current Issues in Training and Education*, Sheffield, Employment Department, pp. 22–8.

ERAUT, M. (1992) 'Mid-career professional education', in PYRGIOTAKIS, I.E., KANAKIS, I.N. and KAZAMIAS, A.M. (Eds) *Crisis in Education: Myth or Reality* (In Greek), Athens, Michael P. Gregory, pp. 310–28.

ERAUT, M. (1994) 'Developing professional knowledge within a client-centred orientation', in GUSKEY, T.R. and HUBERMAN, M. (Eds) *New Paradigms and Practices in Professional Development*, New York, Teachers College Press.

ERAUT, M. and COLE, G. (1993) *Assessment of Competence in the Professions*, R & D Report 14, Sheffield, Employment Department, Methods Strategy Unit.

ETZIONI, A. (Ed) (1969) *The Semi-Professions and their Organization*, New York, Free Press.

FARMER, J. (1981) *Real-Life Problem-Solving Efforts of Professionals and Related Learning Activities*, Champaign, Ill., University of Illinois, College of Education.

FARR, J.L. and MIDDLEBROOKS, C.L. (1990) 'Enhancing motivation to participate in professional development', in WILLIS, S.L. and DUBIN, S.S. (Eds)

Maintaining Professional Competence, San Francisco, Jossey-Bass, pp. 195–211.

FELTOVITCH, P.J. and BARROWS, H.S. (1984) 'Issues of generality in medical problem solving', in SCHMIDT, H.G. and DE VOLDER, M.L. (Eds) *Tutorials in Problem-Based Learning*, Assen, The Netherlands, Van Gorcum, pp. 128–42.

FENNELL, E. (Ed) (1991) *Development of Assessable Standards for National Certification*, Sheffield, Employment Department.

FERNSTERMACHER, G.D. (1980) 'What needs to be known about what teachers need to know,' in HALL, G.E., HORD, S.M. and BROWN, G. *Exploring Issues in Teacher Education: Questions for Future Research*, Austin, University of Texas, R & D Centre for Teacher Education, pp. 35–49.

FLAVELL, J. and WOHLWILL, J. (1969) 'Formal and functional aspects of cognitive development', in ELKIND, D. and FLAVELL, J. (Eds) *Studies in Cognitive Development*, Oxford University Press, pp. 67–120.

FREIDSON, E. (1971) *Profession of Medicine: a Study of Sociology of Applied Knowledge*, New York, Dodd, Mead and Co.

FRIEND, J. and HICKLING, A. (1987) *Planning Under Pressure: The Strategic Choice Approach*, Oxford, Pergamon.

FULLER, F. (1970) *Personalized Education for Teachers: One Application of the Teacher Concerns Model*, Austin, Tex., University of Texas, R & D Centre for Teacher Education.

FURNHAM, A. (1990) 'A question of competency', *Personnel Management*, June, p. 37.

GEALEY, N. (1993) 'Development of NVQs and SVQs at higher levels', *Competence and Assessment*, 21, pp. 4–9.

GEALEY, N. *et al*. (1991) 'Designing assessment systems for national certification', in FENNELL, E. (Ed) *Development of Assessable Standards for National Certification*, Sheffield, Employment Department.

GENERAL MEDICAL COUNCIL (1993) *Tomorrow's Doctors; Recommendations on Undergraduate Medical Education*, London, General Medical Council.

GLASER, B. and STRAUSS, A. (1967) *The Discovery of Grounded Theory*, Chicago, Aldine.

GOFFMAN, E. (1959) *The Presentation of Self in Everyday Life*, London, Penguin.

GONZI, A., HAGER, P. and ATHANASOU, J. (1993) *The Development of Competency-Based Assessment Strategies for the Professions*, National Office of Overseas Skills Recognition Research Paper No. 8, Canberra, Australian Government Publishing Service.

GOODE, W.J. (1969) 'The theoretical limits of professionalization', in ETZIONI, A. (Ed) *The Semi-Professions and their Organization*, New York, Free Press, pp. 266–313.

GRANT, G. *et al*. (1979) *On Competence: A Critical Analysis of Competence-Based Reforms in Higher Education*, San Francisco, Jossey-Bass.

GRUMET, M.R. (1989) 'Generations: Reconceptualist curriculum theory and teacher education', *Journal of Teacher Education*, 40, 1, pp. 13–17.

HAMM, R.M. (1988) 'Clinical intuition and clinical analysis: Expertise and the cognitive continuum', in DOWIE, J. and ELSTEIN, A. (Eds) *Professional Judgement: A reader in clinical decision making*, Cambridge, Cambridge University Press, pp. 78–105.

HAMMOND, K.R. *et al.* (1980) *Human Judgement and Decision Making*, New York, Hemisphere.

HARRIS, I.B. (1982) *Communications for Guiding Teachers: The Impact of Different Conceptions of Teaching and Educational Practice*, March, Conference Paper, AERA.

HERMANN, G.D. and KENYON, R.J. (1987) *Competency-Based Vocational Education*, London, Further Education Unit.

HICKSON, D.J. and THOMAS, M.W. (1969) 'Professionalization in Britain: A preliminary measurement', *Sociology*, 3, pp. 37–53.

HIRSH, W. and BEVAN, S. (1991) 'Managerial competencies and skill languages', in SILVER, M. (Ed) *Competent to Manage*, London, Routledge, pp. 83–100.

HIRST, P.H. (1979) 'Professional studies in initial teacher education: Some conceptual issues', in ALEXANDER, R.J. and WORMALD, E. (Eds) *Professional Studies for Teaching*, Guildford, Society for Research in Higher Education, pp. 15–27.

HIRST, P.H. (1985) 'Educational studies and the PGCE course', *British Journal of Educational Studies*, 33, 3, pp. 211–21.

HOUSTON, W.R. (1985) 'Competency-based teacher education', in HUSEN, T. and POSTLETHWAITE, N. (Eds) *The International Encyclopedia of Education*, Oxford, Pergamon, pp. 898–906.

HOWEY, K.R. and JOYCE, B.R. (1978) 'A data-base for future directions in in-service education', *Theory into Practice*, 17, 3, pp. 206–11.

HUBERMAN, M. (1983) 'Recipes for busy kitchens', *Knowledge: Creation, Diffusion, Utilization*, 4, pp. 478–510.

JACKSON, P.W. (1968) *Life in Classrooms*, New York, Holt, Rinehart and Winston.

JACKSON, P.W. (1971) 'The way teachers think', in LESSER, G.S. (Ed) *Psychology and Educational Practice*, Chicago, Scott Foresman, pp. 10–34.

JESSUP, G. (1991) *Outcomes: NVQs and the Emerging Model of Education and Training*, London, The Falmer Press.

JOHNSON, T.J. (1972) *Professions and Power*, London, Macmillan.

JOHNSON, T.J. (1984) 'Professionalism: Occupation or ideology', in GOODLAD, S. (Ed) *Education for the Professions: Quis Custodiet?* SRHE and NFER — Nelson, pp. 17–25.

JONES, R.T. (1986) *The Development of the Medical Laboratory Scientific Officer Profession: Qualifying Systems, Professional Politics and Technical Change*, D.Phil Thesis, Brighton University of Sussex.

JOYCE, B.R. and SHOWERS, B. (1980) 'Improving in-service training: The messages of research', *Educational Leadership*, 37, pp. 379–85.

KATZ, F.E. (1969) 'Nurses', in ETZIONI, A. (Ed) *The Semi-Professions and their Organization*, New York, Free Press, pp. 54–81.

KERR, E. (1984) *Education for the Professions: The Developing Role of the Public Sector of UK Higher Education*, paper given to Anglo-Swedish Higher Education Conference, Bournemouth.

KORTHAGEN, F.A.J. (1988) 'The influence of learning orientations on the development of reflective teaching', in CALDERHEAD, J. (Ed) *Teachers' Professional Learning*, London, The Falmer Press, pp. 35–50.

KUHN, T. (1974) 'Second thoughts on paradigms', in SUPPES, F. *The Structure of Scientific Theories*, Urbana, Ill., University of Illinois Press.

LANIER, J. (1983) 'Tensions in teaching teachers', in GRIFFIN, G.A. (Ed) *Staff Development*, NSSE Yearbook 1983, Part II, Chicago, University of Chicago Press, pp. 118–53.

LILFORD, R.J. (1992) 'Decision logic in medical practice', *Journal of the Royal College of Physicians*, 26, 4, pp. 400–12.

LORTIE, D.C. (1975) *Schoolteacher: a Sociological Study*, Chicago, University of Chicago Press.

LOWRY, S. (1993) *Medical Education*, London, BMJ Publishing.

MAATSCH, J.L. (1990) 'Linking competence to assessment tests', in WILLIS, S.L. and DUBIN, S.S. (Eds) *Maintaining Professional Competence*, San Francisco, Jossey-Bass, pp. 95–124.

MANAGEMENT CHARTER INITIATIVE (MCI) (1991) *Occupational Standards for Managers, Management II and Assessment Guidance.*

MANSFIELD, B. and MATHEWS, D. (1985) *Job competence — a description for use in vocational education and training*, Bristol, Further Education Staff College.

MARTON, F. and SÄLJÖ, R. (1984) 'Approaches to learning', in MARTON, F., HOUNSELL, D. and ENTWISTLE, N. (Eds) *The Experience of Learning*, Edinburgh, Scottish Academic Press, pp. 36–55.

MCINTYRE, D. (1980) 'The contribution of research to quality in teacher education', in HOYLE, E. and MEGARRY, J. (Eds) *Professional Development of Teachers*, World Yearbook of Education, London, Kogan Page, pp. 293–307.

MCLAUGHLIN, M.W. and MARSH, D.D. (1978) 'Staff development and school change', *Teachers College Record*, 80, 1, pp. 69–94.

MCMAHON, F. and CARTER, E. (1990) *The Great Training Robbery*, London, The Falmer Press.

MCNAMARA, D. (1991) 'Subject knowledge and its application: Problems and possibilities for teacher educators', *Journal of Education for Teaching*, 17, 2, pp. 113–28.

MCNAMARA, D. and DESFORGES, C. (1979) 'Professional studies as a source of theory', in ALEXANDER, R.J. and WORMALD, E. (Eds) *Professional Studies for Teaching*, Guildford, SRHE, pp. 46–60.

MERTON, R.K. (1960) *Some Thoughts on the Professions in American Society*, Providence, Brown University Papers No. 37.

MESSICK, S. (1984) 'The psychology of educational measurement', *Journal of Educational Measurement*, 21, pp. 215–38.

MILES, M. (Ed) (1964) *Innovation in Education*, New York, Teachers College Press.

MILES, M.B. (1981) 'Mapping the common properties of schools', in LEHMING, R. and KANE, M. (Eds) *Improving Schools: Using what we know*, Beverly Hills, Sage, Publications.

MILLER, C.M.L. and PARLETT, M. (1974) *Up to the Mark: A study of the Examination Game*, London, SRHE.

MILLERSON, G. (1964) *The Qualifying Associations*, London, Routledge.

MINSKY, M. (1977) 'Frame-system theory', in JOHNSON-LAIRD, P.N. and WASON, P.C. (Eds) *Thinking: Readings in Cognitive Science*, Cambridge, Cambridge University Press, pp. 355–76.

MITCHELL, L. and CUTHBERT, T. (1989) *Insufficient Evidence, the Final Report of the Competency Testing Project*, Glasgow, SCOTVEC.

MONTGOMERY, J. (1989) 'Medicine, accountability and professionalism', *Journal of Law and Society*, 16, 2, pp. 319–39.

MOORE, W. (1970) *The Professions*, New York, Russell Sage Foundation.

MUNBY, H. and RUSSELL, T. (1989) 'Educating the reflective teacher: An essay review of two books by Donald Schön', *Journal of Curriculum Studies*, 21, 7, pp. 71–80.

MUNBY, H. and RUSSELL, T. (1993) 'Reflective teacher education: Technique or epistemology?', *Teaching and Teacher Education*, 9, 4, pp. 431–8.

NCVQ (1986) *The National Council for Vocational Qualifications: Its purposes and its aims*, London, NCVQ.

NCVQ (1991) *Criteria for National Vocational Qualifications*, London, National Council for Vocational Qualifications.

NISBETT, R.E. and ROSS, L. (1980) *Human Inference: Strategies and Shortcomings of Social Judgement*, Englewood Cliffs, NJ, Prentice Hall.

NORMAN, G.R. (1985) 'Defining competence: A methodological review', in NEUFELD, V.R. and NORMAN, G.R. (Eds) *Assessing Clinical Competence*, New York, Springer, pp. 15–35.

NORRIS, N. (1991) 'The trouble with competence', *Cambridge Journal of Education*, 21, 3, pp. 331–41.

OAKESHOTT, M. (1962) *Rationalism in Politics: And Other Essays*, London, Methuen.

OTTER, S. (1989) *Student Potential in Britain*, Leicester, Unit for the Development of Adult Continuing Education.

PARKER, J.C. and RUBIN, L.J. (1966) *Process as Content: Curriculum Design and the Application of Knowledge*, Chicago, Rand McNally.

PARSONS, T. (1968) 'Professions', in SILLS, D. (Ed) *International Encyclopedia of the Social Sciences*, XII, New York, Macmillan and Free Press, pp. 536–47.

PEARSON, H.T. (1984) 'Competence: A normative analysis', in SHORT, E.C. (Ed) *Competence: Inquiries into its meaning and acquisition in Education Settings*, Lanham, Md., University Press of America, pp. 31–8.

PETRIE, H.G. (1981) *The Dilemma of Enquiry and Learning*, Chicago, University of Chicago Press.

POLANYI, M. (1967) *The Tacit Dimension*, London, Routledge.

RAELIN, J. (1986) *The Clash of Cultures: Managers and Professionals*, Harvard, Mass., Harvard Business School Press.

REDDY, M.J. (1979) 'The conduit metaphor — a case of frame conflict in our language about language', in ORTONY, A. (Ed) *Metaphor and Thought*, Cambridge, Cambridge University Press, pp. 284–324.

REVANS, R.W. (1982) *The Origins and Growth of Action Learning*, Bromley, Chartwell-Bratt.

RICH, R.E. (Ed) (1981) *The Knowledge Cycle*, Beverley Hills, Sage.

ROSS, L. (1977) 'The intuitive psychologist and his shortcomings', in BERKOWITZ, L. (Ed) *Advances in Experimental Social Psychology*, 10, New York, Academic Press.

RUESCHEMEYER, D. (1983) 'Professional autonomy and the social control of expertise', in DINGWALL, R. and LEWIS, P. (Eds) *The Sociology of the Professions: Lawyers, Doctors and Others*, London, Macmillan, pp. 38–58.

RUSSELL, T. (1988) 'From pre-service teacher education to first year of teaching: A study of theory and practice', in CALDERHEAD, J. (Ed) *Teachers' Professional Learning*, London, the Falmer Press, pp. 13–34.

RUTTER, M., MAUGHAM, B., MORTIMORE, P., OUSTON, J. and SMITH, A. (1979) *Fifteen Thousand Hours: Secondary Schools and their Effects on Children*, London, Open Books.

RYLE, G. (1949) *The Concept of Mind*, London, Hutchinson.

SCHANK, R. and ABELSON, R.P. (1977) 'Scripts, plans and knowledge', in JOHNSON-LAIRD, P.N. and WASON, P.C. (Eds) *Thinking: Readings in Cognitive Science*, Cambridge, Cambridge University Press, pp. 421–32.

SCHEIN, E.H. (1988) *Process Consultation*, Vols I and II, 2nd ed., Reading, Mass., Addison-Wesley.

SCHEIN, E.H. (1992) *Organizational Culture and Leadership*, 2nd ed., San Francisco, Jossey-Bass.

SCHMIDT, H.G., NORMAN, G.R. and BOSHUIZEN, H. (1990) 'A cognitive perspective on medical expertise: Theory and implications', *Academic Medicine*, 65, 10, pp. 611–21.

SCHÖN, D. (1983) *The Reflective Practitioner: How Professionals Think in Action*, New York, Basic Books.

SCHÖN, D. (1987) *Educating the Reflective Practitioner: Towards a New Design for Teaching and Learning in the Professions*, San Francisco, Jossey-Bass.

SCHRODER, H.M. (1989) *Managerial Competence: The Key to Excellence*, Iowa, Kendall/Hunt.

SCHUTZ, A. (1967) *The Phenomenology of the Social World* (translated by G. Walsh and F. Lehnert from 1932 original), Evanston, Ill., Northwestern University Press.

SCHWARTZ, M.L. (1978) 'The professionalism and accountability of lawyers', *California Law Review*, 66, 4, pp. 669–97.

SCRIBNER, S. and COLE, M. (1981) *The Psychology of Literacy*, Harvard, Mass., Harvard University Press.

SHERR, A. (1992) 'Professional legal training', *Journal of Law and Society*, 19, 1, pp. 163–73.

SHORT, E.C. (1984) 'Gleanings and possibilities', in SHORT, E.C. (Ed) *Competence: Inquiries into its Meaning and Acquisition in Educational Settings*, Lanham, Md., University Press of America, pp. 161–80.

SIEGRIST, H. (1994) 'The professions, state and government in theory and history', in BECHER, T. (Ed) *Governments and Professional Education*, Buckingham, Open University Press/SRHE, pp. 3–20.

SIGRUN GUDMUNDSDOTTIR (1989) 'Pedagogical Models of Subject Matter', in BROPHY, J. (Ed) *Advances in Research on Teaching*, Greenwich, New York, Jai Press.

SIMON, B. (1981) 'Why no pedagogy in England?', in SIMON, B. and TAYLOR, W. (Eds) *Education in the Eighties*, London, Batsford, pp. 124–45.

SNYDER, B.R. (1971) *The Hidden Curriculum*, New York, Knopf.

SPENCER, L.M. (1983) *Soft Skill Competencies*, Edinburgh, Scottish Council for Research in Education.

STALLINGS, J. (1979) 'Follow through: A model for in-service teacher training', *Curriculum Inquiry*, 8, pp. 163–81.

STEADMAN, S., ERAUT, M., COLE, G. and MARQUAND, J. (1994) *Ethics in Occupational Standards and S/NVQs*, R & D Report, Sheffield, Employment Department, Methods Strategy Unit.

STELLING, J. and BUCHER, R. (1973) 'Vocabularies of realism in professional socialization', *Social Science and Medicine*, 7, pp. 661–75.

SVENSSON, L.G. (1990) 'Knowledge as a professional resource: Case studies of architects and psychologists at work', in TORSTENDAHL, R. and BURRAGE, M. (Eds) *The Formation of the Professions: Knowledge, State and Strategy*, Beverly Hills, Sage.

SWANSON, D.B. (1978) *Computer Simulation of Expert Problem Solving in Medical Diagnosis*, Ph.D dissertation, University of Minnesota, Cited in Boreham (1988).

TOM, A. (1980) 'The reform of teacher education through research: A futile quest', *Teachers College Record*, 82, 1, pp. 15–29.

TUCKETT, D., BOULTON, M., OLSON, C. and WILLIAMS, A. (1985) *Meetings Between Experts: An Approach to Sharing Ideas in Medical Consultations*, London, Tavistock.

TVERSKY, A. and KAHNEMANN, D. (1973) 'Availability: A heuristic for judging frequency and probability', *Cognitive Psychology*, 5, pp. 207–32.

UK GOVERNMENT (1986) *Working Together — Education and Training*, London, HMSO.

UK GOVERNMENT (1988) *Employment for the 1990s*, London, HMSO.

VERRIER, R. (1981) *School-based In-service Education: A Case Study of School Consultancy Relationships*, Occasional Paper 8, Brighton, University of Sussex Education Area.

VROOM, V.H. (1964) *Work and Motivation*, New York, Wiley.

WEISS, C. (Ed) (1977) *Using Social Research in Public Policy Making*, Lexington, D.C. Heath.

WHITE, P. and WHITE, J. (1984) *Practical Reasoning and Educational Theory*, Conference Paper, University of London, Institute of Education.

WIENER, C.L. and KAYSER-JONES, J. (1989) 'Defensive work in nursing homes: Accountability gone amok', *Social Science and Medicine*, 28, 1, pp. 37–44.

WILENSKY, H.L. (1964) 'The professionalization of everyone', *American Journal of Sociology*, 70, 2, pp. 142–6.

WILLIS, S.L. and DUBIN, S.S. (Eds) (1990) *Maintaining Professional Competence*, San Francisco, Jossey-Bass.

WINCH, G. and SCHNEIDER, E. (1993) 'Managing the knowledge-based organization: The case of architectural practice', *Journal of Management Studies*, 30, 6, pp. 923–37.

WOLF, A. (1993) *Assessment Issues and Problems in a Criterion-Based System*, London, Further Education Unit.

WOOD, R. and POWER, C. (1987) 'Aspects of the competence-performance distinction: Educational, psychological and measurement issues', *Journal of Curriculum Studies*, 19, 5, pp. 409–24.

ZEICHNER, K.M. and LIPSON, D.P. (1987) 'Teaching student teachers to reflect', *Harvard Educational Review*, 57, 1, pp. 23–48.

Index